D0500582

C. C. Pyle's Amazing Foot Race

C. C. Pyle's Amazing Foot Race

The True Story of the 1928 Coast-to-Coast Run Across America

Geoff Williams

Rodale books may be purchased for business or promotional use or for special sales. For information, please write to: Special Markets Department, Rodale Inc., 733 Third Avenue, New York, NY 10017.

Printed in the United States of America
Rodale Inc. makes every effort to use acid-free ♾, recycled paper ♻

Book design by Tara Long

Library of Congress Cataloging-in-Publication Data

Williams, Geoffrey, date
C.C. Pyle's amazing foot race : the true story of the 1928 coast-to-coast run across America / by Geoff Williams.
p. cm.
Includes bibliographical references and index.
ISBN-13 978–1–59486–319–6 hardcover
ISBN-10 1–59486–319–9 hardcover
1. Running races—United States—History. 2. Pyle, Charles C., 1882-1939. 3. Sports promoters—United States—History. I. Title.
GV1061.2.W55 2007
796.42092—dc22 2007014440

Distributed to the trade by Holtzbrinck Publishers

2 4 6 8 10 9 7 5 3 1 hardcover

We inspire and enable people to improve their lives and the world around them

For more of our products visit **rodalestore.com** or call 1-800-848-4735

For Susan, Isabelle, and Lorelei

Contents

AUTHOR'S NOTE ix

PROLOGUE: THE AGE OF ENDURANCE xi

Chapter 1
THE BUNION DERBY 1

Chapter 2
BALLYHOO 7

Chapter 3
A DECEPTIVE ROAD 20

Chapter 4
CALIFORNIA DREAMING 25

Chapter 5
ON YOUR MARK 41

Chapter 6
GO! 50

Chapter 7
ODD COMPANY 67

Chapter 8
RACING ARIZONA 92

Chapter 9
ARIZONA ANXIETY 117

Chapter 10
NEW HORIZONS, NEW MEXICO 127

Chapter 11
WEATHERING THE STORM 144

Chapter 12
HOME SWEET HOME 158

Chapter 13
SLOW GOING 181

Chapter 14
ROUGH GOING 202

Chapter 15
INTO INDIANA 224

Chapter 16
FANCY FOOTWORK 235

Chapter 17
LAST LEGS 250

Chapter 18
WAITING GAME 274

EPILOGUE: END OF THE LINE 286
ABOUT NOTES AND RESOURCES 304
ACKNOWLEDGMENTS 307
INDEX 311

Author's Note

The following story is nonfiction. Every bit of it, as ridiculous as some of it may seem, is true to the best of my research. Some anecdotes came directly from the runners' descendents, and some facts from books, court documents, and census records. But by far, most of the information in the following pages is compiled from the nuggets of news left by the reporters covering the story. The sportswriters of that era were known for their creative license, but if the occasional offbeat quote or anecdote came from a reliable source, such as the Associated Press, I chose to assume that the fantastic probably was accurate. After all, perhaps more than any other event, the Bunion Derby embodies the Roaring Twenties, a decade known for being over the top, comically surreal, and plain old fun. Besides, C. C. Pyle would have wanted it that way.

Or perhaps you would rather bowl? In June 1924, Hans Nelson became the world champion of endurance bowling, having won 50 games in a row against five veterans, in 7 hours. In August 1927, Owen Evans, 19, played golf for 17 hours—with no breaks—and used a flashlight to see the ball in the dark.

But endurance competitions weren't reserved only for sports. In the mid-1920s, endurance eating and drinking took the spotlight. At a New York hotel, Kathleen Hayden consumed 36 raw eggs in 85 minutes. Billie Pern, of New York City, drank 27 cups of coffee in a row. That was nothing compared to Gus Comstock, of Fergus Falls, Minnesota, who in 1926 consumed 62 cups of coffee in 10 hours but then was trounced by an Amarillo, Texas, man who drank 71 cups in less than 9 hours. In 1927, Comstock rallied by drinking 85 cups in 7 hours and 15 minutes—only to lose his title to Frank Truckimowicz, of Ray, North Dakota, who pretty much finished the conversation by consuming 90 cups of coffee in 3 hours and 28 minutes.

There were contests that involved devouring sandwiches, flapjacks, hot dogs, and spaghetti. Chicago's Cadarino Nezareno became pasta champion of the world after consuming 7 feet of spaghetti—per minute—for 3 straight hours.

Adults broke records for staying awake the longest and for kissing the longest. Children were recorded flying kites for 2 days and nights and bouncing balls more than 2,000 times, all trying to achieve some legacy among world record holders. Almost as famous as the dance marathoners were the flagpole sitters. Shipwreck Kelly inspired numerous men and women to copy his successful sitting on flagpoles, for days and weeks at a time.

One of the most enduring images of the era is comedian Harold Lloyd, dangling from a clock on a high-rise building in *Safety Last!*, a film released April 1, 1923, that paid tribute to the endurance era. In the film, he climbed up a building to bring publicity to the store he worked for. In real life, a few weeks before Lloyd's film premiered, Harry Young was scaling the side of the Hotel Martinique when on the 10th floor he lost his grip and plunged to his death in front of 20,000 people, including his horrified wife.

That was the fine print of the endurance era: The activities were risky.

No one drowned on January 15, 1927, during the 22-mile swimming race from Catalina Island to the California mainland, but it didn't go well for many participants. One man tied firewood to his back, thinking it would help him float (it didn't). Another man put on layers of clothing and covered himself in swimmer's grease, all designed to keep him warm, but failed to consider how the soaked material would weigh him down. Making matters worse, he tied his shirt sleeves and pant legs securely around his wrists and ankles but forgot about his neck, and so the ocean swept into his clothes, filling him up like a water balloon. In the hours ahead, many swimmers were dragged into boats. As one syndicated newspaper account put it, they were "delirious and raving. Their bodies were numb and marked with purple spots. Their teeth chattered, and they limped like wet rags."

The country loved it. The swimming race was all anyone talked about, especially after 17-year-old Canadian swimmer George Young reached the shoreline at 3:41 a.m., welcomed by a crowd of 5,000 spectators who wanted to get a good look at the young hero. And they got a very good look. A few seconds later, Young dashed back into the water, having just remembered that his swimming trunks had fallen off.

In the aftermath of Catalina Island, and in the midst of flagpole sitting, dance marathons, and rocking chair derbies (where people spent days trying to be the last person sitting and still rocking), one man watching from the sidelines finally decided to step forward. C. C. Pyle, who made his fortune as a sports agent, had an idea.

It would be the mother of all endurance contests. On April 26, 1927, at a Los Angeles press conference full of sportswriters, Pyle proposed a foot race across the United States.

The concept would evolve over a period of months, but his original vision remained more or less intact until March 4, 1928, when 199 men set off from Los Angeles in an attempt to race each other to New York City. Pyle's notion was that any interested man could participate—provided he paid his $125 entry fee, $100 of which would be returned at the end of the participant's involvement, to allow him to have money to return home. Whoever had the fewest collective hours after passing the finish line would win $25,000. It was prize money that matched what George Young received for Catalina, but Pyle's endurance competition upped the ante. Second place would win $10,000. Third-place prize money was $5,000. Fourth, $2,500. And the fifth- through 10th-place winners would each get $1,000. All in all, Pyle promised to award $48,500 in cash, an astounding amount of money in 1928. Using the consumer price index, it would be like doling out almost one-third of a million dollars today.

The thinking was that in between Los Angeles and New York competitors would run or walk anywhere from 30 to 50 miles a day, stopping in a predetermined town (or what they called a night control) to sleep, as was the practice with the cyclists competing in the Tour de France. The next morning, the runners would set out as fast as possible for the next night control.

But if the idea seems surreal now, it was positively ludicrous to 1928-era sportswriters, in an age of crummy roads and shoddy shoes. These men were going to run as much as two marathons every day, for several months.

Pyle, in his typically modest and understated way, told reporters that his race would be the "world's greatest single athletic project."

"Every town through which the race is run will find great profits accruing to hotel men, the restaurateurs, and merchants in general," said Pyle in Chicago a month later. "Thousands will come to town from miles around to see the contestants pass through." Pyle added that he would ask the townspeople to split their profits with him.

Several months later, Pyle's enthusiasm for his project hadn't dampened at all.

"From the way the entry blanks are coming in," enthused Pyle, "I'm certain we will have 1,000 starters."

When a sportswriter in Chicago suggested that what Pyle was planning sounded a bit like a dream, the showman replied, "Sure it does. But I'm the gent who makes dreams come true."

CHAPTER 1

Believed to have been taken 2 years before the Bunion Derby, this photo shows C. C. Pyle taking in the sea air on the ocean liner France. *(Part of the* New York World-Telegram *and the* Sun *Newspaper Photograph Collection, Library of Congress.)*

THE BUNION DERBY

In the 19th century, American cities were full of con artists. Wielding a scalpel and lurking in saloons, barbershops, hotels, and deserted alleyways, they called themselves chiropodists. They gave a bad name to the reputable chiropodist, a precursor to today's podiatrist. If you were unlucky enough to meet one, you were probably already unlucky enough to have corns or bunions. And if you were naïve enough to hire a "chiropodist" to cut off the offending part of your foot, sometimes you were unlucky enough to die from an infected wound.

When C. C. Pyle conceived the course for his race in 1927, podiatry was primitive at best. It was by then a regulated medical field, but shoes were still manufactured in a way that offered little flexibility or support for the wearer, and feet were suffering for it. A Dr. Scholl's ad of the time addressed the severity of the situation when it urged: "Don't neglect your feet. Even a corn is no trivial thing. No matter what foot trouble you suffer from—corns, calluses, bunions, tired, aching feet, weak or broken down arches, crooked or over-lapping toes, weak ankles, tender heels, perspiring or odorous feet—you can have quick and lasting relief."

And now Pyle was promoting the idea of a race in which a group of people predisposed to foot problems would leave Los Angeles and run the equivalent of a couple of marathons a day, every day, until they either dropped from exhaustion or reached New York City. Even coming from a man known for being outlandish, the idea seemed too far-fetched.

For the previous 2 years, one of sportswriters' favorite pastimes was scorning Pyle. He had jumped onto the national scene by officially signing Red Grange as his first client on November 21, 1925. The young collegiate football player became a superstar when, in the aftermath of a phenomenal game, sportswriter Grantland Rice composed football poetry describing Grange as a ghost. It was this poem that led to his nickname, the Galloping Ghost, but it was Pyle who harnessed the Galloping Ghost's energy and made him a star. Pyle had approached Grange in 1924 and, after many months, signed the young man as his first client. It was a bold move for Pyle, who was an obscure theatre manager in Champaign, Illinois, Grange's hometown. In hindsight, it's easy to see why Grange fell under his spell: Pyle was awfully persuasive and had been waiting for a moment like this for much of his life.

At nearly 6 feet tall with broad shoulders, Pyle dressed impeccably, usually sporting a black suit and black derby, hiding a well-groomed patch of yellowish gray hair. The following year, the *New Yorker* would compare Pyle's neatly trimmed mustache to that of W. C. Fields, who used to sport a fake one in his silent films, although he dropped the look by his more famous films of the 1930s and 1940s. C. C. Pyle looked like a man of money and influence, and he was, after years of trying. His initials, sports journalists joked, stood for "Cash and Carry," and Pyle embraced the nickname. Even a few years before meeting up with Grange, Pyle was earning a respectable living, but after representing the athlete, his income accelerated dramatically.

But it wasn't Pyle's appearance that made him so convincing. The man could talk. "He is," one newspaper later wrote, "a Scotch-Irishman with twinkling gray eyes, who immediately takes you in, in the warmth of his greeting and his general good fellowship."

From a financial standpoint, the theatrical manager–turned–sports promoter immediately proved his word was as good as gold. Eleven days into his new career, Grange was richer by $82,000, playing several games with a ragtag operation called the Chicago Bears. On his 12th day, Grange earned another $300,000 after agreeing to appear in the movie *One Minute to Play*, released in 1926. The following year he starred in *A Racing Romeo*.

For $12,000, Grange also agreed to have his name associated with a sweater. His approval for the creation of a Red Grange football doll rang up another $10,000. He then endorsed a brand of shoes for $5,000, a ginger ale for another $5,000, and a cap for $2,500. Pyle even convinced a cigarette firm to pay Grange in the neighborhood of $10,000 to endorse their brand. It didn't matter that Grange was known as a nonsmoker. All he had to say was that if he ever were to take up smoking, he felt sure that he'd like that brand.

From there, Pyle began representing tennis amateurs, turning them professional and laying the groundwork for a professional circuit. He also started to organize a hockey league in March 1927. Finally wealthy and well known, if Pyle had an idea and a spare few minutes, he tried to implement it.

But this plan for a national foot race did little more than make a lot of people shake their heads, some in admiration, others in irritation.

Injury or death was a common argument against Pyle's transcontinental race. One prominent medical expert, Dr. K. H. Begg, predicted that 5 to 10 years would be shaved off the runners' lives. Clarence DeMar, famed for frequently winning the Boston Marathon, declined to participate in Pyle's epic adventure. He believed that no human being could run the equivalent of two Boston Marathons a day, every day, for several months. If their bodies didn't give out, their minds would, DeMar reasoned, from the monotony of running all day for months.

But the thrill of endurance contests was worth the risk, even if you risked all and lost, according to William Hickman Pickens, Pyle's close friend and crucial executive for the past few years. He had said as much in his days as a promoter, in a lengthy 1909 monologue he delivered to the *Los Angeles Times*.

"Well, the boys were a bit unlucky today," shrugged off Bill Pickens when a reporter had asked about automobile racers crashing into fences. "But what do you expect from the automobile racing game? If you cut out the danger and fence-smashing stunts, the crowds would not be attracted, and the sport would be relegated to the bean-bag class. We are living in a fast age, and the professional athlete who is willing to sacrifice his bones and gore on the altar of a highly seasoned sport is the man of the hour in his line.

"You don't believe that Barney Oldfield thinks the crowd comes to see him break records or to witness his wonderful control over a modern juggernaut that goes crazy with the heat, do you? Not on your life. Barney often puffs one of those six-inch perfectos and laughs, and he tells how they all come to the races when he drives, for no other purpose than hoping to see him in a smashup. They have heard so much of his different accidents and have read so often of his supposedly charmed life that they don't want to miss a chance of being 'in at the death.'"

What also appeared questionable to rational people was not just what so many miles would do to the body, but that this race wouldn't be on a running track. It would be *on the roads*.

The federal highway system was still in its infancy in 1928. Ultimately, Pyle selected Highway 66, later more famously known as Route 66. A modern marvel of interstate stretching from Los Angeles to Chicago, it was only 2 years old, largely unpaved, and it wouldn't be completely finished until 1937. The most consistently paved roads wouldn't appear until the runners were deep into Missouri, where it would remain automobile-friendly until Chicago. From there the runners would take a hodgepodge of state routes to New York City, many of the surfaces paved, but some not.

C. C. Pyle imagined runners, with only the poorest footwear, traveling over a highway of pavement as well as dirt, gravel, cement-covered bricks, and in a few stretches, wooden planks. In 1878, a *New York Times* editorial made an observation that was still true in 1928: "It would be impossible to form any accurate estimate of the enormous amount of human suffering that has been caused by boots and shoes. It is true that no man in his senses wears tight shoes, but even the loosest shoe, when new, is stiff and uncomfortable. To break in a new pair of shoes is something every man dreads only less than the annual visit to the dentist."

Shoe companies in 1928 were making a tidy business offering the public everything they could think of to cure their aching feet. Corns, a thickening of skin that collects around the toes, scored high on the foot misery index, but the worst were bunions—a knotting of the muscle and disfigurement of the foot, typically caused by tight footwear. Shoe companies were selling everything from bunion plasters—an application pasted to the bunion—to soothing foot balm. The Coward Good Sense Shoe for Bunions flourished before 1900 and after. In fact, Coward Shoes as a brand thrives in the 21st century.

From building the Erie Canal to inventing flight, Americans had toiled for 150 years to do everything possible to avoid walking, let alone running, across the country. No wonder sportswriters scoffed when Pyle plotted his national foot race. Most people in the country didn't even personally know an avid runner. Only 168 men competed in the 1927 Boston Marathon. In comparison, 40,000 men and women showed up at the Centennial Boston Marathon in 1996.

The journalists' skepticism led to a typical exchange when C. C. Pyle averred that he would have physicians examine the runners before they began the race.

"First, they will examine their feet," said Pyle, prompting a guffaw from someone in the crowd. "What's the idea?" demanded Pyle, who hadn't thought he had said anything funny.

"Well, if a man enters a 3,000-mile foot race, the first thing to examine is his head."

With such snickering, there was no chance that any self-respecting sportswriter could put the wordy, pretentious name in their articles day after day: "C. C. Pyle's First Annual International Transcontinental Foot Race, From Los Angeles to New York."

To avoid Pyle's unwieldy title, a sportswriter came up with a short catchphrase, which everyone else adopted. It was based on the nation's collective experience and history with foot problems. It was a nickname that stuck, that everyone eagerly embraced except C. C. Pyle. They called it the Bunion Derby.

CHAPTER 2

Paul "Hardrock" Simpson was a natural-born runner, but the Bunion Derby was almost his undoing. (Courtesy of the Simpson family.)

BALLYHOO

JUNE 1927, BURLINGTON, NORTH CAROLINA

Twenty-two-year-old college student Paul Simpson was in training, running along the main road in Burlington, when he came to a pothole. He dodged it, but he should have stayed put.

Simpson stepped right in front of a car. Seconds later, he was under it.

It dragged him for "some distance," the local paper reported, until Nellie Jarrett managed to stop her car. Not long after, Simpson's head, which usually sported a crew cut, was wrapped with strands of gauze. Easygoing and honest, he admitted to his hometown newspaper, "It was my fault."

Simpson's speedy recovery more than justified his lifelong nickname. Back in high school, his friends, impressed that in 2 years on the football team he never sat on the bench, had taken to calling him "Hardrock." The name stuck for good reason. A war veteran, Simpson could take a beating. When Hardrock was 15, he lied about his age and joined the army, helping to mop up the mess in the aftermath of World War I.

Anyone who knew Hardrock wasn't surprised that he entered a foot race from one end of the country to the other. The only surprise was that Hardrock was the 37th person to sign up, and not the first.

He was a little late with the entry form and fee probably because he had been immersed in his studies, a year at Elon College behind him. Worried about how he would pay his sophomore year's tuition, he figured that any of the prize money C. C. Pyle was offering could pay for his education—with money to spare, if he finished at the top of the heap. Grover L. Clark, a World War veteran and local fireman, convinced Hardrock that he needed representation if he was going to undertake Pyle's epic race. Clark went to work for his client immediately, signing him up for a local race.

Hardrock could use that race to train for Pyle's grueling challenge, Clark reasoned, and if he won the local race, the $500 prize could pay the expenses he'd likely incur during a lengthy run across the country. After all, while Pyle was promising room and board, a little spare change couldn't hurt. For instance, during the course of the race, Simpson would likely have to buy shoes and socks, which were guaranteed to wear out. And that's how, on September 5, 1927, Hardrock found himself in a foot race against a Texas pony named Maude. They were to run from Burlington to Morehead City and back, a distance of 500 miles. It was a race expected to take several days, and Simpson expected to sleep that night in the town of Clayton, a distance of 75 miles away, though it's unclear if either party was required to run that far on the first leg, or if it was just every man and beast for themselves to determine when and how far they should run each day.

Hardrock showed up at the fire station, where the race was to begin, at 7:00 a.m., an hour before the start time. Maude emerged nearby, in front of the First National Bank, at 7:45. Five minutes before the start of the race, Simpson took his spot, and Owen Faucette led his pony near the young man. Anxious, Simpson stripped off his sweatshirt and pants, revealing shorts and a gauze shirt that read, "Bigger, Better Burlington." There was a short speech reminding the competitors of the route for the race, and moments later, the fire chief shot a pistol into the air. Hardrock took off, "and, like a trans-Atlantic plane, had vanished in half a second," reported his hometown newspaper. Maude began with a walk, but soon she was galloping.

So was Hardrock. The streets of Burlington were mobbed, and 4 miles down the road, in the tiny village of Haw River, young women threw roses at Simpson as he raced up the hill. Maude was still behind, but closing the gap, and soon after, the horse overtook him, creating a substantial lead.

Hardrock kept running, and after several more miles, he barreled forward and passed the pony again, as a stunned Faucette helplessly watched. By Durham, 35 miles away from Burlington, Hardrock had a lead of approximately 7 miles. By evening, 62 miles away from Burlington, in Raleigh, with the traffic heavy, Hardrock and his manager, following in a Chrysler, decided that it was time for the runner to call it a day. Having been hit by a car recently, Hardrock was in no mood to repeat the experience. Besides, Maude was nowhere in sight.

But the next day, as Hardrock ran through Clayton at around 8:45 in the morning, he and Maude were pretty much neck and neck. "Rock feeling fine," wired Clark. Unfortunately, so was Maude. Later that afternoon, in the town of Princeton, Faucette likely felt relieved that Maude was ahead of Hardrock—but only ahead by 2 miles. And for all of those miles, hundreds of cars were lined up against the road, cheering both man and beast on.

Not everyone was enthusiastic. On one street in Raleigh, three thugs began running alongside Hardrock, and one of them grabbed at his shirt. "I'm not a fighting man," snapped Hardrock, and then he sprinted forward, leaving the men behind.

Then, just 5 miles away, in Garner, a mob of people stormed through the village, chasing Hardrock. The suspicious villagers had heard of a sweaty man in shorts and short sleeves running toward their town, alongside a man on a horse, and they had decided that Hardrock must be insane, perhaps an escapee from the Dix Hill asylum in Raleigh. Hardrock's manager wasn't around, but a traveling salesman stopped the crowd from turning ugly. He informed them of the race, and Hardrock was able to slip through Garner unharmed.

Other cities throughout the day provided police escorts, allowing Hardrock to race through red lights. In one town, Hardrock sprinted into a drugstore and, while jogging in place, consumed a glass of milk. "Got no money," Hardrock huffed. "Stop my official car, and Clark will pay you." The drugstore owner, apparently quite impressed, told Clark that the milk was on the house.

Then, on the third day, it came to an abrupt end. Hardrock had limped into Kinston, North Carolina, the evening before, having run a total of 145 miles, and after looking at his foot, Clark suggested that he see a doctor. The next morning, a physician examined Hardrock and insisted that he either quit the race or risk blood poisoning. It was his toe, mostly, that was in such poor shape. An argument ensued, but Hardrock finally came to his senses. Maude was just 5 miles up the road and in no shape to go anywhere either. A truck was sent to pick up Maude and bring her back to Burlington.

Faucette figured it was just as well. He conceded that while Maude had run 5 more miles than Hardrock, she wouldn't have been able to resume a run either. Additionally, Faucette didn't feel too well. "Simpson and the pony are tired all right," he agreed, "but what about me? I was glad to get out of it—that saddle became a very uncomfortable seat."

Hardrock returned to his hometown a hero. He didn't get his $500, and the people who gambled on him lost. But Hardrock would forever be a local legend anyway. In his hometown of Burlington, the story gradually changed over the days and decades, the tale told with a slightly more dramatic ending: Hardrock stopped running after learning that the horse, which was many miles behind him, had dropped dead from exhaustion. Close enough.

And there was no doubt among the townspeople that summer of 1927. Everyone in his hometown and the surrounding areas agreed: This guy was going to win Pyle's race.

1927, Granite City, Illinois

Frank Johnson, a 38-year-old steelworker from Granite City, Illinois, a suburb of St. Louis, was every bit the typical middle-class American. He and his wife, Clara, along with their two children, lived in an unremarkable house and had unremarkable lives. In fact, that normalcy may have been what attracted Johnson to the outrageous idea of running across the country.

Pyle's prize money was also a powerful draw. Johnson was providing for his wife of 17 years, as well as their kids, Alice, 14, and Frank Jr., 9. Clara's father, Henry Grothjahn, 60, a night watchman at the steel mill, lived with them as well, and Pyle's promised thousands teased the family's imagination.

Johnson worked at Commonwealth Steel Company, one of the largest employers in his community, an operation that had existed since the Civil War. They specialized in building locomotive engines, although he primarily worked on automobiles.

Johnson ran marathons in his younger days, and so he felt like he had as realistic a shot of winning the prize money as anyone. He couldn't afford to leave his job for the 3 months that runners were expected to be on the road, however, obliging him and Clara to raise cash from friends, family, and anyone who had a spare dollar, to replace the income they'd lose while he was away. But it was a risk worth taking, Frank Johnson reasoned, if they ever wanted their lives to be anything more than unremarkable.

Clara didn't see it that way. She thought the endurance fads were an affront to civilization.

1927, Columbia, South Carolina

In his second year of college, Morris Saperstein, 21, was planning a career in law, studying at the University of South Carolina. But if he couldn't raise enough money for tuition, he was going to be out on the street.

Morris would have asked his father for advice, but Louis Saperstein was no longer around. Four years earlier, when Morris was 17 and in the midst of preparing for college, his life had detoured into a hospital room with his mother, Fannie, and his five sisters. They spent a weeklong deathwatch with Louis, a Russian immigrant who had come to America in 1902 and begun a home-building business. He had been a hardy soul before suffering a ruptured appendix. The doctors had no way of treating it beyond trying to keep him comfortable, which he wasn't.

After Louis's last gasp, Morris had felt numb and rudderless. When his uncle stepped in with the money to fund 2 years of his college, Saperstein threw himself into his education, making the most of a chance to build a solid future for himself. But now that the money was running out, he was going to lose that, too.

1927, Kerman, California

Frank Von Flue read about Pyle's race with a lot of interest and curiosity. He loved sports and had dreamed of scoring touchdowns or hitting balls out of the park and especially of lunging across the finish line in an Olympic track meet. But the coaches at his high school in Dos Palos, California, had felt he was too small to do them any good, so he had gone through 3 years without participating in any form of organized athletics. Then, as his senior year started in 1920, his family's farm went through a crisis, and Von Flue took a break from schooling to help out at the ranch owned by his parents, Frank and Lulu.

In the fall of 1926, Von Flue finally returned to high school in Kerman, California. The coaches would have liked to have him join a team, but at 24, Von Flue was too old.

After graduation, Von Flue felt aimless. So in the spring of 1927, when he read of Pyle's race in the paper, he immediately began weighing the pros and cons of entering. On the debit side, Von Flue had virtually no experience in sports, and hadn't for about 10 years. On the credit side, he had worked on a farm for years and was in better-than-average physical shape. All he needed was to raise some money for the entry fee and travel deposit home, and he could be allowed in. And if he won, the money could change the direction of his rather directionless life.

But this was all moot if he couldn't figure out how to enter the race. When the summer of 1927 came, Von Flue was still uncertain of the details. Every day, he scanned his hometown newspaper for some new story on the race, some scrap of information, but there was nothing. Then he read of the Redwood Marathon in northern California, along a new highway, and he thought that would at least be a good event to try, to practice for the upcoming nationwide race. Von Flue contacted the marathon's officials and learned that it was a sporting event for American Indians only. Of Swiss heritage, Von Flue accepted this, but he couldn't help feeling frustrated.

1927, Goshen, Indiana

So far, it looked as though the only breaks part-time boxer Dean Pletcher was destined for required hospital stays.

Also a professional woodworker, Pletcher wasn't too thrilled with either of his jobs. In fact, at 25, he felt his entire existence was unfulfilling. Besides being stuck in two unsatisfying careers, he was already divorced and living with his 44-year-old mother, Pearl. His father had died when he was 3, and from then on, it had been Pearl and Dean Pletcher against the world.

When Pletcher learned about Pyle's transcontinental race, he realized that it could catapult him into a new life of what he craved—fame. This athletic odyssey could finally give him the national platform he needed to transform himself into a household name.

It may have been rural Indiana, in 1928, a place and time that were incongruous to lusting for a life of fame and fortune, but there was no shortage of press on celebrities Dean wished to trade lives with. In Pletcher's boxing universe, Jack Dempsey was the towering figure all bowed down to, until 1927, when he was finally flattened in a fight. Babe Ruth was as legendary as they came. In the movies, Douglas Fairbanks, Harold Lloyd, and Rin Tin Tin ruled the box office. Henry Ford was making his cars, Albert Einstein was a star in the sciences, and even crime had its Al Capone. Fame, Pletcher recognized, was a sort of currency. If you had a fortune and lost it, you might be out of luck indefinitely. As long as you had fame, you could make money forever.

Dean Pletcher wanted to be remembered, and his boxing career didn't look promising. After giving it some thought, he decided that Pyle's race might offer him a chance to completely start over. His name and entire persona, however, lacked a certain something. It was too ordinary, perhaps, or too American. So before embarking on Pyle's grand road trip, Pletcher changed his identity. His mother had a habit of lying about her age, so he decided to follow suit. He began telling everyone he was 19, to possibly be regarded as an exciting newcomer instead of a full-fledged grown-up. Then he gave himself a new name, using one that felt more dashing, one that could be said in an Irish brogue. He wouldn't go to the trouble of legalizing it, but from then on he would almost always be known as Mike Kelly. Maybe Dean Pletcher didn't think of the irony as he shed his old identity and prepared for this great race, but it's an unavoidable conclusion: He was running away.

1927, Foyil, Oklahoma

Naturally, there was a girl involved.

Vivian Shaddox was 19 when she entered Andy Payne's life in a most inconvenient way: as his math teacher. Miss Shaddox was only a few months older than Payne, but as his instructor, she might as well have been 30 years his senior.

Vivian was like no one Payne had ever met, though of course she would have to be. Foyil, Oklahoma, wasn't exactly a hotbed of single women. Still, he would have fallen for her anyway. She had wavy brown locks that fell over her left eye if she wasn't careful, and like her shoulder-length hair, Vivian was untamed. As with many young women her age, there was a determination about her, something that set her apart from women of her mother's generation and the generation that followed. She wasn't a woman programmed to submissively follow a man's orders. In the truest sense of the phrase, Vivian was a modern woman. She was a free spirit—or, as everyone called the young, progressive-thinking ladies of the day, a flapper—and she didn't need the Chicago skyline or a Harlem nightclub to prove it either. She drove a car, smoked, and—heavens to Betsy—wore slacks. It's no stretch to imagine the flask of bootleg gin in her back hip pocket.

Payne was smitten.

Even Vivian's career—perfectly logical for a woman in 1928—wasn't an avenue she took because she wanted to fit in with the times. Her younger sister, Olga, was the teacher in the family, the one who found her calling in education and led the more orthodox lifestyle. Vivian came to Northeastern State Teachers College because her parents had asked her to, in order to watch over Olga. Taking the Foyil position was perfectly in keeping with Vivian's personality—it seemed like a good way to achieve some independence from the rest of her family and earn extra money.

Payne was still in high school when they met before Christmas 1926, and Vivian remained in his life until the spring of 1927, when classes ended. She then returned to Tahlequah, a town east of Tulsa, ending their brief acquaintance, even though Andy hoped it had been just the beginning.

Payne, who had Cherokee in his genetic makeup, possessed an easygoing smile and curly hair. Vivian may have found him attractive, but he looked his age, if not younger. He knew his odds of winning over his slightly older, more worldly schoolteacher were slim, but he fell in love anyway. Vivian left after graduation, and so eventually did Andy, although he didn't venture anywhere near her. As he had the previous summer, he hopped a freight train and headed for California. Work was plentiful in the summer, and farmers always needed to hire some help. He would make his way for a time in California, return home for the fall harvest, and ponder his future.

Before Payne returned, however, he saw a poster advertising C. C. Pyle's great race. As he rode the rails back home, he thought about the implications of winning such a race. He could buy a car. He could pay off his parents' farm. He could go to college. Most of all, he would surely impress Vivian. And all he had to do was run across the entire country—faster than anyone else. Payne was just young and naïve enough to think he might be able to pull it off.

He returned to Foyil with a new sense of purpose. He was so confident about his chances that he wrote Vivian to tell her his plans.

Vivian didn't share her first reaction with Andy, which was just as well. After reading the letter she had only one thought: He must be crazy.

Late Spring and Summer of 1927

"Tell her no women will be permitted to run," said Pyle to his secretary, in New York City, where they were squirreled away—likely in his hotel suite—after the promoter heard about an inquiry for race information from a Mrs. Frank Cooley in Springfield, Missouri.

C. C. Pyle was forward-thinking in many respects—all races and ethnicities were welcomed into the race, provided they had their entry fees. The only color he recognized was green, on a dollar bill. But the thought of a woman running across the country in 1928 was laughable, even for many women themselves.

There was scant evidence that women could endure such a grueling physical trial, although one recent accomplishment had proven that they might have been up to the task. In the early summer of 1926, in Chihuahua, Mexico, the Tarahumaras tribe, known for their skill in long-distance marathon running, held a 70-mile competition involving 30 women. They started running at 5:00 p.m., and 14 hours later two women tied for first place.

"The betting was so furious and exciting," the *Los Angeles Times* reported, "that many Tarahumaras lost all their earthly possessions on the result of that great race."

For a brief period, Pyle imagined a race where the male runners would scurry pell-mell and unsupervised as they raced across the United States, leaving it up to the honor system that no one would slip into a boxcar and knock several hundred miles off his run. As interesting as his idea would have been, common sense prevailed: They would monitor the runners.

There was more tinkering with Pyle's ideas. When he announced his race to the world, the event was open to any man. Then, on June 21, Pyle asserted in the *Los Angeles Times* that only professional runners could enter. By the end of July, however, he returned to the original plan: Any man of any ethnicity or degree of athletic experience was welcome.

Pyle spent a good portion of the summer and autumn traveling to Europe to sign up runners. He wanted the finest marathon men available, including the one whom he credited for inspiring his race. It had been one year earlier, April 29, 1926, when an unlikely hero had run an impromptu marathon over untamed Moroccan deserts and roads.

Hammouch Ben Hadge was a Riffian warrior, a native of the Spanish-occupied portion of Morocco. Six years after a 1920 rebellion, Riffian leader Abd el-Krim had a message he wanted delivered to a peace conference in the town of Oujda, in what was then known as French Morocco. Abd el-Krim chose his messenger wisely.

Hadge took off running at sunrise and didn't stop until sunset. When he arrived at Oujda, he delivered the statement just before passing out—"No peace without autonomy."

His message led to the end of the war, but the rest of the world was more taken by the messenger. Everyone was slack-jawed that Hadge had run 70 miles in one day. He was 67.

C. C. Pyle couldn't help being impressed by the warrior's athleticism, but he dwelled on the fact that Hadge hadn't been running in an auditorium, surrounded by a cheering—and paying—crowd. Suddenly, Pyle had his idea for a national foot race.

As it turned out, Hadge was unavailable or uninterested. But it was no matter; Pyle kept working out the details of staging this odyssey, even while pursuing other interests. Charles Lindbergh made his famed solo flight across the Atlantic Ocean on May 20 to 21, 1927, almost a month after Pyle announced his nationwide race. Pyle, like the rest of the nation, was captivated by the performance, but not for the same reasons. He thought about how much money there was to be made by representing Lindbergh.

Within days after the historic flight, Pyle met with Lindbergh's financial backers, offering to become the pilot's theatrical manager.

One idea that Pyle presented was to bring Lindbergh to Yankee Stadium with his airplane, surrounded by an audience of people in the stands and in the infield. Pyle would charge $3 or $4 a head, and everyone would make a fortune. Alas, the investors declined.

"They told me they were going to commercialize his feat in a small way, maybe $300,000 or $400,000, and let it go at that. They talked of putting him in one picture," said Pyle to a reporter shortly after his meeting. "I told them the best they could get was $50,000 and a percentage of the profits. It seems to me that if he wants to do something for aviation, he ought to make as much money as he possibly can in the next year or two and salt it away. There would be millions for him, if he were handled right—millions."

Pyle couldn't resist adding: "Now about this foot race from Los Angeles to New York, I wouldn't be surprised if interest in the winner of that exceeded even the public interest toward Lindbergh. For one thing, it will last more than 2 months, over 3,100 miles, gaining momentum as it proceeds."

In show business lineage, C. C. Pyle considered himself an heir to P. T. Barnum. Every move Pyle made was calculated to attract the public and then convince them to part with their coins and bills. He was an entrepreneur long before the term was popularized, but more than that, he was a showman. Pyle loved money but prided himself on giving the public their money's worth as well. There was certainly money involved with this show.

Pyle would never be mistaken for a humanitarian, but his contest prom
a better future to the small pool of runners who might finish the race.
first-place prize of $25,000 was a lot of income for anyone, but to a l
section of the populace, including men like Frank Johnson, Morris Sa
stein, and Andy Payne, it was much more than that. It was a way out o
darkness.

CHAPTER 3

Along with endurance fads, the flapper epitomizes the 1920s. Flapper *was a term coined to describe a new type of woman emerging throughout the decade, one that was self-reliant and forward thinking, which perfectly describes Vivian, who was much of Andy Payne's motivation for running in the Bunion Derby. (Courtesy of the Vivian S. Payne collection.)*

A Deceptive Road

July 1927, Buffalo, New York

The man on the flagpole waved to the crowd below as he sat on his chair, though it was more of a stool. It was just 13 inches wide and had no back support. If the man ever forgot where he was and reclined, he would have felt a wave of terror as he watched the clouds travel farther and farther away.

The man was Alvin Aloysius "Shipwreck" Kelly, and if the stories about him are true, he lived a memorable life long before he began spending his time sitting on flagpoles for days and weeks at a stretch. Kelly was said to have earned his nickname as a survivor of the *Titanic*, served in the navy during World War I, and had a stint as an airplane stunt performer.

"He knows what he's doing," Kelly's wife promised. "Why should I worry?"

She had a point. He was paid $1,000 per week to promote everything from vaudeville theatres to banks. His latest stunt was on the Andrews Building, near a Loew's theatre. After a week, the plan was to bring the

flagpole sitter to Loew's to discuss his experiences and, of course, to attract a paying crowd. That the public would pay to hear Kelly talk was virtually guaranteed, and had been ever since he scaled his first flagpole in 1924.

One man guaranteed not to be in the audience was Buffalo mayor Frank X. Schwab, who was certain that the public menace was going to fall off the flagpole to his death and that he would be blamed. After Kelly had been atop the pole for over 24 hours, Schwab asked a judge, "What if he would faint in the heat?"

The judge couldn't offer a suitable answer, but Schwab's question was reasonable; a heat wave had killed two people in Buffalo and 33 others throughout New England in the last few days. Schwab ordered a policeman to bring the flagpole sitter down.

Shipwreck Kelly coolly challenged the officer: "Come and get me."

The confrontation only made the public more curious in the ensuing drama. And while the mayor believed Kelly would fall asleep and just fall, the flagpole sitter had a safeguard. He jammed his thumbs tightly into holes in the seat; if he dozed and began to topple off, the pain from the thumbs would jolt him awake.

In his chair, Kelly shaved, ate, and did his business when nature called, behind a little curtain with a bucket.

Kelly was always on his best behavior: unassuming, friendly, and polite—especially to the boys with slingshots. And because of it, when Kelly descended the pole in Buffalo a week later, using a rope that Mayor Schwab would have loved to hang him from, 15,000 newly earned fans were in the streets, cheering and honking horns.

C. C. PYLE wanted to harness the enthusiasm people reserved for luminaries like Shipwreck Kelly and use it to create his own stars, something of a master race of marathon men. He envisioned taking the best of the runners from his cross-country odyssey and showing them off in exhibitions and competitions around the nation.

Pyle was part of a breed of colorful promoters who thrived during the 1920s. They were all aware that their success depended on entertaining the public via the press, telling a compelling story of human drama. Had the promoters of the 1920s been around to see the first episode of CBS's *Survivor* when it premiered in May 2000, they would have enjoyed the drama but also wondered what the fuss was about. The endurance competitions were reality shows that, like the television genre, distorted reality by bringing in a group of average citizens to compete for a prize while being watched by the world. And the surrounding drama of the event was frequently more interesting than the event itself.

Tex Rickard was one of the biggest names in sports promotion, known primarily in the boxing world. His name was splashed on the sports page almost daily since he had promoted the famous James T. Jeffries and Jack Johnson fight in 1910. In more recent years, he advanced the career of boxing legend Jack Dempsey.

Milton Crandall was well known for his dance marathons, getting his experience as a publicist in Hollywood. In 1923, Denver newspaper reporters raced up to Pikes Peak, following a crazy rumor that a whale was beached on top of the 14,100-foot mountain. Sure enough, when they got there, they saw occasional sprays of water shooting into the air, just beyond the peak, with hundreds of people watching and shouting, "Thar she blows!"

Crandall was behind the rocks, spraying seltzer water into the air. But he got what he wanted: publicity for *Down to the Sea in Ships,* a Clara Bow film now considered "culturally significant" and important enough to be slated for preservation in the National Film Registry.

Pyle vaulted himself into the same league, a bigger name than Crandall, though not quite as prominent as Rickard. But that seemed likely to change with Pyle's latest project. For an undertaking this grand, however, he couldn't do it alone.

Red Grange was as much a business partner as a client, but Pyle had another partner of sorts—his secret weapon and close friend, Bill Pickens, an experienced promoter who had been promoting off-the-wall events for more than a quarter of a century. That he was possibly shiftier than Pyle was also a bonus.

Pickens's career in public relations began in 1900, when he was 23 and fascinated with the "999," a race car created by none other than Henry Ford.

Ford hired Pickens, a former bicycle racer, to promote the 999 and hired Barney Oldfield, another bicycle racer, to drive it. Oldfield, who would go on to fame in 1903 as the first driver to ever race a mile a minute, had already become acquainted with Pickens's future business colleague, C. C. Pyle. Oldfield grew up in Ohio and rode in several bicycle races in and around Marion, a town a few miles from Delaware, Pyle's hometown.

Pyle arranged a race between the young Oldfield and a teenager, some outmatched cluck with the last name of Holden. The way Pyle told it, he had plotted out all the details, including Oldfield's travel expenses. When the bicycle race concluded, Holden walked away with nothing, Oldfield took $25 in prize money, and Pyle turned a profit of $7.

Pickens was just starting his career when he promoted the 999, but he was good at what he did, and 4 years later he staged the first international balloon race, sponsored by newspaper magnate Gordon Bennett. Throughout his life Pickens called the balloon race an "artistic success," which was his way of saying that it was unprofitable.

For most of the 1910s, Pickens was involved in promoting stunt flying, always willing to risk a pilot's life as long as it meant a thrilling show for the public. By the time Pickens hooked up with Pyle to help manage Grange and a burgeoning number of tennis stars, his auto and aviation days were behind him. But when Pyle decided to hold a nationwide foot race, they were returning to Pickens's roots. It was an undertaking fraught with peril.

William F. Prouty found this out—that is, if he had any sense of what was happening to him. On December 14, 1927, the 47-year-old sheet-metal worker for a railroad company in Boston spent a long day at the gym, as he had most of the year while training for Pyle's great race.

As early as 1906, Prouty had entered the Boston Marathon and come in ninth. His longest race had covered 598 miles, and in the summer of 1927 he ran 70 miles, achieving a new world record by racing it in 11 hours, 17 minutes, and 32 seconds. Pyle had already said that Prouty was one of his "prize" entrants, and co-workers were so proud and confident that they had already pledged him economic support during the course of the lengthy run.

But Prouty was training for a race more than 3,000 miles long and probably overexerting himself. That December evening, he left the gym and went home, where, quite suddenly, he died.

Your mind might be ready to enter an endurance contest, but that doesn't necessarily mean your body is up to the task. A. F. Conrad was a typical victim. In 1923, he collapsed in Baltimore after dancing for 42 hours. When his partner pulled him to his feet, he snapped, shoving her and swaying toward the orchestra. "Stop that playing! I can't stand it!" he screamed, cursing as dance officials led him away.

Joe "Hold 'Em" Powers was in a class by himself. Though not as well-known as Shipwreck Kelly, Powers had his own fans, who were impressed by his tenacity for flagpole sitting. One of his longer stunts was for the Morrison Hotel in Chicago for part of the summer in 1927.

The man had stamina. Powers lost two teeth when a stiff breeze knocked him into his pole. He sweated in 94-degree heat and stayed on the flagpole even when an electrical storm passed overhead. The storm's powerful winds knocked over a Ferris wheel at a nearby church carnival, and a tent pole impaled a very unfortunate man.

Still, Powers survived it all, remaining on his pole for 2 weeks and collecting his paycheck.

Hopefully, Powers appreciated irony. Several months later, while installing lights at a theatre in his hometown of Lancaster, Ohio, Powers fell off a ladder. He dropped 40 feet, broke both wrists, fractured his left leg below the knee, and incurred a heavy blow to the head, effectively ending his flagpole-sitting career.

CHAPTER 4

Two of England's finest runners, Arthur Newton (left), who by this time was living in South Africa, and Pete Gavuzzi (right). (Courtesy of Guy Gavuzzi.)

California Dreaming

January 7, 1928, England

The roads flooded, the wind smacked against his face, and snow fell. Nevertheless, Arthur Newton achieved a world record, running a distance of 100 miles in the fastest time ever.

Wanting to finish his one-man race in the daylight, the South African began at 2:00 a.m., and by dawn Londoners crowded each other on sidewalks, cheering him on.

Into his epic odyssey, Newton became ill but kept running, pausing to eat a bowl of minced fresh beef but not stopping to drink. In fact, his only sustenance had been his "magic drink," an elixir of lemon juice and salt, which he slugged down before he began moving. When it was all over, his time was 14 hours and 22 minutes, which beat the old record by 20 minutes and 50 seconds. After finishing, Newton flopped to the ground. Everyone applauded, even as he was rushed to a hospital.

One month later, Newton agreed to give up his amateur status and turn professional, entering C. C. Pyle's international transcontinental foot race and aiming to win the prize money.

Of all the admired runners that Pyle had convinced to participate, and there were many, Arthur Newton was the best. Even into the 21st century, rabid runners still revere him. Pyle was elated to be associated with the man, and for Newton, the timing felt right.

Born in Somersetshire, England, in 1883, Newton had moved to South Africa in 1901, following one of his brothers. The next year, Newton began doing clerical work and, after a short career as a teacher, became a cotton farmer. He had only begun running several years earlier because of a land dispute with his government: He wanted to sell some property that the government wouldn't allow him to, and he thought that if he took up a sport like running and became an established figure, he could draw attention to his plight. However convoluted his logic, Newton found his life's passion, establishing himself as one of the world's greatest runners.

Newton's involvement was a coup for the sports promoter, but it seemed like a pragmatic decision for the runner, as he later explained in his 1940 autobiography *Running in Three Continents*: "Naturally enough, I did not want to relinquish my amateur status, but common sense always struck me as being worth more than anything else. As a man of over forty, with no outlook and no pension, it was obvious that, being one of the best-trained men in the world for long distances, I should do well to consider it."

Newton had some tenderness in his tendons, but he signed up for the race, figuring that even if he didn't go very far, he could learn something about the cross-country course. After all, Pyle had said that he wanted to make this race an annual affair.

JANUARY 1928

The autumn of 1927 dragged by for Andy Payne, but he kept busy. Knowing he needed financial backing to travel to Los Angeles and spend months running on the open road, Payne begged the deep-pocketed Oklahoma City Chamber of Commerce to sponsor him, but they declined. Next, he went to Tulsa, hoping they'd bite, since the city was closer to his hometown of Foyil. Once more, Payne was waved away. Finally, he appealed to the mayor of Claremore, a little town next to Foyil.

Claremore had a modest tax base, but unlike Foyil, which was barely a village, it was a thriving community, with a bank, a post office, a library, and a mayor. It also maintained a national presence because of its most famous resident: cowboy, comedian, newspaper columnist, and future radio star Will Rogers, who kept strong ties to the area. There was also a chamber of commerce, and, taken with the young man, its members agreed to help fund Payne's quest to run across the continent. They also believed that putting the spotlight on Claremore would help tourism. The town possessed something special that few other communities in the country had: radium water.

Throughout Claremore were bathhouses, wells, and springs featuring radium water. It was the town's economic engine, drawing in millions of tourists from around the world ever since the city officials began marketing their product in 1903, after a farmer drilling for oil discovered an underground spring that smelled like rotten eggs. It was soon determined that Claremore had radium in its water—hence the nickname Radium Town. Payne, in working out the details to get Claremore's financial backing, happily agreed to promote radium water whenever he got the chance.

Ever since Madame Curie discovered radium in Paris around the turn of the century, the world believed quite wrongly that it had found not just an ordinary mineral but one with medicinal qualities. Rich Europeans started drinking radium water for their health, slowly killing themselves, about the time several Claremore businessmen began raising money to build bathhouses and more wells to entice the rest of the country to come drink and bathe in radioactive water.

Fortunately, Claremore was hopelessly misinformed. There was no serious amount of radium in the water, just a lot of impurities like sulfur. But it certainly seemed like special water. After all, whenever horses, cattle, hogs, and dogs waded into a creek that the well had created, their skin diseases soon disappeared and their cuts and bruises healed.

On the other hand, frogs, turtles, snakes, and the vegetation surrounding the creek were all dead.

But drinking and bathing in Claremore's "radium water" was still far healthier than drinking and bathing in actual radium water.

Andy's father, meanwhile, a busy farmer who was known to everyone as Doc, kept trying to get his son to focus not on the race and getting a sponsor but on completing his chores. One morning, Doc was pleased to see his boy's bed empty at 4:00 and thought he must be doing what he had been asked to do, feeding and harnessing the family's team of horses and getting an early start to plowing.

But breakfast was set on the table, and Andy was nowhere to be seen. When Andy finally emerged in the kitchen 30 minutes later, Doc asked if the horses had been fed. Andy confessed that they hadn't, that the field was still unplowed. Doc, quite reasonably, asked his son what he had been doing. Completing an 8-mile, pre-breakfast run, explained Andy.

This was likely the moment Doc gave up on the idea of his son ever becoming a farmer. The next day, he paid a visit to the chamber of commerce. Flustered, Doc demanded to know when the town officials intended to give Andy his allowance and send him on his way.

The chamber official, taken aback, said that if Doc preferred, they didn't have to sponsor the boy. "No, that's not it," Doc is said to have responded. Then he added that he wanted them to urge Andy on his way as quickly as possible, because the race was the only thing his boy had on his mind.

And so, in early January or possibly in the waning days between Christmas and New Year's, Andy traveled to Los Angeles, taking transportation he had become accustomed to whenever he had limited funds. He found a passing train heading west that had a boxcar with an open door. After giving chase, he tossed in his belongings and climbed aboard.

January 11 to 30, 1928, Burlington, North Carolina, to Los Angeles, 2,490 Miles

Across the country, the runners were coming by car, by train, by boat, and on foot. Hardrock Simpson left his college in North Carolina and made it to Los Angeles in about a month. Writing his college buddy, Wesley "Chop Suey" Williams, on the first day of his journey, he reported:

> Dear Chops:
>
> I didn't get away today until 10:30. I made it to Salisbury by 5:00 o'clock. I am spending the night with my uncle. I picked up 10 rides today for an average of 7 miles per ride. I rode with everything from T.B. patients to sausage salesmen, and in everything from Fords to Cadillacs. And at all speeds from 5 to 70 miles per hour. So far, my trip has cost me only 50 cents.
>
> Aurevoir,
> Hardrock

Only 3 days after leaving home, Hardrock reached Alabama. There, while waiting for a ride at a filling station, a fire broke out in the building, and Hardrock dragged a man from the flames as a crowd looked on. But it was only a moment of glory. He had to walk across much of Texas because most of the cars were going east. His suitcase handle broke, making him an odd sight as he carried it in his arms. But that paled in comparison to his experience in Las Cruces, New Mexico. While he slept in a hotel, someone slipped through the window, stealing $80 worth of traveler's checks, $4.10 in change, a fountain pen, all of his identification, and a set of clothes.

The next morning, an anxious Hardrock wired the mayor of Burlington, who had been in his corner ever since he raced Maude, the Texas pony, and asked him to tell the bank to put a stop order on the traveler's checks. Hardrock's bank book had to eat a few fees: The mayor wired only $70 of his $80 to Las Cruces. But Hardrock saved money and then some. A husband and wife who owned the Deluxe Café adopted him for a day and gave him breakfast and dinner. When Hardrock's money was wired in, he tried to pay them back, or at least for the cost of the telegram to the mayor, but they refused.

The marshal in Las Cruces also helped out, arranging a ride for Hardrock with a Nebraska gentleman who was headed to Phoenix. They set out in a sporty Chrysler, and the man paid for Hardrock's room in Lordsburg, New Mexico. If Hardrock's faith in humanity had been shaken, it was stable once again.

January to February 1928, Kerman, California

Frank Von Flue finally began seeing more articles about Pyle's race in his newspaper. Then he learned that two young men from Fresno, close to Von Flue's town of Kerman, had signed up for the race. That did it. Von Flue decided to participate as well. He wrote the *Los Angeles Times* to find out how to enter the race, and not long after, he received an entry form.

Von Flue sent it in, along with his entry and deposit fees. Meanwhile, his parents thought he was certifiable. They kept trying to persuade him to give up the idea and get his money back. Von Flue ignored them and began training for the race. It didn't go well. For starters, he trained at night, after working at his family's farm. As he ran past houses, dogs barked and chased him. Passing cars flashed their headlights. People around here didn't jog—and not at night. They, too, thought he had lost his mind.

Then, 2 days before he was to report to Pyle's 3-week training camp, Von Flue injured his right foot while training. Although he was told that the injury wasn't too serious, he wasn't allowed to run for a few weeks. Sickened at the prospects of being barred from entering a sporting event once again, Von Flue sent word of his situation to Pyle. To Von Flue's surprised pleasure, he received permission to come to the training camp 12 days late, in order to let his foot heal. Still, this type of luck didn't make his parents any more confident in his decision. Frank Von Flue hadn't even begun the race, and he already was off to a bad start.

February 12, 1928, Los Angeles

The runners who showed up at Ascot Speedway, as instructed, were asked to return the next day, because of a previously scheduled automobile race. The plan had been to bring the athletes into the arena once the dust had settled, but someone—presumably at Ascot—requested that Pyle bring everyone in a day later, on February 13. Which they did.

Although Pyle made an exception for Von Flue, anyone else living in North America was supposed to arrive at his training camp 3 weeks before the race. International travelers were allowed to come later, provided they arrive by March 4. For Pyle, there were some benefits for having weeks of training at the Ascot Speedway. He was able to use the time to meet the runners and set up operations, but let's not kid ourselves. Primarily, it allowed the newspapers plenty of time to churn out stories about the athletes and publicize the race—and because Pyle charged room and board at his camp, he made some easy cash. It was a hallmark of his personality. For instance, he had a magic trick he liked to play in which he would ask for a quarter and make it disappear. Whoever volunteered the coin never got it back.

But there were some benefits for the runners as well. They did get to train without major distractions, and they could eye their competitors and get a sense of their strengths and weaknesses. One advantage that perhaps half the runners seemed to have was a trainer.

Just as a boxer wouldn't think of getting into a ring without a trainer handing him water and whispering advice between rounds, or a race car driver wouldn't hit the track without a pit crew, many athletes came with backup support. A trainer could give a runner a much-needed rubdown after a long day or before a grueling race. A trainer could fetch water or find a new pair of shoes to replace the broken-down ones.

Most, if not all, of the international runners were accompanied by trainers, usually provided by their own governments, and numerous American runners were similarly equipped. For instance, Nick Quamawahu, a

Hopi Indian and one of the race favorites, had several trainers. Those who didn't know trainers or couldn't afford them asked their family members to step in.

Some runners, however, pish-poshed the idea. Among them, Hardrock, Frank Von Flue, Frank Johnson, Morris Saperstein, and Mike Kelly jettisoned the notion of looking for a trainer. They were already at the camp; they were ready to run; they couldn't afford one; they didn't need one; there was no time.

Basically broke himself, Andy Payne didn't have a trainer, but the concept of having one seemed reasonable. He started chewing the idea over.

THE MOOD OF THE FIRST DAY at Pyle's training camp was akin to summer camp. There was a festive feeling as athletes from around the country arrived at the speedway. Dr. Robert Burgess Gordon, from Jefferson Hospital in Philadelphia, brought a small cadre of physicians and nurses to give the entrants a physical. Anyone failing his tests was shown the door, in theory; years later, runner Norman Codeluppi recalled that the physicals were extremely cursory. Von Flue, who came later, didn't even get his.

Dr. William "Bill" O'Brien presented the first of several daily lectures. An osteopathic physician, ex–professional baseball player, and a former accountant—not to mention a champion marksman during World War I—the pudgy 33-year-old had been the physical supervisor for the last three Davis Cup teams, one of the most prestigious tournaments in tennis, and he instructed the athletes on caring for their bodies and maintaining a proper diet. Meanwhile, Dan O'Leary, an 87-year-old world-champion long-distance walker, was scheduled to tell the athletes what he knew about keeping their feet in proper shape.

Of all the guests and speakers, O'Leary, a wiry, mustached man, was the most unique. The Irishman had been walking in contests for almost 75 years. He considered it his greatest accomplishment when, at 66 years of age in 1907, he decided to walk 1,000 miles in 1,000 consecutive hours. It was a stunt that had been attempted before by other champion walkers, but always by people much younger than O'Leary. And it was quite a stunt. O'Leary would walk 1 mile, usually in about 15 minutes, and then have 45 minutes to recover. In the beginning of his stunt, at a walking track adjacent to the Norwood Inn in Cincinnati, this obviously wasn't a difficulty, but the continuous nights of broken sleep eventually took their toll. In the middle of the night, O'Leary might sleep for 40 minutes but then be aroused by the Norwood Inn staff and volunteers, trudge outside to the track and walk a mile while judges and timekeepers monitored him, and then retire to his room, only to be woken up at the start of the next hour.

When O'Leary began his walk on September 8, 1907, he was 144 pounds. When he finished on October 20, he was 122 pounds. By the last week, O'Leary was periodically suffering from some form of dementia—when woken up in the middle of the night, he thought he was a younger man, back in the mid-1800s. Then one Tuesday at 3:00 a.m., as the *Ogden Standard* in Ogden, Utah, described it, O'Leary "was suddenly attacked by spasmodic derangement of the intestines, which threatened to prostate him and from which he was relieved by the administering of restoratives." It was the most polite way possible of observing that O'Leary had diarrhea.

On his last day of walking, sores formed on his left foot.

For his troubles, O'Leary received $5,000 from the International Tuberculosis Association, which asked him to conduct the stunt to raise awareness of their organization.

As difficult as that walking trip had been, in 1921, at the age of 80, O'Leary tried something more ambitious. He decided to walk to every state capital in the country (Alaska and Hawaii hadn't yet been admitted into the Union, making his feat slightly more possible). O'Leary spent the next decade periodically tramping from one capital to another, or sometimes starting anew from his home in Chicago. Eight years into his journey, almost finished with his goal, he introduced himself to the runners of the Bunion Derby to provide insight and inspiration.

Lectures were only part of the runners' training; practice races were also conducted. Four days into the training camp, Pyle organized a 15-mile run for the approximately 200 runners and a 10-mile walk among the championship walkers. In the 15-mile run, Payne came in sixth place. He felt good about that, but he could see why having a trainer would be important. They had been standing on the sidelines and splashing cups of water on their athletes during the race. When it was over, Quamawahu, who had several trainers, won the 15 miles, earning a cash prize of several hundred dollars. Pyle handed out a total of $1,000 in prize money for the walkathon and running race, a pleasant start to a 3-month event that promised daily cash prizes to runners, on top of the final grand prize of $25,000. A talented runner—with a trainer—could clearly clean up over the next few months.

Payne decided to look for a trainer first and worry about the finances later.

He found Tom Young, from Miami, Florida, who had planned on running until he contracted influenza after coming to California. He emerged with his health intact but realized he was too weak to try running across the country. So Young worked out a deal with three runners to serve as their trainer. He had a motorcycle, and the thinking was that he would zip along to each runner, delivering water and reporting the distance to the next town. Like the other trainers, Young would also give the runners rubdowns and help them recover during the hours that they weren't on the road. Because Young was spreading himself between three competitors, or four with Payne, he could be had cheap.

Payne wanted to hire Young, but to do that he needed money, and the stipend he received from the Claremore Chamber of Commerce was virtually depleted. Not knowing where else to turn, he sent a telegram to his benefactor:

> G. A. Rogers,
>
> Mayor of Claremore
>
> Have placed sixth in a race of 15 miles from a field of 200 of the best long distance runners in the world. Distance too short. Have been training for four months for long jumps of 50 to 60 miles per day. I have run 60 miles in 8 hours and 32 minutes. I have excellent chance of winning

> this race from Los Angeles to New York, if the people of my home town will back me. I have spent all of my money training. I must have the services of my trainer in this race.

Exactly what the mayor wired back no longer exists apparently, but the reply was positive. Additional funds were sent, and Payne was able to hire Young. What Young was paid isn't known, but it was really the promise of winning that kept all the trainers acutely interested in their clients. If the runner won any prize money, the standard deal was that the trainer received 10 percent.

FROM HIS TENT in the middle of the grassy field, which was in the middle of a dirt track that hosted races of every kind, from horses to motorcycles to cars, Hardrock wrote letters in his spare time. He penned his daily memoirs mostly to Staley A. Cook, a reporter at the *Burlington Daily Times*, who covered his running exploits with Maude. Hardrock was clearly awed by the new world he had discovered. Despite his time in the service, he was still basically a country boy, a point amply made in his letters to Cook.

"I saw my first Japanese woman barber," wrote Hardrock, who was astonished at the city's steep prices. "I went into the cheapest barber shop I could find, and they charged me fifty cents for a haircut." Later, he observed that the traffic was heavy and that "the people don't look where they're going and will walk over you if you don't get out of the way. I learn something now every day and see something new."

Hardrock also raved about seeing a movie that had come out the previous year and was still playing in the theatres: the silent film classic *Wings,* with Gary Cooper in a bit role, about World War I flyboys.

On February 14, Hardrock wrote to Cook and described what it was like to bunk with a couple hundred other men:

> It sure was cold last night, and all we had was a thin mattress and two thin blankets. I don't think I slept any more than half an hour, for the fel-

lows raised Cain until 10 o'clock. Then it was too cold to sleep. The fellows began to crow for daylight at 4 o'clock.

They serve plenty to eat here. I walked and ran together over the hills and on the track from 9 to 3 o'clock except when I was eating. Then the newspaper reporters made us jog around while they took our pictures. I am sunburned almost black.

We have a man with one arm entered in the race. At present, there are 304 entries. Pyle is charging an admittance fee of 50 cents for adults and 25 cents for children to watch us stroll around the track . . .

This was a little disturbing to Hardrock, who wouldn't have minded Pyle spreading the wealth around. As it was, Pyle was charging all of the runners 50 cents a night for a bed and 50 cents for each meal, and if they wanted to participate in the race, the rules stipulated they couldn't lodge or eat anywhere else. It was like living in a prison, only everyone paid rent and asked to be locked up. Hardrock went on to say, "If I don't get some money soon, I ain't going to eat no more."

The following day, Hardrock penned another letter to Cook:

. . . today, it was cool, and the wind blew so hard it blew the tents down. I ran and walked together for 30 miles today. Pyle is sure cleaning up on us. He charges us 50 cents for beds and only furnishes us with a thin mattress, and two blankets for bed clothing, and if you don't sleep with all your clothing on, you will freeze. He charges us 50 cents a meal and serves us the very things a runner shouldn't eat, such as steaks, baked potatoes, white bread, pies and coffee. He has no baths for us, and we have to furnish our own towels and soap . . .

Hardrock didn't discuss why he was complaining about having to furnish his own towels and soap when there were no baths. But on the plus side, Hardrock was enjoying the camaraderie:

This is one jolly bunch of fellows in this tent. They keep you laughing all the time, by their jokes and hot air. An Englishman sleeps next to me, next to him is a Scotchman. He said my name is Scottish. The rest of the

> fellows are from different states. We have a poet, an opera singer, two milk testers, a milker, a blacksmith, a hobo and a lawyer in our tent.

In general, the tents were filled with men who looked or sounded alike. The African Americans were in one, and the Americans, English, and Canadians grouped in tents. The Italians bunked together, as did the Finnish runners. So did the Native Americans.

Hardrock liked the fellows he was rooming with but realized that he would have to be on guard even at the speedway: One of his track outfits was stolen from the tent.

But the day after the theft, Hardrock wrote that things were looking up, particularly because Cook had sent $50 that the newspaper had raised from concerned readers after Hardrock was robbed en route to Los Angeles:

> . . . I received your $50 today and I sure do thank you for it. It sure did come in handy, for I had just spent my last penny. Where did you raise it? Please thank every one that had a hand in it. It sure gives me new courage to face whatever may come. I covered 43 miles in my workout today. The fellows quit eating and sleeping in the camp, and Pyle got wise to himself. He gave us three blankets, a shower bath and changed our diet to the things we should have . . .

The money Pyle made off runners like Hardrock helped his bottom line, but it was a pittance compared to what he eventually would generate off them—or so theorized *Seattle Post-Intelligencer* sports editor George Scherck, who wrote a lengthy story several days into the race, explaining how Pyle figured to get rich. To that point, skeptics concluded that he couldn't turn a profit off the race because Pyle's management promised food, lodging, and medical attention. These things, of course, cost money.

But as Scherck explained, Pyle had found one company to furnish all of the runners with $5,000 worth of bacon and ham. Another enterprise was furnishing $7,500 for the right to provide foot powder to all of the runners. A cereal company was paying $6,000 for the honor of feeding the competitors breakfast. The names of the companies, Scherck didn't mention, probably not wanting to give Pyle's sponsors any free publicity. It was well publicized, however, that the buses carrying Pyle, some of his crew, and journalists were donated and constructed by the Faegol Company, which also paid Pyle $2,500 for promotion of their vehicles. Pyle was true to his word, heaping lavish praise on Faegol in the programs that he sold in each town. The programs, which sold for a quarter each, were booklets with mini-biographies of the runners. Pyle didn't invent corporate sponsorship, but he had branded Red Grange in an innovative way that sports fans were unaccustomed to, and now he was taking the same business model to his race.

Meanwhile, as Scherck noted:

> The race is being run over the U.S. 66 Highway. And that cost someone something. Any city village or metropolis through which the runners pass pays for the privilege. Not only does the community pay Pyle, but it also agrees to allow the sideshow to exhibit each evening, besides paying prizes for the first five to finish at its control point. Pyle has complete control of the output of his winners. Thus he will cash in on the vaudeville contracts, on advertisements for shoes, food, clothes and other articles used on the route.
>
> Yes, Mr. Pyle will cash in and carry away much gold. He gambled, and it looks as if he should win along with the victors of the race.

Scherck was far from the only sportswriter commenting on the race. As March 4, 1928, came closer—the marathon's start date—newspapermen gravitated to the Ascot Speedway. The Associated Press also sent a journalist there, as did other news bureaus like United Press, the Newspaper Enterprise Association, and the International News Service, which was run by newspaper magnate William Randolph Hearst. Meanwhile, in the palaces, jammed in among *Felix the Cat* cartoons, Buster Keaton shorts, and features, was newsreel footage of the training. The general public was starting to notice that a race was afoot, and as the word spread, some interesting characters capitalized on Pyle's growing notoriety.

Dr. John J. Seiler, of Augusta, Georgia, was one such individual. Also known as the Flying Yank, Seiler was a long-distance runner who traveled from town to town promoting good health, and on occasion he penned a fitness column that ran in newspapers. Three years earlier, in 1925, he gained attention after he challenged five opponents and trounced them in a race at Cermak Park in Chicago.

But many of Seiler's exploits were more or less hearsay—said by Seiler, who in 1927 claimed that every month for the last 3 years, he had run approximately 100 miles at a time. He made this boast shortly after a 1927 run, in which he was said to have run from Danville, Illinois, to Miami, Florida, a distance of 1,380 miles, the longest distance ever hoofed on foot by one man, Seiler claimed. Later that year, he made a dash from Atlantic City to Pasadena, California.

According to the news accounts, Seiler put in 9 hours a day on the road, wearing out seven pairs of shoes and passing out at the end of 3,052 miles. So it's no wonder that a few months before the Bunion Derby began, Seiler issued a challenge that Pyle couldn't refuse.

John Seiler announced that he would start running 1 week after the start of the race, on March 4th (as Pyle liked to quip, the start date was "March Forth"), and he would follow its exact route. The Flying Yank then promised that he would beat all Pyle's racers to New York. Whether Pyle was pleased or not, he couldn't refuse the challenge because he didn't own the roads. If Seiler wanted to pursue them on foot, there was nothing to be done about it. Pyle simply went about his business in Los Angeles and ignored the fellow.

Seiler wasn't the only hotshot looking to become the fastest runner in the West. There was a man who called himself Levett, also known as the Human Dynamo. In 1903, on the high school track team in Salem, Illinois, Levett ran a 25-mile race, then 44 miles the following year, 60 the next, and 81 the year after that. More recently, he had run from San Francisco to Los Angeles in under 2 weeks.

And now Levett announced that he would run across the entire country several months before the beginning of the Bunion Derby. Levett declared that he would depart Los Angeles on September 1, 1927, and arrive in New York 60 days later, which, if accomplished, would rob Pyle's event of much of its drama.

At the last minute, however, Levett didn't run. Instead, when Pyle's runners left the starting line, Levett traveled with them, as an employee of Pyle's. Embracing the concept of keeping your friends close and enemies even closer, the showman persuaded Levett to drop his solo trip and instead write running commentary, which Pyle's organization could submit to newspapers. It was a shrewd preemptive strike. C. C. Pyle already had enough enemies.

CHAPTER 5

In front of the bus that carried the runners' luggage, sometime early in the race. As it turned out, many of those pictured didn't make it very far. (Courtesy of Guy Gavuzzi.)

On Your Mark

February 24, 1928

Every day, it seemed, C. C. Pyle added another esteemed official to his staff. Ralph Goodwin, one of the era's best-known automobile race timers, came on board to time the runners each day. Goodwin came complete with a staff of six assistants to help with timing the athletes, who were believed to number 275.

Another celebrity official was the race's physical director, Hugo Quist, known for being the trainer of legendary Finnish gold-medal Olympian runner Paavo Nurmi. Meanwhile, Arthur Duffy had been named the race's official referee.

Aside from being a respected sports editor at the *Boston Post*, on May 31, 1902, Duffy became the first man to run the 100-yard dash in 9.6 seconds, beating John Owen's record of 9.8 seconds, which he had set in 1890. Duffy was highly regarded as a runner, even after it was learned 3 years later that he had won some money in races in England the summer before his famous sprint. Since he was thus considered a professional, staining the purity of amateur athletics, his name was stripped from the record books. But 26 years later, it almost didn't matter. Duffy was still well respected by many, and a catchphrase was still in use for anyone doing a mad dash for, say, a trolley car. A person would look at the other knowingly and say, "He's doing an Arthur Duffy."

Pyle certainly respected him and promised that Duffy, and only Duffy, would be in charge of the runners' welfare.

But despite the well-known staff, they were almost an afterthought compared to the one true star accompanying the Bunion Derby. He was a sensation that Pyle had helped create, a man guaranteed to draw attention to the race in town after town: Red Grange.

He was ruggedly handsome, with short, dark hair; piercing eyes; and a winning smile. He walked with a bit of a limp, his knee having been injured a few months earlier in the previous season. Damaging his knee was almost inevitable. Football in the 1920s was a tough game, almost an endurance sport in itself. In one game during the previous year, a player had broken his right leg, another man had dislocated his shoulder, and another had had his nose smashed in and left the field with blood covering him. A guy playing tackle had gotten five stitches under his eye and then went back to the field. Brick Muller, Grange's nemesis, had had his arm thrown out of its socket—but his teammates were able to lodge it back in place so he could keep playing. Another player had been knocked unconscious twice and left the game unsure of what day it was. Grange was described as "being broken almost in two" by *Los Angeles Times* sportswriter Braven Dyer, who added that player "Wealey Fry was ruined early in the game and never returned."

So Grange was in the off-season and not sorry about it. That he was with Pyle during this race wasn't surprising to anyone who knew the two men. Always wanting to protect his investment, Pyle kept Grange close to him, ever since he had taken him on as a client. Pyle constantly worked on building their friendship, intertwining their lives wherever he could. Pyle worked out a deal for Grange to purchase a large swath of land in his brother's 5,000-acre ranch in Santa Rosa, California. The football star turned most of his newfound land into a hunting preserve and a smaller section into grazing land for sheep.

Pyle had lived with Grange during the summer of 1926, when the football star filmed *One Minute to Play.* Around that time Pyle had even tried to make Grange a family member, suggesting that the 23-year-old romance his 19-year-old daughter, Kathrine, but that apparently never came to fruition. And during the Christmas holidays of 1927, Grange had spent at least some of his time in Santa Rosa with Pyle and his mother. By the winter of 1928, if Grange hadn't accompanied Pyle, it almost would have been odd, and with his bum knee, what else was the football star going to do?

Besides, Pyle knew that making Grange the race's assistant director would attract people to the race.

He kept adding more and more staff. Pyle hired football players to be his police and enforce the rules. He had a camp manager and another man in charge of the crew that set up and took down the tents every day. There was a hospital, with two doctors and a few nurses to monitor and care for any of the runners' medical needs. A former army cook staffed the mobile kitchen—a glorified truck. Pyle even saw to it that there were cars equipped with laundry facilities and a barbershop.

Pyle wasn't paying everyone. Dr. Gordon and his colleague, Dr. John Baker, were at the Ascot Speedway, observing the marathoners for a study that they were planning, to determine if the effects of running every day over an extended period of time had any negative effects. Dr. Gordon was planning to travel with the runners only for a short time; Dr. Baker, however, was going to be in for the long haul, apparently bartering his services for the chance to study the runners.

There was also a freelance shoemaker, who made his money on whatever the runners could afford.

Of all the people on Pyle's payroll, however, there was a contingent of employees who were truly unique—those who staffed what Pyle called his carnival. Most folks referred to it as a freak show.

Late February 1928

Arthur Newton traveled by ship for a week and, after a few days in New York, embarked on a 4-day, 5-night train trip to Los Angeles, stopping for half a day at Niagara Falls, which he found "pedestrian" compared to Victoria Falls in Rhodesia.

Newton admired the infrastructure that Pyle had put together for his race. There were 16 "marquee" tents housing the runners at night, and during the day, numerous athletes were running on the track or climbing the nearby hills. But as he probed further, he realized that most of the athletes weren't as all-powerful as they should have been. "The great majority of the men were quite unaware of the magnitude of the task ahead of them and were not sufficiently trained," lamented Newton in his autobiography. "Those who, on one occasion only, had done as much as fifty miles in a single day could almost be counted on the fingers of a single hand."

Hardrock also noticed that they seemed an unlikely group of runners. In a letter to his university, Hardrock wrote, "Our biggest curiosities are a one-armed entry and a man from the House of David with a beard a foot long," referring to Roy McMurtry and Dick Frost.

McMurtry, 32, was a one-armed runner who seemed to function perfectly fine, whether he was running, playing billiards, driving a car, or riding a motorcycle. His parents were farmers, and so, too, was Roy. He registered for the draft on June 5, 1917; but the fact that he had "lost an arm," as he put it, accounted for why he did not fight in World War I.

Perhaps because of the loss of his arm, McMurtry focused on his legs. Whatever his motivation, he belonged in Pyle's race. His mini-biography in the program noted that in 1922 McMurtry had run from Indianapolis to San Francisco in 20 days.

Frost, 56, usually dressed in khakis, was a Hollywood bit actor. Billing himself as R. Lucien Frost, he had a peculiar gait that developed when his feet were frozen during a stint as a mail carrier in Alaska. His reddish gold beard was often tied to his belt when he ran. It was long because Frost was a member of the House of David, a cult that prevented its members from trimming their hair. The organization, which formed in 1903, also mandated lifelong celibacy, even among married couples, which may explain why there are so few members around today.

Frost did his part to preach the word of the Lord while earning his keep as an actor in biblical stage plays. Celibate or not, though, Frost was no prude. In the after hours of a race, Frost could often be found at the center of a small crowd, leaning back in a chair, telling dirty jokes.

"There are some of the craziest fellows in this race that I ever met out of an asylum," concluded Hardrock. "With their queer ideas and the other fellows' hot air, you are kept laughing all the time."

Newton couldn't help wondering how any of his competitors could possibly run more than 3,000 miles. For all he knew, the 27-year-old runner Wildfire Thompson was the best there ever was, but you'd never guess it. Thompson was decked out in bright red long underwear.

He was also a few weeks past his last boxing match, in which he was hammered six rounds before being declared the loser. Like Mike Kelly, Patrick De Marr, Sammy Robinson, Harry Grimmett, and numerous others in the Bunion Derby, Thompson frequently boxed. But then, who didn't? During the 1920s, boxing was the nation's second most popular sport, following baseball. In 1924, the *Indianapolis Star* reported that there were 11,440 boxing matches held around the country. Thompson was also a wrestler.

Other careers were well represented in the race. One entrant believed the walking requirements in his job in the postal service would help him be victorious; a bill collector who walked from house to house felt the same way. There was an Oklahoma cowboy, a streetcar operator, and a baker. The latter was Alexander McMillian, 37, who proclaimed, "I shall show the field of about 228 contestants that a pie-eating pastry patter can put pep into this bunion derby. I eat a whole apple pie every day. You know, the old saying of the proof of the pudding and keep the doctor away?" (A tad overconfident, he lasted approximately 2 weeks.)

Despite the varied careers, what many men had in common was that each wasn't much of a runner. Before the race started, Pyle put together the program containing the mini-biographies and photos of the runners, which he planned to sell at each town. His description of James F. Gleason, of Los Angeles, was typical: "Gleason will be one of the many runners representing Los Angeles. He is a veteran without a mark in the record book but can be counted on to do his best. He is 44 years old and was born in England."

John Cronick, a 24-year-old from Saskatchewan, Canada, who had never even run the 100-yard dash, probably spoke for many of the men when he explained why he entered: "I thought it would be a good chance to see the country, get some experience, and I had a chance at making some money."

All in all, the field was quite a mix of occupations and social classes, with scattered elite runners among them. As the Associated Press's Russ Newland recalled years later, "There were cooks, laborers, bank clerks, night watchmen, fishermen, truck drivers, prize fighters, wrestlers, and others all trying for the $25,000 . . . "

Like Newton, Dr. Baker wasn't awed by the runners. Of the 199 men who were to compete, he felt that approximately 40 of them "appeared capable of withstanding strenuous athletic competition. Six runners were found to be suffering from acute respiratory infections, 9 had gastrointestinal symptoms, 1 had signs of active pleurisy, 4 had chronic bronchitis, 11 had moderate emphysema, 1 had a morning temperature of 102 degrees Fahrenheit, and 18 had more or less serious contusions of the feet, legs or knees."

Still, they were allowed to race, which seems to give credence to some runners' memories that the physicals weren't taken too seriously.

Dr. Baker had more prerace observations: "Approximately 50 percent of all competitors were underdeveloped physically and could scarcely be compared with long-distance runners usually seen in universities or athletic clubs. It was found that only six runners, in preparation for the race, ran over 25 miles daily, and comparatively few had competed in important long-distance races."

Newton was one of those six and had a biography any runner would envy. As it read in Pyle's program: "Holder of every amateur running record from 29 to 100 miles. He is 44 years of age and was passed up for the last two Olympic Games because the 26-mile marathon was too short for him."

Newton did have some formidable competition. Nestor Erickson, a well-known marathon racer, was predicted to win Pyle's race by Paavo Nurmi, a Finnish runner with eight gold medals so far. Juri Lossman, who earned a silver medal in the 1920 Olympics, was expected to finish in the top 10; Guisto Umek was a prominent speed walker, and his fellow Italians Joe Conto and Paolo Bruno were among the best runners in their country.

Despite being the oldest entrant, 63-year-old Englishman Charles Walter Hart was a threat. Hart, sporting a reed-thin mustache, was 5 feet 3 and 138 pounds and looked 10 years younger than his age. Hart could half-walk and half-run "almost indefinitely," one sportswriter claimed, and he had several long-distance records to his credit. One of those, for the fastest time over 100 miles, Newton had shattered the month before. Hart planned to avenge himself by beating Newton in the Bunion Derby, and his odds of doing so weren't bad. He was hedging his bets, though. He had teamed up with fellow British runner Pete Gavuzzi, sharing the same sponsor and deciding that they would share the prize money, if one won and the other didn't. Meanwhile, they would also increase their odds of bringing in cash by sharing the daily prize money. After all, Gavuzzi was fast, but Hart had more experience as a distance runner.

Still, Hart had plenty of potential to win without help. He had recently challenged three men to a 100-mile race, with some unusual ground rules: He would run the entire distance alone. The three, presumably younger, runners conducted a relay race, each going a distance of approximately 33 miles against the older man's 100. Hart won.

But of all the runners, only Willie Kolehmainen could be considered Newton's equal.

A native of Finland still trying to get his American citizenship, Kolehmainen looked every bit of his 40 years, with sunken cheeks and a receding hairline. A short man, he didn't appear to be a daunting opponent, but he had won numerous running medals since 1910, the year he moved to New York City.

His most glorious win was a prestigious marathon in Edinburgh, Scotland, in 1912, finishing in 2 hours and 29 minutes, seizing the title of the fastest human being alive. Willie went on to train his brother, Hannes, a gold-medal-winning runner at the 1912 and 1920 Olympics.

In 1924, Willie decided to try to become an American, but, because of an unfortunate 1917 incident, he was roundly rejected. During World War I, Congress amended the draft to include foreign-born residents who declared an intent to become American citizens. Kolehmainen was ordered to appear at a draft board in Quincy, Massachusetts. A pacifist, however, he didn't show up, so he was charged with desertion and tossed into a military prison called Governors Island in Upper New York Harbor.

He was released a year later.

Kolehmainen was a little testy about the experience, remarking, "People on the job in 1916 called me a dirty foreigner. When the war came, I am no longer a dirty foreigner. They want me to fight."

By 1928, Kolehmainen was still without American citizenship and holding down a career as a bricklayer. He had given up marathon running, but the Bunion Derby called to his soul. Three months before the race, Kolehmainen put down his trowel and resumed training. It was clear to all of the sportswriters who watched him fly around the track that he was the man to beat.

He would be an intimidating competitor. But otherwise, Newton couldn't help feeling quite good about his chances.

Pyle valued Newton's star power and experience and asked him to speak to the other men a few days after his arrival. "Naturally I had no time for small details," wrote Newton, who also likely didn't want to give away too many trade secrets, "but I warned them one and all that we were in for a 'desperately serious affair,' and that only those who used their heads to some purpose, and who also enjoyed remarkably good luck, could hope to come in prominently at the other end."

Newton wasn't being melodramatic. For the next several months, each man would be engaged—body, mind, and spirit—in a furious battle against each other and himself. Something out of the ordinary was bound to happen.

For now, Pyle wanted to focus on preparations. The day before the big day, Pyle called all of the runners for a meeting. He informed them of what he promised was a minor matter. The first five races wouldn't offer prize money at the end of the day. The runners digested this bit of alarming news. Part of the allure of racing across the country for months had been that even if you didn't win the prize money at the end of the road, you could win cash in the daily laps.

The towns were supposed to furnish the daily prizes, but these first several wouldn't, apparently unfamiliar with how the race was going to be conducted. Pyle assured everyone that other communities were on board, and by the sixth day, the daily prizes would kick in.

The runners murmured approval.

Pyle also informed everyone that the food served during the race would be much better than what had been served in the weeks of their training and that the medical attention and accommodations would improve. Some of the runners, those who hadn't been around as long, shrugged. Not everyone felt the camp had been a negative experience.

"Be on deck tomorrow at 3 o'clock for the start of the race," Pyle told his runners on March 3.

Frank Von Flue later recalled that he hardly slept that night.

The excitement was palpable. Hardrock captured everyone's mood in one of his letters to Elon College: "Tell Professor Martin I am not studying history now, I am trying to make history."

CHAPTER 6

C. C. Pyle confers with Thomas Ellis, a gifted Canadian runner. (Courtesy of the El Reno Carnegie Library.)

GO!

DISTANCE SO FAR: ZERO MILES; 199 RUNNERS

MARCH 4, LOS ANGELES TO PUENTE, CALIFORNIA, 17 MILES

In theory, the heaviest runners woke up first.

All through the night, the rain had been relentless, and around dawn, the iron cots began sinking into the earth. As the athletes awoke, cursing in various languages, they grabbed their belongings, from their money to their all-important shoes.

Andy Payne brought with him five pairs of Spalding leather shoes with reinforced soles. Hardrock created his own special shoes, made of cork (for padding) and asbestos (for keeping his feet protected from the heat). Frank Von Flue felt confident about his footwear, having removed the spikes from his baseball shoes.

But no one recognized the wisdom in sporting a pair of heavy logging boots, except, of course, for the one man who decided to wear them: Eugene Estoppey. Once upon a time, he was a near-legendary runner who, during a career of odd jobs, like that of a lifeguard and a salesman, had been running for almost 40 years, since 1890, racking up impressive records (he once covered a mile in 4 minutes and 44 seconds). But the year before, he showed up at the Catalina Island swimming race dressed in an aviator's helmet, sandals, and (covered in a special swimmers' grease) underwear and several sweatshirts. He almost drowned, and now he was entering the Bunion Derby in almost equally questionable attire.

The runners haphazardly collected their belongings as the camp was hastily taken down. The start of the race wasn't scheduled until midafternoon, but it felt as if there was no time to waste.

Everywhere C. C. Pyle walked, he saw almost-managed chaos. Trainers and runners hoisted luggage into the official bus intended for baggage and tents. The truck housing the mobile kitchen was stuck in the mud, and the driver couldn't dislodge the wheels. One of the athletes, speed walker Guisto Umek, stormed up to Pyle and in a furious mix of Italian and English explained that one of his shoes had been stolen. Pyle assigned two men to help Umek and continued surveying the havoc that had overtaken Ascot Speedway.

It was actually worse than he realized. Pyle wouldn't know it for at least another day, but his carefully constructed organization was under the impression that 275 runners had signed up. There were, however, actually 199 participants—meaning that his accounting books would soon reveal that he had made far less money at the training camp than he had imagined, and that for a brief time, Pyle's crew believed that 76 men dropped out the first day after the introductory 17-mile lap.

As Bill Pickens rounded up a dozen runners to help push the truck out of the mud, and as two football players found Umek's shoe underneath a suitcase, one has to think that some of the athletes or race officials like Red Grange looked at the panoramic mess before them and thought, "What am I getting myself into?"

THE STADIUM began filling with people, as a multitude of residents and tourists filed in. It was such an intriguing event that George Haehn, the police chief in Warren, Pennsylvania, who was in town to pick up a suspected forger and escort him back to his state, took the time to sit in the audience and watch the runners begin their long journey.

Near the sidelines was a young man, probably around 20, his cheeks scarlet red from a fever. His $100 travel deposit had been returned. Although too sick to run, according to the doctors, the young man refused to leave. He just kept watching the runners and looking forlorn.

Next to him was another young man, an unkempt sort who looked as if he hadn't eaten a meal in a week and must have drifted over to the festivities. The unshaven vagrant had two dogs with him and was carrying a banjo. He was a 17-year-old known around the neighborhood as Ukulele Jake. He begged strangers to give him $125 so that he could enter the race. No one took him up on it.

The contestants finally gathered on the muddy track, and Pyle organized everyone in rows of 20, separating the men, as much as possible, into groups by nationality. There were 24 countries represented, and many athletes were adorned in gaudy, colorful uniforms and carried flags representing their respective nations. Even so, it was also a motley collection of runners, from men in normal running attire like shorts and tank tops to Wildfire Thompson in his red long underwear to Estoppey in his logging boots. Another man likely stood out: John E. Pederson, a jeweler from Spokane, Washington, regularly ran in a business suit—it was his normal athletic attire, and it seems unlikely he would have changed for the occasion. An avid runner, he claimed to have never paid a cent for a doctor's visit in his life. He also had another eccentricity: "I don't wear underwear because I don't believe in binding the body up in anything like that."

At 3:04 p.m., Grange lit what reporters described as a starter bomb. It exploded with a deafening bang, and the spectators in the stands began cheering and shouting.

With that, the runners were off.

"It was," described Braven Dyer of the *Los Angeles Times*, "a sight worthy of the greatest movie director in the world."

Russ Newland of the Associated Press agreed, determining that the Bunion Derby was "at one and the same time, the most cuckoo, fantastic and fascinating enterprise ever carried out by a sports promoter. Sue me if I am wrong."

Men moved en masse as the starter-bomb smoke drifted across the mud-covered track. Everyone was supposed to be released 20 at a time in order not to overwhelm the roads, but the athletes just started running, as did numerous newsmen, like Newland, Dyer, and Maxwell Stiles of the *Los Angeles Examiner*, who sprinted to a cream-colored luxury motor home that Pyle had named the *America*.

Pickens and Grange joined the reporters and Pyle in the camper, as the runners circled the speedway twice before starting down the road.

It was a stumbling, halting start, because they were ankle-deep in the soupy track. Estoppey's boots were already cumbersome, weighted down with mud. Straggling through the swill were two favorites to win, Willie Kolehmainen and Gunnar Nilson, who quickly demonstrated why many figured they were the men to beat. As soon as they finished with the track, Kolehmainen and Nilson sat down on the pavement and quickly removed muddy stockings, which they had put over their shoes to protect them from the elements. Tossing the socks aside, they sprinted past the other runners slogging about in mud-clogged shoes, boots, and bare feet.

As Hardrock, Frank Von Flue, Morris Saperstein, Andy Payne, Frank Johnson, Mike Kelly, and dozens of others dashed onto the road, they were met with shouts and encouragement from thousands of spectators. The public numbered in the hundreds of thousands, and for the next 12 miles, well-wishers from all over Los Angeles poured out of their automobiles, parked three to four deep, to see the runners off. The whole thing felt a little like a parade—runners and 61 vehicles, including trucks, cars, buses, the giant camper, and a vehicle carting a giant container that looked like a coffeepot. The lettering read: "Maxwell House Coffee. Coast-to-Coast."

The idea was that Maxwell House would travel along with the Bunion Derby athletes and give free coffee to the runners. Much to the chagrin of the runners, this plan ended well before the race did.

After a few miles, the crowds thinned out until near the first night's stop, a little town called Puente.

C. C. Pyle, along with Pickens, Grange, and several other race officials and journalists, motored ahead of most of the runners. Meanwhile, spectators filled the roads, forcing the slower runners to jockey for space among the people and extensive traffic. One Los Angeles reporter took to a car shortly after the race had begun, and by the time the journalist arrived in Puente, 6 hours had passed—4½ hours after the first runner crossed the finish line.

Many of the official race vehicles were old clunkers, like the Model T, but one in particular was clearly the headquarters of the operation: Pyle's luxury camper. The *America* cost $25,000 to build and was more luxurious than most houses. The floor was carpeted to match the plush, blue mohair upholstery and interior paneling, which was bordered with hand-finished mahogany. There was a fold-in table, a writing desk, a combination phonograph and radio receiving set, three reclining chairs, and a double Pullman-type seat, which could sleep two. Pyle's expensive toy had hot and cold running water, a bathroom with a shower, a kitchen with an electric refrigerator, a sink, a gas stove, and a water heater. Especially impressive was the air-conditioning, supplied by Frigidaire.

A door at the rear of the camper opened to an observation platform, and stairs led to the upper deck, where six people could sit—even while the vehicle was in motion—underneath a collapsible awning and protected from dust and debris by a windshield. In case anyone forgot who owned this piece of majestic machinery, Pyle's monogram appeared in gold letters on the rear license plate.

One paper referred to the *America* as "the most pretentious land yacht ever built." Pyle loved that.

He had reason to be proud. Much of Pyle's life had been spent pursuing affluence. Pyle was 8 when his father died, and from then on, the family struggled to bring in money. Pyle's mother, Sidney, paid the bills as a dress-maker, and as her three children grew, they quickly found ways to earn money. In 1894, when Charley was 12 and his brother Ira was 14, they served as something of a travel agency for one of their father's churches and accompanied the tourists as train butchers, a common term in the 1800s to describe the people who sold passengers candy, fruit, and cigarettes. By 1900, 22-year-old Anna was a telephone operator, 20-year-old Ira was employed at a grocery store, and Charley, going on 18, worked as a telegraph operator at the train station.

Small wonder Pyle invited not only his wife, Effie, from Chicago to see the *America* after purchasing it in San Francisco but also his 21-year-old daughter, Kathrine. Family history repeated itself in a way: Just as his father had done to him, albeit unintentionally, Pyle deserted the first Mrs. Charles C. Pyle and their baby daughter. But in recent years, he had made amends with both Dot and Kathrine, and it was a glorious personal victory for Pyle when Effie christened the *America* with a bottle of grape juice with Kathrine watching on. The first thing they did, after waving good-bye to the reporters Pyle invited to the event, was to climb aboard and drive to Santa Rosa, California, where he could show off their new digs to his mother, brother, and sister.

THE RACE TO PUENTE was more ceremonial than anything else. It was only a 17-mile journey, the shortest distance that the runners would travel during the entire trip. Still, even on that day, some personalities began to shine through. At the head of the pack were the men who adapted so well to the muddy track, Kolehmainen and Nilson, and a well-regarded Hopi Indian, Nick Quamawahu.

Not far behind was Payne, jockeying for a decent position among his competitors, and yet he knew full well that he needed to heed his trainer's advice: "Don't overdo it," Tom Young said. "Six and a half miles an hour.

That's the pace you set." Payne listened, watching a handful of athletes easily pass him by. Even if it felt a little demoralizing, he was ahead of Arthur Newton.

And by the end, Young seemed to know what he was talking about. Payne was in ninth place. Two slots behind was Hardrock. Newton came in 29th that day but couldn't have cared less. A 17-mile race was hardly worth the effort and, compared to what was ahead, barely a drop in the bucket.

Far behind them was Charles Hart, the 63-year-old Englishman, and Roy McMurtry, the one-armed runner from Indiana—a little surprising since both men had long records of achievement. Kelly, Johnson, and Saperstein also didn't crack the top 50. Despite wearing logging boots, Estoppey miraculously beat several of the younger runners. Von Flue arrived in 62nd place, but he could live with that. Two days before, Von Flue had run 3 miles past Puente and back as a practice run. He performed well, but he developed shin splints on the way back and, from that, would have soreness in his legs for the next several days. Once again, not a great start to the race.

WITH THE RUNNERS, Pyle's crew, the trainers, and all of the spectators, Puente's population "was swollen to many times its normal size," reported Braven Dyer. The townsfolk needed this diversion, maybe more so than any other community the Bunion Derby would pass through. Everyone was unnerved by the discovery of a young boy's headless corpse a few weeks earlier, left in a ditch alongside a road.

What no one knew was that Puente was being stalked by a relative rarity in 1928—a serial killer.

His name was Stewart Gordon Northcott, and in the coming months the 21-year-old rancher would make headlines in the region: Several weeks after Pyle's race left Puente, Northcott struck again, murdering two more local boys and a 19-year-old youth from Mexico. Later in the year, authorities discovered a torture room in his ranch—the *Los Angeles Times* called the entire spread a "human butcher farm." There were other oddities to his story—the murderer had a peculiar fondness for tapioca pudding. His mother cooked it every week and took it to the ranch. During the autopsy of the 19-year-old victim, an abundant quantity of the dessert was found in his stomach.

Northcott was hanged October 2, 1930, for using an axe on three young boys. One can imagine that on the evening of the first stop along the Bunion Derby trail, the most exciting event to possibly have ever passed through here, Northcott may have mingled with the cheering crowd, less concerned about watching the runners than finding his next victim.

A JUBILANT MOOD prevailed in Puente that evening. For 2 hours, a parade of athletes cascaded through the town—and then the finish times became more sporadic. Many of the runners, especially those at the front, were grinning. Only occasionally was there a man with a grimace or a wobbly knee, a signal that perhaps not everyone was up to the task of running more than 3,000 miles. As the runners came in, Ralph Goodwin and his staff jotted down their times as an announcer shouted each man's number. The athletes' names weren't declared, at Pyle's request; the only way the fans would know which runner was which was to buy a program.

It was shrewd thinking. With 199 men in the race, it was impossible to keep track of all of them. It would have been difficult enough *with* a program, and it wasn't easy to follow the runners' progress in the sports pages. After all, especially at the beginning of the race, how could you know who was worth getting to know? Would it be the one-armed runner? The senior citizen? The doctor? Any one of them might drop out by the end of the day—or last several months in the race.

The program that Pyle had written up was full of praise for the runners, but the man who received the most admiration and acclaim was—himself. The first page made it clear who the public should be watching: "From obscurity to international prominence in a few short years is the accomplishment of the man responsible for the greatest foot race of history," the page began. The next paragraph concluded that Pyle was a man "who is now known as the greatest promoter of the age." He wrapped up his biography in his usual modest way: "At first a dream—then a reality. Runners from every nook and cranny of the world responded to the call. Today, hundreds of the greatest and fleetest are traversing the route from Los Angeles to New York. Today the eyes of the world are watching the greatest, most stupendous athletic accomplishment in all history. From obscurity to fame. Hail C. C. Pyle."

Sportswriters snickered, but they also admired how Pyle thought things through. As soon as the competitors passed the finish line, they were ushered into the tent city that Pyle's personnel had erected. If fans paid admission into the walled enclosure, the entertainment continued. Otherwise, the show was over.

Inside the tent city, families bought popcorn, peanuts, soda pop, and pink lemonade, and the runners who Pyle cajoled onto the stage made for unique entertainment. Red Grange emceed, and that first night, Ed Gardner, one of four blacks in the race, made a sound that resembled the whistle of a steam locomotive, and English runner Pete Gavuzzi, an agreeable singer, likely entertained the crowd.

Most runners kept their distance from the show. Von Flue rested in his tent, changed into some clean clothes, ate the dinner that was served at 7:30, and was pleased to note that it was considerably improved upon the gruel served to them during the training. He met up with some other runners to stroll through Puente. Then he called it a night and went to bed, where he lay awake on a back-breaking cot, wondering if, as his family suggested, he really was crazy for trying to run across the country. Von Flue thought about the first group of runners—Kolehmainen, Nilson, and Quamawahu—who had covered the first day's 17 miles in less than 2 hours. They were seasoned runners who probably knew what they were doing, and if they did, Von Flue realized that he had very little chance of making much of an impression during the race.

Newton wasn't sleeping well either, but not because of nerves. The entertainment Pyle was providing was overwhelming the thin tent walls. The circus would have embarrassed P. T. Barnum—no elephants, tigers, or clowns to be found—but Pyle was proud of it. Anyone who came into their giant tent found Egyptian belly dancers, a two-headed chicken, a five-legged pig, a glass-eating man, and a tattoo artist whose body was slathered in collegiate mottoes.

There were two female musicians, one who claimed to be the world champion in ladies' slap-tongue saxophone, a style of playing that involves putting more tongue than usual on the reed of the instrument, and another who said she held the top title of women's bass drummer. There was Piu, a plump, elderly matron in a dress who happened to be a snake charmer—and performed in drag. A manly figure during the day, Piu drove one of Pyle's trucks, helped set up the tent city, shot craps with the best of them, and often was asked to escort drunk or excitable guests out of the carnival.

And yet, because Effie and his daughter didn't travel along with Pyle, Piu was practically the most feminine face at the Bunion Derby. The Egyptian belly dancers didn't last long. Many men watched the women dance and remained in their tent for the rest of the night—never getting around to the other money-making attractions, like the games of chance. After a few California towns, Pyle sent the belly dancers packing to Los Angeles.

Kah-Ko was a trained police dog that, according to Pyle's usual understatement, was the smartest canine in the world. There were also caged tropical birds, reptiles, a human skeleton, and a dried-up human corpse, mummified by arsenic, that Pyle called "the Oklahoma outlaw."

The two-headed chicken was a normal bird with an artificial chicken head attached to it. Every once in a while, the chicken would scratch the fake head and pull it off, to the surprise of the crowds.

At least the mummified outlaw was authentic. He was also Pyle's favorite staff member, the showman claimed, because the Oklahoma outlaw never complained of his billing and accommodations or asked for money.

The runners called the corpse Oscar, but his name had once been Elmer

McCurdy, a 31-year-old luckless bandit. His last haul was $46, after he and his gang haplessly blew up the safe in the wrong train, resulting in a theft that one newspaper reported was "one of the smallest in the history of train robbery." A posse caught up with the robbers, and McCurdy, surrounded in a barn, fired the first shot and then was quickly exterminated. He met his untimely end in October 1911, but McCurdy was never buried. He was given some embalming fluid, perhaps to keep him around until a family member could identify him, and then languished in an undertaker's parlor for several years, where he became something of a local celebrity at the Johnson Funeral Home in Pawhuska, Oklahoma. Then in 1916, two con men convinced authorities that McCurdy was their kin—and soon began displaying him in West Texas, charging the public to see his body. Ultimately, McCurdy wound up in a wax museum in Los Angeles, where Pyle rented him out to use in his carnival.

The mummy's owner, Louis Sonney, sent his son, Edward, along with Pyle's caravan to accompany their embalmed bandit in a Single-O, carnival slang for one attraction under a tent. It was here that crowds came to gawk in wonder at the corpse.

McCurdy's life wasn't much to brag of, but considering his current position—mounted in an upright coffin and an unwitting player in C. C. Pyle's sideshow—his afterlife was worse.

March 5, Puente to Bloomington, 34.7 Miles

The noise from the carnival didn't fade until around midnight, and then it rained, and the tents leaked.

In the early-dawn downpour, Pyle's crew began taking down tents and packing up everything: 15 tents, 250 cots, 500 pillows, and 700 blankets, among other items. Pyle called the runners together to take roll call and give a pep talk. Sporting his familiar black derby, Pyle stressed, "The runner who wins this big race must have guts and stamina."

He told everyone that he was going to make the Bunion Derby an annual affair—that as the years continued, he would bring in even more of the greatest runners from foreign lands to compete, and that in a few years, the prizes every year would collectively amount to half a million dollars.

The runners hung on his every word.

Except for Elton Haynes. He had been gung-ho about running across the country when he first arrived from Akron, Ohio, but on the first race day, he just went through the motions of running. He decided that there were too many talented marathoners in the race for him to waste his time on this and felt that other matters were more important.

While training in Los Angeles, Haynes fell in love, proposed, and lined up a job. Having already won something from the race, Haynes quit, becoming the first runner to drop out of C. C. Pyle's First Annual International Transcontinental Foot Race.

After Arthur Duffy blew his whistle, Kolehmainen sprinted like a man trying to get out of the way of a runaway train. Despite the rain, which put much of the paved highway under water, it took him only 4 hours, 12 minutes, and 30 seconds to travel just over 34 miles. His nearest competitor, Ed Gardner, came in 30 minutes later.

The sportswriters called Gardner "The Sheik," because of the white clothing he wore wrapped around his head. It was a compliment, even if there were racist overtones. Sports journalists of the era, most of them hailing from metropolises filled with immigrants, generally respected athletes for what they had to offer and didn't seem to care what they looked like. Certainly there were glaring exceptions. Occasionally a quote from Gardner or another African American would be written in a dialect resembling that of one of those wide-eyed, half-witted porters or butlers who now bring the storylines to a jarring halt in so many classic, black-and-white Hollywood movies. And although Nick Quamawahu was usually referred to as the "Arizona Hopi Indian," he was sometimes "the grand little Indian," "the little brown Injun," and that runner with the "weird name." But then there were sportswriters like Braven Dyer, who observed in an article that when it came right down to it, the only true American in the race was Nick.

THE REST OF THE PACK dribbled in over the finish line, hidden under rain slickers, long pants, overcoats, sweaters, and hats. Many of them were slipping and stumbling, wiping the rain out of their eyes. They had little choice but to continue. They could stop and shiver in the bitter cold or push toward the finish line and a warm shelter.

Six racers had had enough, including Percy Smallwood, who traveled all the way from Wales only to give up on the second day. Eli Sanchez had trained by running 40 miles a day for 2 months; then, 45 miles into the race, he broke one of the arches in his foot. Whoever said life wasn't fair may have been thinking of the Bunion Derby.

One odd man, oddly, wasn't out. The teenage tramp, Ukulele Jake, decided that, official or not, he was going to run in the race, and to C. C. Pyle's chagrin, the police informed him that the athletic hobo had as much right as anybody to use the public streets. Splashing through puddles with abandon, Ukulele Jake and his two dogs cheerfully outran several of the elite runners.

Nevertheless, Pyle was pleased. The crowds in Bloomington were as enthusiastic as in Puente, and the programs were selling briskly, meaning that the carnival appeared capable of paying for the upkeep of the race and then some. Pyle's only concern was that Kolehmainen would outpace everyone, eventually boring spectators and making the race a foregone conclusion. After his run, Kolehmainen didn't even pant, though he was dripping with sweat. He made the comment that he could have run another 25 or 30 miles. His only complaint was that his legs were cold, because he hadn't worn anything in the rain other than his normal running attire.

That evening, Kolehmainen made his way to a drugstore, where he knew he could get a cold soda pop and a little food. He sat at the counter and was waited on by a young woman with dark eyes. He flirted with her as he polished off a meal of corned beef with cabbage and then devoured two slices of pie. In his small talk with the reporters, perhaps thinking of how Gunnar Nilson had trailed him the day before, Kolehmainen promised that anybody who followed him too closely the next morning would soon be lost in a cloud of his dust.

Kolehmainen needn't have been concerned. Nilson had already developed a sore knee and finished the second day by hobbling 34 miles in the rain.

HARDROCK wrote a letter to his hometown newspaper that night, nicely encapsulating his experience so far:

> Willie Kolomanein [*sic*] won today's run in 4 hours and 12 minutes. It was 38 miles from Puente to Bloomington. I was eleventh in about 5 hours. It was cold and rainy all day. I had to run on the hard surface nearly all the way. I walked about 5 miles of the distance and finished fresh. I am in fine shape except for a little skin off the toes. I am running with a little Italian by the name of Joe Canto [*sic*]. He is a veteran runner and knows pace, so I am sticking with him. He throws his arms around my neck at the end of each day's run. The sportsmanship is fine in this race.

By the end of the second day, Kolehmainen's main threat was Olli Wantinnen, a Finnish runner who barely spoke English. A reporter with the *Los Angeles Evening Herald* attempted an interview with the help of an interpreter, Hugo Quist, one of the race officials.

Quist translated the first question and then replied to the reporter that Wantinnen, who was resting on his cot, did not feel tired.

"Have you lost any weight?" the reporter asked. Wantinnen, 97 pounds, gamely answered that he couldn't afford to.

"Can you keep up this pace clear across the country?" Wantinnen shot the reporter a look that needed no translation: He could.

"We're a queer lot, we Finns," someone said from nearby, sitting on his stiff mattress. "We run because we don't know any better. There's nothing else to do in our country. If we ever started thinking, we'd quit running. A man with too much imagination can't stand this punishment."

The man speaking was Arne Suominen, a 28-year-old who seemed to have everything going for him. He was extremely physically fit, with a keen intellect to match. Eight years earlier, when he had come to America as an exchange student, one of his first accomplishments was to win a marathon in Worchester, Massachusetts. Even after he settled in Detroit and opened a doctor's office, he still found time to win marathons.

After Pyle announced his race, Suominen knew he could win. Entering, however, required some sacrifice—he gave up his medical practice.

The *Los Angeles Evening Herald* reporter forgot all about Wantinnen. Instead, he peppered the doctor with questions, and Suominen did his best to answer. "No, I don't get a second wind, as you call it," said Suominen. "Just the same old first wind."

Suominen also held forth on hydration and hunger: "I don't worry about water on the way—that's bad for you," he asserted. "But I do get terribly hungry. Those orange groves along the road today," he grinned, "they came in mighty handy for the boys. I'll bet there's a trail of orange peels for miles back."

March 6, Bloomington to Victorville, 45.4 Miles

The next morning, Kolehmainen was once again the Invisible Man, leaving everyone else to compete for second place.

At least the morning finally provided perfect temperatures for running—it was cool and cloudy, with no drizzle. The runners needed Mother Nature's help, because they were tackling the Cajon Pass. The scenic mountain trip was recommended by the Automobile Club of Southern California, but it was not nearly as accommodating for pedestrians—a grueling road that wound its way mostly upward for many miles and 4,200 feet.

Oxygen was scarce. Muscle cramps set in. The afternoon sun grilled the pavement, making the barefoot runners shriek.

Some men fared quite well. Suominen kept his pace steady and was the 10th runner to reach Victorville. Far behind the doctor, Von Flue alternated between walking and running, and after crossing the peak, he was in good enough shape to run the remaining 12 miles. Sam Richman, a New York runner, made it over the Cajon Pass in fine shape, but 3 miles from the finish line, he wrenched his ankle. For the last 3 miles, he limped and hopped his way to Victorville. It took everything he had, but he came in 15th place for the day.

According to the Associated Press, every runner slowed to a walk at some point except Hart, the senior marathoner. Several men lost the battle with the Cajon Pass and dropped out of the race altogether.

C. C. PYLE was in Victorville, decked out in khaki pants with leather puttees—strips of material wrapped around his legs to keep them warm, in the fashion of World War I soldiers. Clutching field glasses, he was watching Willie Kolehmainen.

Much earlier in the day, Kolehmainen cleared the town of Verdemont and then sprinted as he entered the rocky terrain of the Cajon Pass. Suddenly, his groin muscle gave out.

Kolehmainen slowed from a run to a walk, battling against some of the worst pain imaginable: a stabbing pain cutting through his inner thigh and then ricocheting into his pelvis. With every step, Kolehmainen's agony increased. He ended up on his back, his facial muscles contorted as his trainer gave him an alcohol rub.

Somehow, Kolehmainen limped over the Cajon Pass and eventually into Victorville, ahead of most of the runners, since he had reached the mountains long before most of the others. But Kolehmainen's victory no longer seemed preordained. In one day, he dropped from first place in elapsed time to 15th place.

Kolehmainen didn't sound as if he thought it was over. That night, he told sportswriter Leland Lewis, "Sure, I'll go on. I'll take things easy for a time. My leg will be all right soon, and then I'll make up for lost time."

He had reason to be optimistic, despite his misfortune. According to

Lewis, the rest of the field was struggling terribly, as the "Cajon Pass with its 4,000-foot altitude claimed a score of runners as its victims. Patrol cars covered the region until after midnight—picking up stragglers who for hours had stubbornly defied fatigue, sprained muscles and ligaments, cramps, heart palpitation and other ailments."

Some men were reduced to practically crawling up the road. Everything Payne's trainer had told him was forgotten for now. There was no running 6½ miles an hour. Payne just inched up the pass as best he could. Years later, he would say, "The Cajon Pass hurt me more than anything."

The elevations were overwhelming everyone. Gavuzzi was alarmed to see that many of the runners were bleeding—from their noses and ears.

After the Cajon Pass, Hardrock stopped writing his hometown newspaper regularly. Picking up a pen required too much physical and mental energy.

As night fell, over half of the athletes were still scaling the Cajon Pass, and what really burned Pyle up was Ukulele Jake. The musical bum with the two dogs was still among the runners, looking quite cheerful.

In fact, as *Los Angeles Times* reporter Paul Lowry headed back home, driving past the worn and forlorn on the Cajon Pass, he noticed Ukulele Jake's unflagging condition: "He was strumming the uke and humming to himself, apparently in far better shape than the poor devils who plodded on ahead, their heads hung on one side, their tongues gasping and a look of woebegone agony on their faces."

CHAPTER 7

Morris Saperstein, in the 1930s, on his wedding day. He holds the distinction for probably being the last Bunion Derby runner alive. He died in February 2005 at the age of 98. (Courtesy of Fred Saperstein.)

ODD COMPANY

DISTANCE SO FAR: 97.1 MILES; EST. 150 RUNNERS

1900 TO 1905, DELAWARE, OHIO, TO CALIFORNIA

Charley Pyle was 18 years old when he learned that he had the lungs and heart of an 81 year-old.

Pyle told the *New Yorker* that he developed pleurisy from injuries he had received in a basketball game when he was 16 years old, which is possible, though such injuries would have had to be quite severe. More likely, Pyle didn't want to admit to a reporter, the public, or himself that he had inherited his father's poor constitution. However he caught the ailment, his family doctor thought an arid environment would help and advised the young man to go west.

In 1900, Pyle packed his bags and boarded a train, gainfully employed. Before leaving Delaware, Ohio, he was hired by Western Union. He earned a $2 commission for every time-service clock he sold, but it must have been a sorry piece of equipment; Pyle, a born salesman, couldn't convince people to buy them. The farther west he traveled, the more broke and hungry he became.

What seems to be clear—according to Pyle's accounting of it—is that he began selling the railroad passes that he had collected on his travels, creating a little travel agency. It was a brief career, but it earned him some money, and the man who would later be called Cash and Carry took his earnings to a tiny California outpost called Trinity, a community that existed because of the Trinity Gold Mining Company. Pyle quickly fell in with the wrong crowd and lost his travel agency profits in a card game. The way Pyle explained it, he had won, but his opponent didn't see it that way. The man pulled a gun, and moments later Pyle was penniless.

Desperate, Pyle had to earn some quick cash. He thought of the bicycling race as well as a wrestling match that he promoted in high school and decided that there had to be a sporting event he could whip up. He settled on boxing and organized a fight that pitted himself against a miner.

Boxing isn't meant for someone with a weak chest and lungs, but Pyle, who would eventually fill out to around 175 pounds, had left nothing to chance. His opponent was a senior citizen who weighed 118 pounds and had back problems.

Pyle played up the match, attracting an audience of 210 miners willing to pay $1 admission, with half the proceeds going to the winner and the other half to an injured miner nursing a sore thumb. Pyle, who spent his life in pursuit of profits, had just created his first, and probably last, charity show benefit.

Punches flew, and Pyle found himself in the fight of his life. It isn't known if prior to the match Pyle knew the elderly man's former occupation—or if he figured it out during or after the match. In any case, Pyle was battling a former boxer.

The miner couldn't stand straight, his body bent from a lifetime of stooping over a drill, but that turned out to be his greatest asset: Pyle couldn't get a solid punch at the man's face or chest. Pyle, meanwhile, was hit relentlessly and was in danger of leaving the ring bloodied, battered, *and* broke. But he rallied, and the match was declared a draw. Pyle and his opponent received $52.50 each, and the miner with the sore thumb walked away with just over $100.

Pyle, weary but wealthier, trekked north into Oregon, where he met up with the Margarita Fischer Company. This theatrical troupe of approximately a dozen actors of varying ages and talents performed in vehicles featuring the former childhood actress, Margarita Fischer, who had made her debut when she was 8, under the name "Babe" Fischer. Margarita's father, John, had owned a hotel in Oregon when a theatrical agent convinced him to let her appear in a small role in a play, *The Celebrated Case*. Soon, John sold his hotel and created an acting company. He performed, so did his eldest daughter, Dottie, and, of course, Margarita was the star. Margarita's and Dottie's mother looked after them all.

The Fischer company's specialty was theatrical plays, which they performed for nights at a time at an opera house or some other venue. They also lent out particular actors to a vaudeville revue, which performed as a band of musicians. And somewhere around 1900 or shortly after, the Fischer company was in Silverton, Oregon, where Pyle somehow met them. However it happened, he got in good with them, and soon Pyle not only had a job but also met the woman he would eventually marry.

He almost certainly noticed his future sister-in-law first. Her name was on the marquee, after all, and Margarita Fischer was a stunning creature. But she was 15 years old and under the watchful eye of her father. Her older sister, Dorothy, whom everyone called Dot, was 17, attractive, and available for marriage. They wed in September 1905 in Aberdeen, Washington. There's a mention of it in the paperwork for Pyle's divorce. It's almost the only reference remaining that pertains to their unhappy union.

The Margarita Fischer Company hired Pyle to be the theatre troupe's advance man. For $10 a week, Pyle traveled ahead of the actors, posting placards in prominent spots in town, alerting the public to the show's arrival. He also painted, repaired, and shifted scenery; blew a tuba in a band; took tickets; did a drunk act; and made the hotel and stagecoach arrangements for the cast, among other things. One of Margarita Fischer's souvenirs from this period was a written agreement that Pyle made with a hotel in Albany, Oregon, which agreed to offer first-rate service to the acting company as well as furnish a breakfast of "ham and one egg."

During this time, Pyle was learning tricks of the trade that would later serve him well when he became America's first modern-day sports agent. Pyle even functioned as the company's theatre critic. His reviews, always glowing, frequently appeared in the papers of northern California and southern Oregon.

Pyle and his wife traveled with the theatrical group until the spring of 1906, when John Fischer died in Eureka, California. Pyle's survival instinct seemed to have kicked in then. With a businessman named F. W. Parker, he purchased or rented a theatre in Eureka, which Pyle renamed The Theatre Margarita to capitalize on Margarita Fischer's fame. And yet, oddly enough, within weeks, he and Parker were drafting a letter to Pyle's old troupe, saying that their services weren't needed.

In trying to generate business, Pyle allowed guests to see movies and pay for them later, a financial strategy that didn't pan out then but would eventually be figured out by the time MasterCard and Visa took over the world. The strategy may also be why, in 1907, Pyle and Dot moved to Oakland, a suburb of San Francisco. Pyle took a job as a business manager for two theatres in Oakland and San Francisco. He was grateful to get the job, especially because he was about to become a father.

On August 21, 1907, Dot gave birth to Kathrine. Apparently, agreeing on her name was a difficult task. Several years later, in court records, Pyle referred to her as Gladys Catherine Pyle. Even if that was her name, Pyle apparently didn't know that Dot had been spelling Catherine as Kathrine. Odder still, her birth records show that the daughter of Charles and Dorothy Pyle was born Mary M. Pyle.

Beyond the arguments over their daughter's name, Dot and Charley's marriage was disintegrating. The pregnancy was difficult—from the moment Kathie was born, Dot was chronically sick, though no family member understood what her condition was. The 25-year-old Pyle wasn't well equipped to deal with Dot's sickness, fatherhood, or his mother-in-law.

Six months after the baby was born, Pyle's mother-in-law, Kate Fischer, called the police. Shortly after being arrested, Pyle was informed in court that he was accused of improperly providing for his baby daughter.

Pyle talked the judge out of giving him jail time, but several weeks later, he was arrested again, thanks to his no-nonsense mother-in-law. This time the charge was not providing for his wife.

Again, Pyle protested to the judge, this time producing letters that he had written to Dot, pleading for her to live with him. She was, Pyle explained, an invalid living at a local hospital. Pyle even hinted that his wife had refused to share her bed with him.

Given his future regard for the truth, it's easy to suspect that Pyle was just telling the judge what he believed the man wanted to hear, but he may have had a case. Dot *was* sick. Margarita Fischer mentioned her sister's "illness" to a business associate in a letter written in October 1907, and wrote about it again in the 1960s, noting that she had to provide for her ill sister and her niece for years because Dorothy wasn't well enough to work.

Pyle was frustrated. Dot was, too. They were in a stalemate, sharing a life they no longer had an interest in.

March 7, Victorville to Barstow, 36 Miles

At 9:27, on the morning after braving the Cajon Pass, the whistle blew, and C. C. Pyle took off in the *America* as the runners hurriedly left Victorville behind. Among those runners was Willie Kolehmainen, who for the first time wasn't in a hurry. He was planning to walk the next 36 miles.

But Kolehmainen's inner thigh muscles were racked with pain, and the arches in his feet were broken. It felt as if a marble were stuck inside his foot every time he took a step, and so 3 miles into the day's race, Kolehmainen had enough and surrendered. An automobile took him the remaining 33 miles to Barstow, and by nightfall he was on a train bound for New York City. The pain lasted for weeks.

Kolehmainen didn't know it, but his days as a champion runner were over. Eight months later, he competed in a 16-mile race against three other world-class long-distance marathoners, including an Olympian. Kolehmainen came in last.

Sportswriter John Kieran of the *New York Times* was sympathetic, if sarcastic. "Willie Kolehmainen was unfortunate," he noted shortly after he folded. "Willie is a good runner, but he comes from Finland, where the running is done either on frozen ground or on skates. If Mr. Pyle had laid out the course from Haines, Alaska, to the east coast of Labrador, Willie would have been far in front by this time and gaining distance every day on a diet of frozen fish. But warm weather cooked him completely."

Gunnar Nilson fared no better. His arches fell, and a car sped him to Barstow to be examined by the doctors. If the doctors could treat him, Nilson vowed he would resume the race. But they couldn't, and he didn't.

Nick Quamawahu was also struggling. The gifted runner, short and stocky, tried gamely to keep up his pace despite cramps and sore feet, but he needed an hour to cover 3 miles. Around nightfall, he withdrew 14 miles from the finish line and was shuttled to a hospital in Oro Grande for an operation. The barefoot Quamawahu had cut his heel, and it was believed that an infection had spread throughout his bloodstream.

The struggle wasn't against only the distance and the terrain beneath the runners' feet. Another enemy gunning for them was the heat, with the mercury frequently topping 90 degrees. Many runners were actually eager to reach unpaved roads and were anticipating the next day's lap, when they could contend with anything from dirt and gravel to boards—none of which trap warmth like the sun-baked pavement.

ONLY ED GARDNER appeared to have no problems the day after the Cajon Pass. He raced past the finish line, with a time of 5 hours, 15 minutes, and 10 seconds. Ten minutes later, the second runner of the day, Arthur Newton, swooped into Barstow, putting him in fourth place overall. In third place was Olli Wantinnen, who was now in first place altogether. It was Day 4, and everything had changed since the first 48 hours. The front-runners were now memories, replaced by Gardner, Newton, Wantinnen, Finnish runner Nestor Erickson, and New Jersey's John Salo.

Andy Payne paced himself per his trainer's advice and came in a respectable 17th place for the day, bringing his total time to sixth place.

Most of the others dutifully plodded down the road. Charles Hart didn't break any records, but he reached Barstow well ahead of many younger competitors. Speed walkers Guisto Umek and Phillip Granville finished in 21st and 27th place, respectively.

Ukulele Jake never received rankings, but he reached Barstow in fine health.

At 10:30 that evening, as many of the reporters scattered to search for a telegraph operator, 10 runners hadn't clocked in. By midnight, they still hadn't arrived, making it seem probable that they had given up, along with numerous runners who had surrendered earlier in the day. Sportswriters were having trouble keeping up with everyone dropping out. It's estimated that in the first few days of the race, more than 70 runners were defeated by either the desert or the Cajon Pass. Pyle never expressed any worry or doubt—that wasn't his style—but if the athletes' ranks continued to hemorrhage at this rate, no one would be running by the time they reached Texas.

His greater concern, though, was the race's finances. The runners' travel deposits—$19,900—were supposed to be seed money used to pay the 70-some people that Pyle had on staff. But every time a runner dropped out, Pyle had to give back $100. The runners had bleeding feet; Pyle was bleeding cash.

March 8, Barstow to Mojave Wells, 32.5 Miles

Confounding everyone who had given up on him, Quamawahu announced that he was still in the race. As a brass band tuned their instruments, preparing for a rousing 8:55 a.m. send-off, Quamawahu was being dropped off 14 miles to the west, well behind his peers at the starting line in Barstow. Quamawahu was starting the day's race where he had left off the previous day. It had been decided that if anyone dropped out the day before but wanted to stay in the competition, he would have to knock off the remaining miles to the night control that he hadn't yet reached before racing to the next finish line. And so Quamawahu would get to run 14 miles and then another 32.5 miles to the isolated community of Mojave Wells.

Except that, of course, running was out of the question. With his heel hurting and his feet beginning to blister, Quamawahu walked. Yet, he felt that he could still prevail, making up the lost time over the course of the next 2 months.

Only he couldn't, not really. Frank Johnson learned the horrors of slipping behind, later telling the *St. Louis Post-Dispatch*, "If you have a day's run of 25 miles and quit at 3:00 in the afternoon with five miles to go, your time goes on to midnight and to that is added the time it takes you the next day to cover the five miles."

In other words, if an athlete quit running at 3:00 p.m., *9 hours* were added to his *total* time. And he still had to run those extra 5 miles the following morning. It was like collecting a debt that was almost impossible to pay off.

IF THE OTHER RUNNERS hadn't already noticed him, Brother John would have looked like a mirage—even though it sounds appropriate, no one really expected to see a prophet roaming the desert.

Like the indefatigable Ukulele Jake, Brother John hadn't filled out the application or paid his deposit money, but he was participating in the race, anyway. He had no chance of giving Pyle the $25 entry fee and $100 in travel deposit money. When the race began, he had 97 cents.

Brother John's real name was John B. Nash, but he told reporters that his name was Jonas Israel. He was from Elk Garden, West Virginia, and 58 years old. Israel had a long beard and was deeply religious, fancying himself "the Lord's entry" and running the race in sackcloth. (He was wearing shoes at this point in the race, which he hastily found after the hot pavement burned his bare feet.)

If Israel was to be believed, he had once spent 4 years in the army, in field artillery, and had been preaching since 1914. He also married twice and was the proud papa of nine children fanned out across the country. Since he began preaching, he claimed he had been arrested 47 times, jailed on 21 occasions, and confined for various periods in 17 different insane asylums. Brother John explained, "They always had to let me go, because I convinced my keepers that their minds were equally distorted as mine."

Pyle didn't fret over Brother John's unofficial inclusion in the race as much as he did Ukulele Jake's. After all, how long could the aging religious zealot last? Israel had a bizarre plan to win the cross-country competition, intending to fast periodically during the race. Brother John bragged to a newspaper correspondent, while in the middle of a hurried walk: "I have taken neither food nor drink since Wednesday night, and I will continue my fast until nightfall on Saturday. In spite of the hardships of the desert, I am supported and given strength. I may fall behind the runners for a time, but will catch up with them again and again, and finally come into glory in New York."

Brother John had a reason for suspecting he might fall behind the runners: "From sundown Friday to sundown Saturday, I observe my Sabbath and will be off the trail," he said. "I will draw my robes about me and lie down under a clump of sagebrush, hopeful and unafraid. Once I went eight days in the desert without water as a penance. If I can guide a few souls aright, my journey will be worth while."

Then Brother John pulled out what sportswriter Leland Lewis described as a small fish horn and blew into it, releasing a blast that shattered the calm of the desert.

ARTHUR NEWTON was the front-runner on the way to Mojave Wells, 20 miles ahead of his nearest competition. He performed at his business-as-usual pace, nonchalantly passing lava beds, cactus, and barren wasteland. He drank a little here and there, but he always waited until after the daily race to quench his thirst. It was his routine; he was well aware that he wasn't invincible. His Achilles tendon in his left leg was still hurting, and now he had other nagging problems, including a cold he couldn't shake and a bad sunburn.

"In everyday life you don't realize that your skin is a comfort," wrote Newton in his autobiography, "but when the sun removes many square inches of it in patches all over your anatomy, you wake up to the fact all right."

His skin felt like wallpaper without enough paste. He also needed a good scrubbing. He managed to get a bath the first two nights from kind strangers willing to open their homes, but he had no such luck in Mojave Wells. The town, if it could be called that, had no electricity and one water well that pumped 200 gallons an hour, but it wasn't enough to meet the needs of the townspeople and Pyle's army.

As it were, the initial plan was to run from Barstow to Ludlow, but Arthur Duffy scotched that idea, citing the 52-mile distance and the heat. Instead, Duffy settled on Mojave Wells, shaving off 22 miles and a fair bit of humidity.

"I want to get into Chicago with 100 men," explained Duffy. "I can't do that if we continue to kill them off with long jumps."

Pyle wasn't exactly delighted—extra days increased his costs—but the runners must have been pleased, particularly the oldest and youngest of them. Charles Hart straggled into town second-to-last, just ahead of 15-year-old Tobie Joseph Cotton.

Cotton was desperate to run in the race, telling officials he was 16, pretty certain they wouldn't allow a 15-year-old to enter. Actually, he turned 15 only 2 days before the start of the race. Cotton's reasons for wanting in the race were understandable. It must have appeared to be his best chance to save his family.

Tobie's father, Henry Cotton, had had a career as a blacksmith, but in recent years had become an auto mechanic in Los Angeles. He did well with his new vocation until a jack slipped and a 3-ton truck pinned him underneath it. Henry survived but was paralyzed from the waist down. He was unable to work, at least as an auto mechanic, and odds were, that the jobs for a paraplegic African American in 1928 weren't plentiful. It was the last thing Henry Cotton needed—he had a wife and seven children to support.

Tobie's family agreed to help the boy enter the race. They cobbled together his entry fee and required travel deposit.

Henry, Tobie, and two younger brothers, Wesley and James, piled into their old Ford Star touring car that they had bought for $50. The family would follow Tobie, to look out for him.

Hardrock, meanwhile, who had no one trailing after him, learned that one of his newfound friends was out of the race. Veteran runner Joe Conto, who Hardrock described in an earlier letter as someone who threw his arms around him at the end of each race, had dropped out a few hours earlier that day. He had water on the knee, a generic term used to describe a terribly painful swelling. Conto ended up traveling with the group, working for Pyle by selling race programs to the crowds.

It was a hard day for a lot of the Bunion Derby gang in Mojave Wells, particularly Tom Gallery.

Gallery was a well-known boxing promoter, not to mention the husband to silent-era heroine Zasu Pitts and occasionally an actor who appeared in almost two dozen silent films in the 1920s.

Gallery wasn't in the race as a runner. But he was taken with this notion of running across the country, and his friend Pyle invited him to ride along in his caravan. Gallery readily agreed to come along, at least for a while. But in Mojave Wells, as night fell, Gallery realized he had lost some keys near the official bus that carried the blankets, cots, tents, and baggage. He pulled out a trick pocket flashlight that looked like a gun and crept about. Just as he found them and was slipping his flashlight in his pocket, the town constable hauled out a Colt 45, jammed it into Gallery's ribs, and slapped a pair of handcuffs on him.

"Caught ye dead to rights," the constable snapped. "Don't try to do any explaining. Just tell it to the judge."

Gallery didn't argue—and was marched to the jail. As the jailhouse door clanged shut, Russ Newland of the Associated Press and several others came into the police station to vouch for Gallery. Within minutes, they convinced the constable that the arrest was a mistake. But Gallery, shaken to the core, decided that the Bunion Derby was a "lot of nonsense." He left for Los Angeles on the next train.

March 9, Mojave Wells to Bagdad, 41 Miles

They started running at 7:29, squinting in the morning sun. As he had 2 days before, Ed Gardner left the competition in the dust.

Twenty-one miles later, in Ludlow, confident that the other 120-odd athletes were far behind him, Gardner reached Pyle's caravan, settling in for lunch, and stopped to quench his thirst. As Gardner caught his breath and his handlers washed his feet and changed his socks and shoes, Newton came by, waved off the invitation for a drink, and dashed off into the desert. Soon after, Gardner was trailing after him.

The other runners arrived in Ludlow before too long. Concluding that Wantinnen was a good choice to cheer for, local schoolboys began pelting him with bouquets of desert flowers, shouting, "That's the boy, Olli!"

"Thank you, little folk," replied Wantinnen, in broken English. Then either feeling no urgency or needing a break, he added: "I must stop and shake your hands." It wasn't much longer, however, before he disappeared. Everyone had a good incentive to run a little faster and harder. As Pyle had promised, this was the day that those who won the lap would start receiving daily prize money.

TWENTY-EIGHT YEARS EARLIER, the town of Bagdad had had a 200-ton capacity ore mill, a mining camp, and a railroad servicing the bustling small town. But the railroad improved its grade and tracks, which meant the extra crews that had been stationed in Bagdad were no longer needed. And in 1918 a devastating fire destroyed most of the wooden buildings in town. By 1923, the post office had closed. The dying town was slowly being swallowed up by the desert, brick by brick.

The Bagdad that the Bunion Derby passed through still had a library, numerous restaurants, a telegraph office, and a sheriff, but it wasn't very crowded, and so Pyle sent his carnival to the nearby town of Needles, even though the runners wouldn't be there for another 2 days. Better to generate excitement about the race than waste his showmanship on a few sparse citizens in a ghost town.

Indeed, by the 1950s, Bagdad consisted of only a few remaining houses, some guest cabins for the few tourists passing through, a gas station, and a popular eatery called the Bagdad Café, the only place in the region to have a jukebox and dance floor. It was a favorite stop for passersby, and the inspiration for a 1985 movie called *Bagdad Café*. Today, there is no town, just a flat, barren stretch of sand.

When Newton arrived in Bagdad—in first place, 3 miles ahead of Gardner—he was mortified to find that his search for a bath had again come up empty.

Newton wasn't the only man who missed soap. "We always hoped that the night would find us in a town, as we all wanted to get a bath," recalled Frank Johnson, although he was being generous toward some of his fellow runners, for there were some, like Wildfire Thompson, who never seemed to bathe. "The hotel keepers usually stuck us pretty hard for such service, and a dollar was the usual charge, though if you put up a hard-luck story, you might get by for half a buck."

But at least on that day, Newton made it to Bagdad. Not everyone could say the same.

Eugene Estoppey finally gave up, after logging approximately 200 miles in his logging boots. Although the 57-year-old, a lifelong runner who once was a formidable athlete, had something to be proud of, especially after his ill-fated attempt to swim the Catalina Channel, it was his last hurrah. Estoppey's slide into obscurity and humiliation continued.

The following year, Estoppey challenged a Japanese runner to a race, all the while boasting about his past accomplishments. During the week before the run, Estoppey bragged that America was about to beat Japan, ascribing more importance to the competition than it merited, especially since only 100 people showed up to watch and the mayor of Fresno refused an invitation to fire the starting gun.

It was a 10-mile event, but Estoppey collapsed after 5, falling onto the track, unable to move any farther. "My ankles are no good. I'm through. My hat's off to Japan," he said.

As 1929 drew to a close, Estoppey ran for 9 days, with a total of 37 hours to cover 180 miles—impressive, but a far cry from his old days of glory; he carried a message to the major of San Francisco from the mayor of Fresno, who probably felt sorry for the guy after ignoring his race earlier in the year.

It was a worthless stunt, since either mayor could have called the other on the telephone, but Estoppey simply needed to be a man in motion. A few months later, with the Great Depression in full swing, Estoppey was employed as a waiter at a work camp in Ahwahnee, California, and frequently he would put down his tray without warning and run down the road and back, unnerving everyone. The *Fresno Bee* reported that the local sheriff was asked to take away the running waiter. When the *Bee* last commented on his condition, Estoppey was in a county jail, awaiting word on whether authorities were going to declare him legally insane.

THE RUNNERS who reached Bagdad gathered around Pyle, who revealed that the community leadership hadn't agreed to pony up money for the daily prizes. There was a lot of grumbling, and Pyle assured everyone that the daily prizes would definitely, eventually be coming. He said he was going to send one of his representatives forward, to make positively sure that the upcoming towns would be cooperating.

TEN MILES AWAY, as the sun disappeared, Walter Ricketts, from Southampton, Ontario, was still on the road. As Ricketts was about to learn, running at night meant putting your life in someone else's hands.

The faster athletes always had two distinct advantages over the slower ones. If they could make it to the town (or what they called the night control) relatively early, they had the rest of the day to recover and relax before going to bed and recharging for the next day's journey. And the fastest runners weren't forced to run in the dark.

In the 1920s, roaming along a lonely countryside or mountainous road at night was a death wish. It wasn't just the lack of streetlights. Dust clinging to the headlights obscured a driver's vision, as did a dirty windshield, since cars had wipers but no washer fluid. Wrecks at night were common, because a driver's vision was obscured by the light from another auto, causing him to instinctively swerve and hit something else. Two drivers going toward each other in the night resulted in a game of blindman's bluff.

The *Los Angeles Times* 2 years earlier explained that most headlights created a window of light ranging from 6 to 15 degrees, "which leaves a dark area on both sides of the car for a considerable distance, making it difficult to see the ditches or judge intervals in passing other cars or to see pedestrians, at short range, stepping into the line of travel."

That is what was about to happen to poor Walter Ricketts. An automobile, pitching from side to side, rocketed toward him. Whether or not the driver had narrow, dusty headlights to guide him, it didn't matter: Ricketts was invisible.

After Ricketts was knocked senseless, the car didn't stop. Ricketts suffered two fractured ribs and withdrew from the race as police issued bulletins for the public to be on the lookout for a yellow Studebaker.

March 10, Bagdad to Danby, 31.9 Miles

C. C. Pyle liked what he was seeing. For not the first time, Pyle declared, "This race is going to be an annual affair. When I see the thrilled folks fairly springing from the ground to watch the boys go by, I feel I have received a real calling . . . even though the multitude gets to see the high points of the extravaganza without contributing to the box office."

But pleased as he was, the race already had logistical problems. From Bagdad, Pyle had plotted a course to a town called Fenner, 44 miles away. But then, at the last minute, Pyle decided that they would converge on Essex, 42 miles away. But when a water delivery to Essex was delayed, Pyle hastily made Danby the destination, which was even closer. Because of that decision, reaching Needles would require a whopping 57-mile trek through the desert the following day.

Confused? Think how the runners felt. The decision to run to Danby in lieu of Fenner and then Essex postponed the 7:00 a.m. start time by a few hours—regrettable, because that ensured that even the fastest runners would be in the sun during the day's warmest hours.

Again in the lead, Newton had the honor of being the first to check out their latest night control. Uncomfortable, sunburned, and filthy, he was again disappointed to learn that Danby had no available showers. "Many of the stopping places and villages in the desert had apparently never heard of such a thing," lamented Newton. All Danby had to offer was a general store and a few scattered houses.

But later in the day, Newton probably finally received his wish. There was enough water to set up what Frank Von Flue remembered as a "bath house," where people could shower. One can only hope Newton learned about it before it was taken down.

It was a miserable day overall. Von Flue developed such a devastating sunburn that it would leave scars that wouldn't heal for 10 years. Meanwhile, the scenery was monotonous—nothing but sand, with occasional sagebrush dotting the landscape. The road beneath them was a mix of dirt and gravel, the latter effectively chopping up their shoes and feet. Leroy "Doc" Freeman, from Oklahoma City, pulled a tendon in his left ankle, but that didn't prevent him from staggering toward Danby.

Everyone kept moving, encouraged by trainers supplying water to every runner. It was definitely an asset to have your own personal aid, though. For instance, Rod Ellsworth, a runner from Pennsylvania, had his brother-in-law and a friend as trainers, trailing him in a Ford touring car that they had bought in Los Angeles for $30. Every 10 miles, Ellsworth would change his shoes to refresh his feet and prevent blisters—impossible without a trainer's assistance. Nevertheless, Ellsworth found the slog through the desert a generally miserable experience.

Whatever strategy a runner used, it could only help so much. The ground was rough, the heat was excruciating, and for some, the hunger and thirst unbearable.

And there was little chance of quenching your thirst. Harry Sheare, a runner from San Francisco, later recounted that during this period, they rarely were able to find water to drink, even in the towns. They were usually grabbing a bottle of soda pop at the local gas station, and the opportunities to do that were scarce.

George Rehayn devised his own clever method for staying hydrated. A German American just a month older than Pyle, Rehayn was a colorful character who had been a bicycle racer in earlier years and was still in excellent physical condition when he decided to enter the race. He frequently belted out tunes as he ran, which earned him the nickname "the Singing Dutchman." To stay hydrated during the race, whenever he reached a gas station, he snatched the watering can, having figured out that invariably there would be refreshing, lukewarm liquid waiting for him, even if it was really for an attendant to add to a car's radiator.

One day about this time, Newton later recalled, Rehayn grabbed a bright tin watering can and started drinking. He had about a pint before he stopped, spitting out what he could.

It was gasoline.

He kept running, but he became violently ill, and it took several days for him to recover.

Everyone was aching, but they all had their own motivations for not falling to the ground and surrendering to the elements. Morris Saperstein kept going because he knew that a college education was his if he could make it to New York. Teodocio Rivera, a Filipino dentist, planned to turn his prize money into an institute that would further dental research work in his homeland. Andy Payne had a family farm to save and a girl to win over.

But some couldn't go on, simply because of bad luck. Sometime that afternoon Pat Mahoney, a 32-year-old from Long Beach, California, was hit by a car and was later discovered by several walkers, who found him lying unconscious in the middle of the road. They propped him onto his feet, and Mahoney somehow navigated the remaining miles to Danby.

SAPERSTEIN WAS FLOUNDERING. After 7 days and 240 miles, his body, particularly his feet, was giving out. He had run in high school, but the longest of those races had been maybe 5 miles.

Saperstein had nothing to feel bad about. By the time the Bunion Derby reached Danby, more than one-third of the original number of runners had dropped out. As Dr. Gordon and Dr. Baker wrote in their report:

> The general appearance of most runners after completion of the daily mileage was that of exhaustion, with cold perspiration, dyspnea, drawn facial expressions, hunger, thirst and a desire to sleep . . .
>
> As the race progressed, other complications in addition to those previously noted were as follows: boils (one rectal abscess), diarrhea, tympanitis [inflammation of the inner ear], sudden elevation in temperature while running, nausea, acute upper respiratory infections with fever of 100 degrees to 101 degrees F., loss of toe nails, blisters of the feet . . .

The list droned on.

Saperstein suffered from swollen arches, although the official diagnosis probably should have been posterior tibial tendonitis. The skin underneath Saperstein's arches likely swelled, which is common among runners overexerting themselves, especially those with flat feet. Once the foot swells, the base of the foot is painful to touch. Assuming Saperstein ran for some time with posterior tibial tendonitis, every step would have been agonizing.

The idea that he could keep running for the next 3 months was patently absurd, and Saperstein did the only reasonable thing he could do. On the train back to New Jersey, he kept his feet propped up—and continued to for the next several weeks.

Saperstein's dreams of a college education were finished, although he would go on to have a healthy, happy, and long life. Saperstein is believed to have been the last surviving participant of the Bunion Derby, passing away in February 2005 at the age of 98.

He didn't initially surrender his goals of finishing college, but after the Great Depression went into full swing, it eventually became apparent that he was destined for other things. He became a store manager and later a successful tailor living in Port Arthur, Texas.

During his long life, Saperstein occasionally regaled his wife and children with stories of his dance marathon days and of how once he was in a dance contest with comedian Red Skelton. He talked about a high school classmate who went on to become the well-known MGM studio head, Dore Schary.

He revealed quite a few layers of his personal past. But Saperstein never spoke about his own athletic performance as a runner—despite an impressive showing of scaling the Cajon Pass, crossing miles of deserts, and outlasting several world-champion marathon runners.

For reasons no one will ever know, Saperstein went to his grave without mentioning a word to his family about the nightmarish race and the showman who organized it. His son, Fred, learned about the very existence of the Bunion Derby from his own son, who stumbled upon the information after looking up his grandfather's name on the Internet.

March 11, Danby to Needles, 57 Miles

Arthur Duffy kept reassuring the runners that they would get a day of rest, but Pyle would have none of it.

The runners were resting plenty, as far as he was concerned. Every day the race operated—profits from the towns and carnival notwithstanding—was another that Pyle's enterprise spent money. Besides, the shortened daily runs had already caused some nationwide disenchantment among sportswriters, a group of people Pyle needed in his corner because they could generate excitement among the communities his race would pass through.

But his hope for cheerleading in print wasn't coming to pass. In the waning days of the California passage, with 10 more states on the itinerary, *New York Times* scribe John Kieran wrote, "Before the transcontinental caravan started on its way, Mr. Pyle announced that the runners would average 55 miles per day and would arrive in the Yankee Stadium on or about May 10. But he neglected to say what year. The way the race is progressing now, this was a serious omission."

The criticism stung. Pyle prided himself on staging a show that no one would or could forget. He envisioned his race as the type of spectacle he had enjoyed in high school when he was an impoverished, sickly teenager daydreaming of a better life. The college football games at Ohio Wesleyan University had been a welcome respite from the rest of the week. Wesleyan's brilliant coach, Fielding Yost—also known as Hurry Up Yost—made a particular impression on Pyle, who later recalled: "When things looked dark, he would jump in and play the last half himself. That was laudable in a coach in those days." By 1928, Yost had retired from coaching but was still the athletic director and a living legend at the University of Michigan. Not surprisingly, when Pyle led the charge to truly professionalize professional football, his hero, Yost, was infuriated.

Another man on the football field dazzled Charley—Charles Lloyd Barney, a noted strongman who lifted grand pianos and held them at arm's length over his head. He picked up trolley cars. He once held a horse over his shoulder.

Newspapers around the country throughout the 1890s and the first decade of the 20th century reported on his exploits. Nebraska's *Lincoln Evening News* reported in 1895 that Barney routinely killed cattle by hitting them with his fist and once lifted a wooden beam—loaded with eight men—over his shoulders. He used to astonish the citizens of Des Moines by picking up cows and horses and carrying them across the street.

In 1897, after the obligatory stint in vaudeville, Barney became a student at Ohio Wesleyan and quickly joined the football team. Charley Pyle, 15, thrilled to the sight of the 204-pound football athlete crushing opponents, with Yost coaching. Over 30 years later, Pyle felt that he was masterminding an athletic event every bit as entertaining and compelling as the athletics Yost and Barney delivered. It's just that in the desert, no one was around to see it. Not yet.

There would be no rest for the weary on Sunday. In fact, that day would see their most lengthy jog yet, beginning at 5:00 a.m. The early hour would shield them from the day's most brutal heat for a time.

Despite yesterday's meeting with a speeding car, Pat Mahoney was at the starting line. The whistle blew, and he ran, but his badly wrenched hip betrayed him. He wobbled and then toppled to the ground. Mahoney was going home.

The *Los Angeles Examiner*'s Maxwell Stiles summed up the perils the runners faced, remarking, "A dangerous trail, it is. One might class it with automobile racing and football. Only in this instance, it's a game between the pedestrians in the race and the motorists out of it."

As usual, Newton started his run slowly, with approximately 80 men ahead of him, but as the day wore on, he steadily cruised past the field.

A few hours later, the show-off Dr. John J. Seiler took off running from Ascot Speedway, still intending to eventually pass the runners. When he reached Bloomington for his first night's rest, he was at the Bunion Derby's second stop. Seiler had run 2 days' worth of his competitors' distance in a single day, although, to be fair, the first leg of the Bunion Derby was a relatively brisk 17 miles.

DURING SOME DOWNTIME in the evening, Hardrock managed another letter to his hometown newspaper, the *Burlington Daily Times*: "I have never seen so much suffering in all my life as men have endured on this race. How I admire the nerve of some of these fellows, with the ailments some of them have. I don't see how in the world they drag their bodies along! The Lord has blessed me through, outside of a little soreness, tiredness and blisters." What Hardrock didn't know was that his shoes with the cork and asbestos were responsible for his blisters and soreness. He hadn't realized the shoes' flaw—they were a little narrow in the ball of his foot.

And the blisters, which covered his feet, were quite a problem. When one burst, he had to limp the rest of the way to the finish line.

But Hardrock didn't have a monopoly on suffering. Years later, Nick Anthony, who had been a 16-year-old runner from Long Beach, California, revealed to a reporter that on the trip to Needles, "two runners went out of their minds from the heat of that day. The promoters somehow managed to keep it out of the papers."

Even if unaware of the men going out of their minds, the sportswriters had a sense of what the men were enduring. During one restless moment, Russ Newland hopped out of the official bus and jogged behind it for 200 yards—and then got back on the bus, sweaty and humbled.

Newland and the other sportswriters got a kick out of the fact that as challenging as the terrain was, the oldest runners were outdoing their juniors. Charles Hart was still barely besting Tobie Cotton. Dick Frost, 56, was still a contender. Sixty-year-old Charles Gallena was hanging in there.

So was Ukulele Jake—to C. C. Pyle's utter frustration. At the rate he was going, the unofficial runner could place first, making a mockery of the whole race.

JOHN CRONICK WAS FIRST into Needles, jogging in on a wide gravel road. Cronick had run for 8 hours and 44 minutes. He averaged nearly 7 miles each hour under clouds that leveled the temperature a bit, but the rolling desert hills still provided ample difficulties. Most troubling was the sand that had settled over the road, as speeding cars sprayed and kicked up clouds of dust that enveloped the runners.

Cronick was welcomed with cheers and applause. Much of the public present, especially on the outside of town, were Native Americans who came to see Nick Quamawahu, who came jogging in very slowly, due to his wounded heel. If his speed was disappointing to the crowd, they didn't show it. A 12-Indian marching brass band accompanied Quamawahu for the last 2 miles into Needles, and for the first time since his injury, he broke into a spirited run.

Five minutes after Cronick's arrival, Newton appeared, annoyed by the road conditions—gravel kept getting stuck in his shoes—but he was otherwise fine and still in the position of first place. Payne followed Newton shortly after, lifting the young Oklahoman to second overall. Ten places after that, in 13th place for the day, was Hart. "Thirteen may be my lucky number," the veteran runner quipped.

Newton was delighted to be in Needles, a community where he could take a bath. The city was an oasis, with a movie theatre, restaurants, and comfortable lodging. It had a city council, a Needles Recreation Hall, and a weekly newspaper called the *Needles Nugget*, which you could subscribe to for $2 a year. There were plenty of businesses around to advertise in it, selling gas to lumber to landscaping services. There were even popular saloons and pool halls around town—perhaps too popular: A few weeks earlier, nine squads of prohibition officers had conducted a large series of raids in Needles, arresting 10 men and three women for selling mash and bootleg whiskey.

But of all the industry in Needles, the trains were what really kept the city in business, and Saturday was payday for the railroad workers. C. C. Pyle had set up the carnival on Friday, with little revenue to show for it, but on Saturday, a full day before the runners limped into town, business was brisk. Even the next morning, church services couldn't completely compete with the Bunion Derby's two-headed chicken and Elmer McCurdy.

When Pyle found his hotel room and had a moment to think, he couldn't have been more pleased. After several questionable showings in towns, Needles was a windfall for the carnival. When it was all said and done, the First Annual International Transcontinental Foot Race had brought in $1,350, of which the Needles Chamber of Commerce received only $135, which resulted in a $76 profit for them, after incurring expenses such as hiring a police force to keep the traffic at bay as the athletes hobbled into town.

The *Needles Nugget*, like a number of local papers, expressed a little concern that the town didn't quite see as much money as Pyle had promised. The cash registers were making a lot of noise at the hotels and restaurants, the *Nugget* reported, but otherwise, most of the other businesses didn't see greater activity. "But, anyway," the paper concluded, "we have seen the international transcontinental footrace, Colonel Cash and Carry Pyle, the great 'Red' Grange, and that's something. Just how much, each citizen can best decide for himself."

AS FOR THE BUNION DERBY TROUPE, no one wanted to leave Needles. General stores carried lotions that trainers could buy for their runners and hot meals were plentiful. Von Flue probably wasn't the only one who used the city as a chance to buy some new footwear: patent leather street shoes. He figured they had to be better than his original pair, which had pretty much disintegrated.

Compared to the desert outposts they had stayed in, Needles was practically a utopia. The runners felt so refreshed that no one dropped out that evening or the next morning; they all decided to continue the race.

Two familiar faces, nonetheless, weren't there when the whistle blew the next morning. The Sabbath had been 2 days earlier, and that's likely when Brother John finally lost sight of the Bunion Derby runners. However, Brother John didn't wither up in the desert and die. He kept walking.

A couple months after the Bunion Derby ended, he turned up in Edwardsville, Illinois, still tramping across the country. He was wearing an all-white outfit, clean-shaven, bald, and holding a staff. He refused car rides, insisting he would walk across the entire country, and he revealed to a reporter that he had wandered in the California desert for 4 days without food. He was still preaching, collecting dimes from anyone kind enough to give them to him, and blowing his trumpet.

The other athlete missing in action was Ukulele Jake. He and his dogs frustrated Pyle to no end—allowing a road clown to run with the best athletes in the world threatened to turn the event into a laughingstock. And the way things were going, that seemed likely to occur without Ukulele Jake's help. Something had to be done, and Pyle decided to make his last stand in Needles. When Ukulele Jake arrived with his two dogs, the SPCA was waiting for him.

The animal rights organization had been thriving since before Pyle was born, and just as the puppet master had hoped, the association came and swiftly took the dogs away, seizing them at a moment when Jake wasn't watching them. Pyle's plan worked even better than he could have dared hope, because when Ukulele Jake began combing the town for his missing dogs, he was picked up by the police for vagrancy. By the time Jake extracted himself from the clink and stared down the long and desolate stretch of Highway 66, Pyle and his runners were deep into the dangerous desert sands of Arizona.

CHAPTER 8

A scene that could have been in any town, any day of the race. Here, the runners are waiting for the whistle before running 33.5 miles to Oklahoma City. (Courtesy of the El Reno Carnegie Library.)

Racing Arizona

Distance So Far: 295.5 Miles; Est. 100 Runners

March 12, Needles, California, to Oatman, Arizona, 20.5 Miles

The Bunion Derby runners left at 10:00 a.m. Whether the decision to leave so late was conscious or not, no matter: It meant another long day of running in the desert heat to finish another stage fraught with confusion. Down the road a ways, no one could quite agree where they were going to next.

The original plan had been to set the course so that it utilized a bridge 12 more miles down the road, which led to Topock, Arizona. But when the runners reached the Colorado River, a number of Mojave Indians were waiting with boats, offering to ferry the runners over the water.

C. C. Pyle wasn't sure what to do. The runners could go approximately an extra 24 miles and continue following Highway 66. That was the original plan, and it made sense. But by taking the Mojaves' ferries, Pyle guarded against having his population of runners plunge. The route from Needles to Oatman through Topock meant a 48-mile run across more harrowing, mountainous desert. Many of the runners wouldn't be able to hack it. If they crossed the Colorado River now, it was only 20 miles to Oatman, which still made for a grueling day. Of course, they could run to Topock and spend the night there. But that meant staying the night in yet another desert outpost where few dollars would come in, and in the process earning still more criticism from sportswriters convinced that the race was going too slowly.

Another benefit of running through Topock, however, was that the runners wouldn't be charged. The Mojave Indians wanted money.

Pyle set the course through Topock, but then everyone complained so loudly that Pyle quickly relented rather than risk a mutiny. Pyle reluctantly paid the river operators, and soon after, the Bunion Derby was on its way once more.

The caravan didn't miss much by skipping Topock—it existed primarily because its port and railroad station aided in shipping gold from the nearby Oatman mines. Today, virtually nothing remains of Topock.

For Pyle, leaving California was vastly different on this occasion as compared to when he left 20 years earlier. Last time he snuck way; this time, it was a victory march.

CHARLEY PYLE moved eastward in 1908, without his wife and daughter. Did he tell his wife he was going out to buy some cigarettes and never return? Did he slip out in the middle of the night? Was there a fight, before he stormed out of Dot's hospital room? We'll probably never know, but Pyle eventually made amends with his daughter, who had a warm relationship with her father by the Bunion Derby years, and by then, he even had restored his friendship with Dot.

In 1908, however, Pyle was establishing a pattern that he followed for the rest of his life: He was incapable of an enduring, monogamous relationship.

When Pyle left California, he bought a projector and some films and traveled around the Northwest as an impromptu movie exhibitor. Moving pictures were a curiosity, and Pyle managed to attract crowds. By 1910, he was in Boise, Idaho, where he once toured with the Fischer theatrical troupe, but this time he was broke and bottomed out. He had to pawn his projector's lens to get a meal, which then meant he needed to take his career in a new direction.

He set his sights on an empty store on Main Street and, despite his financial situation, he signed a lease, obliging him to pay $100 rent every month for the next 2 years. Pyle then hired a carpenter to put in seats and build a new façade with a ticket booth. The carpenter, naturally, asked for a deposit so he could buy the lumber.

"Come with me," said Pyle, who led him to the office of a lumber dealer. Pyle looked at the lumber dealer and gestured to his new friend, the carpenter. "Give this man everything he wants."

Pyle told the lumber office to bill his new movie theatre. Then, as his new theatre was constructed, a local capitalist tagged after Pyle, wanting to know what was being built. Before the investor knew what was happening, he was a 50-50 partner and paid Pyle $2,500.

Pyle used that money to pay off the carpenter and lumber office, and then—before the movie theatre even opened—he sold the other half of the business for another $2,500 and left town.

He settled in Pocatello, Idaho, investing his new fortune in an amusement park and vaudeville theatre, but his mini-empire was quickly threatened when a new law mandated that amusement parks close on Sunday. Business took a big hit, and Pyle was in serious trouble again. Another payday arrived, and his entire vaudeville troupe demanded the money owed them—a total of $750—or they would walk out. That very day, however, a theatre producer from Pocatello walked into Pyle's office and asked him if he could hire some vaudeville acts for his grand opening.

"I can let you . . . for $750 down," said Pyle.

The producer agreed, and they went into partnership for a brief time.

When Pyle left Idaho for Chicago in 1910, he had $1,900 in his pocket. Within weeks, though, he was in court, defending himself against Dorothy's lawsuit. A devout Catholic, Dot decided she could live with the stigma of a divorce and asked for one and financial support. By the time Pyle was finished talking to the judge, Dorothy received only the divorce.

If it bothered him that he was leaving Dorothy and Kathie to fend for themselves, Pyle could comfort himself with the knowledge that his ex-sister-in-law was increasingly popular on the vaudeville circuit. Between Margarita Fischer and his overprotective mother-in-law, Dorothy and Kathie would make out just fine. Indeed, in 1911, Margarita married film director Harry Pollard, and by 1914, he was directing himself, his wife, and 6-year-old niece, billed as Kathie Fischer, in a series of now mostly forgotten motion pictures.

Pyle, meanwhile, was 28 and had a clean slate. One way or another, he was going to do everything he could to find his own path to fame and fortune.

ALONG THE BANKS of the Colorado River, there were 14 boats that were slightly wider than canoes, each able to seat six men. They couldn't quite haul everyone across at once, and no one was allowed to resume the race again until the last man was across. Steve Owen, a 6-foot, 270-pound hulk of a man, made sure that the runners obeyed Pyle's edict.

Owen was the captain of the Bunion Derby's two-man police force, and he wasn't just some bouncer who made sure only the right people entered a speakeasy. Owen was a former wrestler and a tackle with the New York Giants. Owen pulled in $100 a game, but as it was the off-season, Pyle's invitation for some steady work must have seemed promising. Pyle, in fact, promised to pay him every day.

If Owen was the sheriff, Roy "Bullet" Baker and Ray "Red" Flaherty were his deputies. Like Owen, both were football players, professional, intimidating, and talented. Baker threw the first touchdown at the 1923

Rose Bowl game. Flaherty would become a member of the Football Hall of Fame, most notably as a coach for the Boston Redskins. In 1934, when the Giants played a game on frozen turf that saw players slipping everywhere they went, Owen devised a plan to destroy the other team. Before the game, he had sent out a fellow to borrow basketball shoes from a nearby college. Owen and his teammates, with better traction on their side, crushed their opponents, 30 to 13. Owen later became the coach of the Giants—a position he kept for 23 years. Ironically, years before his beefy days as a football player and Bunion Derby cop, Owen had hoped to become a jockey.

Even if Owen wasn't around, no runner in their right mind would have slipped away during the river crossing. Everyone was always grateful to take any opportunity to relax. While the first group of runners waited for the subsequent boats to transport the rest of their mates, they dangled their blistered feet in the muddy waters. Inside the boats, the runners dunked their heels and toes over the sides—at least for a while. The boat crossing was less than idyllic; Pete Gavuzzi later recalled that he and many runners had to get into the water and help push the boats over sandbanks.

Not helping anyone was a heavy fog drifting over the river, and for a time, seven runners were even believed to have fallen out of their boat and perhaps carried away by the current, but in the end everyone made it across. Andy Payne was particularly interesting to the Mojave Indians, who were excited to learn that his heritage included Cherokee. They offered him his own personal boat ride, while the others struggled with sinking canoes.

Once across the Colorado River, the runners received two oranges, courtesy of F. F. Gunn, father of one of the runners, and were warned that the oranges would be their only form of liquid or nourishment until they came across Pyle's caravan. "Lord knows when we were going to see them," Gavuzzi remembers thinking, "because they were all going a completely different way than us."

The men as a group were thrilled to be across the river and into new territory. "Good-bye, California! Hello, Arizona!" several shouted. Owen blew his whistle, and the tough grind started again.

"The roads there are described as the very poorest in the state of Arizona," wrote Maxwell Stiles of the *Los Angeles Examiner,* "and Arizona is more famous for its gila monsters than its highways." He unfortunately added, "In this case the runners with the swollen feet and ankles who bring up the rear are the heela monsters."

Stiles's penchant for comedy aside, he was correct about Arizona's roads, and Pyle's missing caravan made the situation worse. In California, at any unusual turn, red arrows marked the way for the runners, but now they were ahead of Pyle, left to figure out the wilderness for themselves. The runners dubbed that section of the journey "The Jungle Run."

Arthur Newton had left the others behind in a hurry, but he soon slowed down and stopped, hurriedly trying to determine where the road, covered in brush, led. He was still waiting when a lanky 23-year-old, Pete Gavuzzi, caught up with him.

"Peter, where are we?"

"I don't know," admitted Gavuzzi, who probably took this opportunity to light up. He was frequently seen on the road, in mid-run, smoking cigarettes. Gavuzzi scaled a small tree, attempting to spy something that would point the correct way. But he saw nothing. Behind them, there were no other runners—yet.

Newton and Gavuzzi finally settled on the same path. It resembled a goat trail, Gavuzzi later said, although it was actually an abandoned stagecoach route.

Newton ran, quickly leaving Gavuzzi behind. But soon after, he became disoriented in the sagebrush, desert sands, and multitude of paths, any of which might be the main road. Newton stopped, waiting until Gavuzzi again appeared on the horizon. The men held a quick meeting about the next direction they should be heading. They settled on one, and once more, Newton left Gavuzzi behind—this time for the rest of the day's race.

Gavuzzi had short, untamed hair and a thin mustache—with a week's growth of beard—and a lean frame that made him appear taller than he was. He was born Pietro Gavuzzi to an Italian father and French mother in

Folkestone, England. His accent was Cockney, though he frequently spoke Italian and was fluent in French as well. Newton liked him, writing that Gavuzzi was "always supremely good-tempered and happy." Gavuzzi was one of the best runners in the group, and "he seemed to just glide over the ground as a swallow glides through the air without a suspicion of effort or concern."

Because he was a slight fellow, Gavuzzi had left school at 14 to train as a jockey, but 5 years later he weighed 112 pounds, still a lightweight but too heavy for the saddle.

Gavuzzi had been boxing and long-distance running in his spare time, but with his days as a jockey behind him, he decided to pursue a career outside of sports. Wanting to see more of the world, he joined the White Star liner *Majestic* as a steward. Still, he stayed in shape because competitive running was a sport that many ocean liner crews participated in, which captains and management encouraged. Even his serious smoking habit couldn't change the fact that Gavuzzi was a remarkable runner.

ANDY PAYNE, despite consistently coming in the top 10 for the day, never seemed to be in much of a hurry. "Just keep stepping from day to day. Maybe speed up when we pass through the home country, and save a sprint for the Yankee Stadium, New York. That's my motto," he told reporter Leland Lewis. The "home country" referred to his home state of Oklahoma, and if Payne was worried about his pace, Lewis would have had to pry the information out of him. Like his father, Andy was guarded. You just didn't share your problems with strangers.

Payne's "stepping from day to day" strategy was hatched by his trainer, Tom Young, who chastised him whenever he ran too fast. Andy assumed it was good guidance. As a boy, Andy had read sports magazines and carefully analyzed any of the articles that featured foot racing. Young's recommendations seemed sound: Run hard, but not too hard. If you're going to burn yourself up during one of the daily runs, do it when you can most afford to, near the end of the race.

Even if Payne never thought of it in this way, he was a big believer in the tortoise and hare story: Steady and sure wins the race.

He hadn't always been that way. In previous summers, Andy hadn't been lazy, but he wasn't focused either. He and his younger brother, Hensel, traveled the rail lines, drifting from town to town. On at least one occasion, somewhere in California they approached a police station, asking if the sheriff would lock them up for the night, since they had nowhere else to stay. The marshal did, and Andy and Hensel had a night of free room and board. Then, during the days, they soaked in the endless sunshine.

Andy came by his wanderlust naturally. His father, Andrew "Doc" Payne, left home in 1887, when he was 11. According to family lore, Doc didn't like his stepfather, who seemed like a lazy sort of buffoon. Doc found his way to Claremore, where—and this part is true—he worked on a ranch for Clem Rogers, father of 8-year-old eventual superstar Will Rogers. The two boys were close, until Doc eventually moved on.

Doc had a tough life, and he drummed his work ethic into his own children. If there wasn't work to be done on the farm, Doc would invent chores for the kids, like moving rocks. Andy, however, usually elected to supervise his brothers and sisters rather than be a principal worker. As a result, Doc wondered and worried about that boy.

He needn't have worried, though. In the Bunion Derby, Andy displayed a supreme work ethic, and his father, keeping up with the race in the papers, took notice.

EVERYONE had their own plan for winning the race. Shortly before tackling Arizona, Phillip Granville, a speed walker from Toronto, told Stiles that he believed Newton was going to tire out. "I'll really start running when I hit Chicago," explained a confident Granville in cool, crisp Oxford English. "I can run 26 miles a day without tiring myself, if I have to. I prefer to walk until all the runners are out or half dead. Then I'll start running, and I think that between Chicago and New York, I can pass every man in the field and win by as many hours as I care to win by."

Harry Gunn was also a speed walker, but unlike many of the walkers, he was determined to stay that way, even if that meant losing the race. Gunn, 25, stood out from the crowd not only because he was always moving in swift walking strides but also because he was a millionaire's son—and brought his millionaire father along with him.

The richest man traveling with the Bunion Derby was not Pyle, but Freeman Fremont Gunn, more commonly known as F. F. Gunn, and simply Dick to his friends and neighbors back in Ogden City, Utah. He owned the Gunn Supply Company, which provided labor to the Union Pacific lines from Seattle to Kansas City, and Los Angeles to Omaha. He also spent several thousand dollars building a restaurant, later known as Dick's Café. By utilizing his eatery, he had an interesting way of combining charity and capitalism. He routinely offered free meals—generous and well-cooked portions of food—to the needy and unemployed, and then when the men came in, he offered them the chance to do some temporary work on the railroad.

F. F. Gunn, 53 years old, a husband and the father of six children, decided to use Harry's adventure as an excuse for a vacation for himself and his family. He traveled in two luxury campers, one that housed his sporty roadster, and if the rumors are to be believed, he also brought along a personal trainer, who gave Harry a cold soda pop every 30 minutes. It seems like a plausible scenario, since little expense was spared to help Harry. The elder Gunn confirmed it later at a Rotary Club meeting that Harry drank only Ogden water on the trip: It was shipped by express to various cities along the route.

Of all the runners, Harry needed the prize money the least, which explains why he had little interest in winning it. He simply wanted to promote his passion and set a world record in his beloved sport. He wouldn't have minded winning the race, but it would only be accomplished by speed walking.

Since its earliest origins, speed walking had been a much-maligned activity in the sports pages, but papers readily covered it, nevertheless, since at least as early as 1878, when the *New York Times* did a story about the results in the Amateur Walking Championship of America. Competitive walking was becoming extremely popular into the early 20th century, and by the time Harry Gunn discovered it, it was an industry. Still, that didn't stop sportswriters from grousing. One *Times* columnist in the 1920s sniffed that walking races were "unnatural and abnormal. As long as we have races to see how fast a man can walk, why not add a few events to see how slowly a man can run?"

If Gunn had his way, people were going to stop mocking his chosen sport, though certainly Stiles was a convert to Granville's walk-then-run strategy. Before he made a long drive back to Los Angeles, he concluded to his readers: "If Newton can last, Newton is certain to win. There's an 'if' there. Granville can and will finish, and there's no 'if' about that."

ARTHUR NEWTON was the first of the Bunion Derby runners to jog into Oatman. He couldn't have been happier to be in civilization, even if the town had seen better days. When Newton came into Oatman—with Granville far behind him—he hurried past a quaint icon even for the 1920s, a town crier, who immediately reported Newton's arrival to anybody within earshot.

The mining town, established after gold was discovered in 1902, was already in decline, as great quantities of gold hadn't been found there in years. Until 1901, the town was known as Vivian (like Andy's elusive schoolteacher crush), named after the first gold mine.

Newton and the others came to a town bloated with saloons, restaurants, and hotels, but the community was decaying. In 1915, a $14 million gold strike caused the population to swell from a few hundred to more than 3,000 miners, speculators, merchants, saloon keepers, and restaurant and hotel operators. At the time the Bunion Derby came to town, the Oatman

Eastern Company announced that they had located a small vein of ore and had high hopes of finding more.

Today, Oatman is another ghost town along Route 66, but it hasn't been forgotten. It's a tourist attraction where visitors come to feed the wild burros that roam the street and to watch staged gunfights on the weekend. Movies like *How the West Was Won* have been filmed here, and the Oatman Hotel is famous for the suite where Clark Gable and Carole Lombard honeymooned on March 29, 1939.

Oatman was no Needles, but the runners were relieved to see that it wasn't Bagdad, Mojave Wells, or Danby either. It would do. Pyle, though, was disappointed; Oatman had only 800 residents. Although the whole town pretty much turned out for the race, and the carnival was something of a hit, it needed larger communities to really turn a profit.

With several hours of daylight to kill, Newton wrote some followers in England to tell them that his leg probably couldn't hold out much longer. Newton predicted that in a matter of days he might have to drop out.

One player in the Bunion Derby drama had done that in a most anticlimactic fashion. In Rialto, some 60 miles from the starting point of the Bunion Derby, Dr. John J. Seiler gave up his quest to overtake the Bunion Derby runners. His infuriated financial backer, Barney Lubin, angrily declared, "I'm not a runner, but I could do better myself."

Seiler did his reputation no favors when the following year, he was arrested with a partner, Pascal Juliano, for stealing $4,500 worth of diamonds from a jewelry store in Quincy, Illinois. The *Decatur Herald* speculated that Seiler was likely not a doctor, and added that shortly before the jewel heist, Seiler and his "secretary" Pascal visited towns throughout Illinois, offering their services to food companies, including bakeries, ice cream companies, and milk dealers, trying to work out a deal for Seiler to promote the health benefits of their products.

In the late 1930s, Seiler was written up in a Nevada newspaper, which mentioned that he gave a speech about running to some high school athletes and stated that he was prepping for a local race. Otherwise, he seems to have dropped off the running map.

AS MANY OF THE RUNNERS SLEPT, one of the more unusual incidents of the Bunion Derby was occurring. Here's how Associated Press sportswriter Russ Newland told it years later in a letter to a friend: At some point early in the race, he chatted with a middle-aged runner who looked out of place. It turned out the runner was a lifelong golfer, but not quite good enough to win awards and make a living from the sport. He entered Pyle's Bunion Derby.

When the runner didn't arrive in Oatman, the Bunion Derby police force went searching for him. They finally found him on a ledge in the Black Mountains with a rubber inner tube around his neck. He was strumming it like a guitar and singing at the top of his lungs. As Steve Owen, the head of the police force, tried to figure out how to retrieve him, the man shouted that it wasn't necessary.

"Never mind, fellows. I'll come down," the man said excitedly. "I'm not nuts. I've discovered what's making me slice!"

There were a number of similarly surreal moments that most of the runners missed along the route. Owen reported to Pyle that one of his patrol cars, responsible for monitoring the progress of the runners, had skidded off a cliff. The showman was horrified, until he learned that no one had been hurt and, even better, no one planned to sue him. Ever enterprising, Pyle wanted to go to the wreckage site to collect the scrap material and sell it, but Owen said that nothing remained except a smoldering heap.

In another instance, Pyle's advance men came into one town—probably in Arizona—drumming up support and interest in the race before the runners came through. They mentioned the names of some of the runners to one of the newspaper editors, who perked up when he heard about Phillip Granville. "That is rather coincidental," the editor said. "He is Canadian, and so am I. His name is Granville, and by jove, so is mine. I wonder if it could be. . . ."

The editor guessed that Granville might be a cousin, and Pyle's men didn't dissuade him. Before the race, the editor wrote a lot of articles about Granville, giving him a ton of publicity and making it seem that he was the finest athlete in all the land, which was not a wholly outrageous statement. Granville, the editor, bragged to his friends that Granville the runner was his cousin. After whipping the town into a frenzy, the editor stood with a group of his friends as the runners came through, anxiously waiting to welcome his would-be relative.

The editor, who was white, was unaware that Phillip Granville was black, an Oxford-educated Canadian born in Jamaica. It was never recorded exactly what happened when everyone saw Granville run through the town, but one imagines, given the thorny race relations in 1928, that there were a lot of anxious faces and then derisive laughter—at the editor's and Granville's expense.

March 13, Oatman to Kingman, 28.8 Miles

Hours before the runners drifted in, the carnival came. Townspeople watched tents unfold and mattresses unroll. According to the local Kingman paper, quite a few residents from Oatman showed up to investigate the runners' progress. The society pages mention several affluent families, including an owner of a gold mine, who came specifically to Kingman to watch the race.

In that regard, C. C. Pyle was proven right. Kingman was a relatively prosperous town of 3,000 residents, not including surrounding communities. This was not some anonymous desert outpost. Pyle's carnival would do well here.

The *Mojave County Miner* reported that "there was a large influx into the town that day, which made business for the garages and gas stations, hotels, restaurants, meat market and others." The paper went on to say that the chamber of commerce verified that while the carnival made money, the town made more.

Hardrock scrambled up and down long stretches of dirt road in a desolate part of the desert. The day before, he had placed ninth, and now he was in the lead, finally living up to his standards. Hardrock wasn't used to having trouble running. It was part of his life. When he was 8, his mother started sending him on errands to the grocery store to help channel his energy. It was a 2-mile journey, and young Paul would race to the store, make his mother's purchases, and run back to their farm. Then in the military, he started running with the encouragement of a fellow soldier who was also a boxer. "It makes the eggs taste better," the boxer said of running before breakfast, and they would go at it for 4 miles every morning.

When Simpson returned to high school and earned his nickname, Hardrock, as a football player, he was also a member of the track team, winning the state championship in the mile. Upon graduating, Hardrock was admitted to West Point, but he opted to attend nearby Elon College. Hardrock joined Elon's track team and competed in the 100-yard dash, low hurdles, javelin throw, and 2-mile run. He was captain of the cross-country team and set a state record in the 6-mile run.

With a history like that, Hardrock expected more than what he had to show for his efforts so far. He was much like a small-town valedictorian going to Harvard and realizing that he hadn't been the only straight-A student in the world. Maybe now, though, he could vault to the head of the pack.

On the other hand, most of the runners did better that day, though no one felt that he had conquered the land.

It was about this time that Frank Von Flue decided he was out of the race. His patent leather street shoes, which he found in Needles, were not a smart purchase, and now, with severe bruises on his heels, he decided to quit as soon as he found a race official to share the news with. There was no way he could keep running; most of his toenails had fallen off. He kept limping along, though, toward the next desert community. Fifteen minutes later, he entered a small town with a water pump. After dousing his feet, he felt so good that he suddenly threw on his shoes and broke into a hobbled run after the others.

"God it was terrible," said runner Mike Joyce weeks later. "Not a breath of air. Blistering sand, rocky roads, with those mirages dancing up in front of us."

Alfred E. Gauvin seconded that. The 23-year-old from New Hampshire gave up after he sprained an ankle and both arches in his feet collapsed. He later told a Pennsylvania newspaper, on his way hitchhiking home, "You've never tried anything until you try the grind across the desert country under the tropical sun. I don't mind running 25 miles a day at a grinding pace once in awhile, but to keep it up day after day is physically impossible."

Gauvin vowed that this was his last try at running across the entire country: "Never again."

By mile 18, a sweaty, gasping Hardrock was slowing down slightly, enough so that Newton, running at his usual machine-like steady clip, overtook him. Newton jogged into a town of 3,000 residents, many of whom were cheering and applauding. Flags and bunting hung from doorways and light posts.

Hardrock came in second. It was quite a performance, especially considering that he was still wearing his narrow-heeled, asbestos-insulated shoes. They were constricting his feet into positions that no normal foot should be put in. These were shoes that, if he had been less active, were perfect to form the race's namesake: a bunion. That didn't happen, but Hardrock would pay dearly nonetheless.

HARDROCK had even beaten two solid runners who accidentally took a shortcut. Harry Rea and Billy Busch traveled down the wrong road for a time, cutting miles off their route. Arthur Duffy determined that it was an honest mistake but penalized them, adding an hour to their overall scores to "maintain the spirit of the race."

Meanwhile, the merchants of Kingman tried to maintain the Bunion Derby spirit as well. Days after the runners were gone, the Kingman Drug Company offered "Bunion Derby Specials." The ad that ran in the *Mojave County Miner* said, "We all have bunions, and all have corns, so avail yourself of these wonderful bargains."

Most of the runners flopped down in their cots, but William Kerr was not among them. A strapping navy man from Minneapolis, Kerr had more than just his rugged build going for him; he had friends helping him along the way. For instance, when he ran into Kingman, Kerr was met by Commander E. E. Wishon, who had been in Oatman the day before and who made sure that Kerr received a shower, food, and anything else the lad needed.

Kerr was smart enough to be sponsored by the Los Angeles American Legion. Periodically throughout his journey, in communities large and small, American Legion members would look out for him.

Not a stickler for details, Pyle had already forgotten that he had issued a mandate 2 days before the race that all runners would sleep in tents. Several millionaire backers offered to furnish their own runners with luxury motor homes, but Pyle turned them down.

"All runners will be placed on an equal basis on the trip," declared Pyle, who possibly didn't want his own luxury home overshadowed. "And everyone will be accorded like treatment. They will all sleep, eat, and run under the same conditions, in order to make it fair for everyone."

In the next town, though, Kerr was given the best room at the Beale Hotel, where he was able to shower and dine on a specially prepared meal. Kerr also received a rubdown.

Commander Wishon, the future justice of the peace for Kingman, was well-connected among his American Legion brethren. He made calls to Peach Springs, Seligman, Williams, and Flagstaff, ensuring Kerr's needs were covered throughout Arizona. The American Legion couldn't run for

Kerr, and they couldn't always help him out in the most unpopulated of places, but in the towns where they were represented, they made sure he could recuperate in style.

Somewhere in Kingman, the other athletes shivered in their tent city. The humid night temperatures had been exchanged for the March mountain air. Each morning, as they climbed to altitudes of 5,000 and 6,000 feet, frost covered the grass, and patches of snow clung to the edges of the road.

But in taking advantage of the American Legion's largesse, Kerr didn't do anything unsportsmanlike; he was just luckier than most of his competitors. At least half the runners had a trainer or some sort of network helping them, creating a disadvantage for those not fortunate or wise enough to bring someone along. Tobie Cotton's father and brothers offered not only moral support but also cold drinks whenever they could. Harry Abramowitz was supplied with shoes, courtesy of his financial backers, the YMHA (Young Men's Hebrew Association). Numerous international athletes, like Guisto Umek, were put up in hotels during the race, and no runner, if he was given the chance, turned down the opportunity to sleep somewhere besides what Pyle was offering.

Kerr was working within the framework that Pyle created. That the infrastructure didn't make for a completely level playing field was one of those lost details. When it came to details, Pyle was like a farmer carrying too many eggs from the henhouse. Invariably, a few always splattered on the ground. Kerr undoubtedly slept well that night—and who could blame him?

MARCH 14, KINGMAN TO PEACH SPRINGS, 51.7 MILES

From the moment everyone woke up, a sense of dread overcame the camp. This was going to be a long run, double what it had been lately, and through the desert. Even though it was a race, it was difficult for a lot of runners to think of anything except making it across another stretch of land, let alone trying to beat anyone to a far-off finish line. But that, of course, was what one had to do if he were going to reach New York in first place.

Frank Von Flue began the numbingly long run with what he called a slow dog trot, a pace that he maintained until he learned from race officials that about half the distance had been covered. Then he slowed to a walk, traveling that way for a few miles, and then he started running, picking up as much steady speed as he could for the rest of the lap, passing many runners but never overcoming some of the others, like Newton, who came in 20 minutes earlier than anyone else that day. A storekeeper presented Newton with a mat, handmade by a local Native American. These weren't exactly the daily cash prizes that Pyle had promised—and which still hadn't materialized—but Newton appreciated it nonetheless.

Once Von Flue finally reached Peach Springs, well after Newton, he was told that he was in 16th place overall. Considering that on the first day of the race, he had been in 62nd place, he was quite pleased.

FRANK JOHNSON was trailing badly. He now fully understood why he should have hired a trainer. He had passed on one not just because of the cost—for he could have probably come up with an arrangement to share his winnings—but also because of what Pyle had promised. "Conditions as outlined to us before we started sounded fine," said Johnson to the *St. Louis Post-Dispatch*. "But when the race began, things changed. For instance, we were told that all our bedding, blankets, pad and cot would be numbered, and that the numbers had to be painted on the outside of our suitcases. The suitcases were loaded on a truck each morning before we started to run and were to be deposited at the next control station."

Even better, each runner's grip, as a suitcase was more frequently called, would be waiting for him at his bed in his tent. "Then we were supposed to go to the bedding station and get our individual equipment," said Johnson. "But when we started to run, the system went flooie."

The blankets they received each evening weren't washed and weren't their own individual blanket, so night after night, they were more and more gamey. Compounding Johnson's problems, "Frequently, the baggage truck was delayed. One day I waited two hours for my equipment because of a delay of this kind, and you can imagine how my feet felt after running all day, and then standing around for two hours, hoping for a change of shoes and socks."

If the baggage truck arrived early, Johnson was equally doomed. "The grips, instead of being placed on the bunks, would be thrown out in a great heap, and it was up to each individual to go scrambling into the heap for his baggage."

Johnson watched wearily and enviously as the trainers rooted through the pile, looking for luggage. "If you had an assistant, you could rest after your run, while your trainer obtained your baggage, and then he could rub you down and nurse your wounds," said Johnson, who miserably concluded, "A man without a trainer or assistant was helpless."

It was 32 miles outside of Peach Springs when Johnson decided it was time to surrender. The usual contenders—Newton, Gavuzzi, Payne—were far ahead of him. Johnson knew he had no chance and no energy. He had given it his all, but enough was enough. He flagged down a passing vehicle and was driven to the night control point, where he sought out Pyle.

Pyle wasn't pleased with Peach Springs, a little trading post on the edge of a reservation that was home to 300 Haulpai Indians. Pyle looked at the thin crowd and, as he had in many of these tiny western towns, wondered what he had been thinking, bringing the race here. And now another runner was informing him that he'd had enough and would like his $100 travel deposit.

But, when Pyle looked up Johnson's number to record the latest runner exiting, he realized he had something in his bag of tricks that might keep another participant from departing. Pyle had received a wire for Frank that day—a trainer from Granite City, Illinois, was coming to help him. "You'd better reconsider and remain in the race," advised Pyle.

Frank Johnson was in little mood to hear this. His feet were badly blistered. But Pyle suggested he see Dr. Baker, who looked him over and said he would be fit to resume running the next day. Johnson was doubtful, but he said he'd think about it.

March 15, Peach Springs to Seligman, 38.3 Miles

In the early hours of the morning, Steve Owen led a search party: Osmond Metcalfe, a young, struggling Canadian actor–turned–speed walker, was missing.

He hadn't appeared at the finish line at midnight, and no one knew where he was. Owen organized a search party, and around dawn, they found Metcalfe wandering in a field. He was cold, tired, and clutching a bouquet of wildflowers.

As one newspaper put it, Metcalfe suffered "a nervous shock," a diplomatic way of suggesting he had lost his marbles. Owen offered a ride back to camp for Metcalfe, who promptly refused. He did, however, want to discuss food. Metcalfe demanded a meal in a way that unnerved even the burly Owen. The football star and the others agreed that locating breakfast should be the first item on their agenda, and they accompanied him to a diner in Seligman, where he consumed four sandwiches, three cups of coffee, a double order of ham and eggs, and four large hotcakes.

"I feel better," Metcalfe finally said, "but I've lost my appetite for long-distance hiking." He dropped out.

FRANK JOHNSON thought about quitting. Then, half-questioning his own sanity, he decided to stay, which meant that while his competition went to the starting line, preparing for a 38-mile run, he boarded a bus. Traveling with him were at least two other runners, Pennsylvania's Rod Ellsworth, who had dropped out of the race the day before with a bad foot, and Charles Hart, who had simply been exhausted as the altitude slowly began climbing. Ellsworth and Hart each were dropped off approximately

10 miles from Seligman, where they had given up the day before, but Johnson stayed in his seat. In fact, he remained sitting for 22 more miles, traveling 32 in all until reaching the spot where he had quit the previous day. As grueling as the day before had been for the runners, the mileage had been approximately 51 miles. Today, if he completed the distance, Johnson was looking at 32 miles plus another 38. All in all, just over 70 miles.

Johnson left the bus, his feet tenderly touching the road. "I couldn't run," recalled Johnson, "but I shuffled."

Usually, Johnson wore size 8 shoes. On that day, he had a shoe 2½ sizes bigger, and he wore several pairs of stockings and cotton packed between each sock.

He kept shuffling, throwing out his arms and legs into a swinging gait that didn't cause him too much agony. Later, in a moment of bravado, he would tell a reporter that it didn't matter that he was 100 hours behind the leader of the race—not when in a race expected to last 100 days. Johnson told the reporter that he believed the others ahead of him would burn out. Johnson, though, knew he was only fooling himself.

But he kept thinking of Pyle's suggestion, almost a warning, really: *A trainer from Granite City, Illinois, is coming to help you. You'd better reconsider and remain in the race.*

Johnson didn't want to disappoint Granite City, not to mention Clara and the kids. He kept shuffling, all the way to Peach Springs, which must have been gratifying and sickening to reach. He had covered 32 miles, and he wasn't even halfway to his destination.

TRAFFIC CONTINUED to be a problem. Ten miles out from the starting point, Giacomo Clarizo, an Italian runner, was struck by a passing motorcycle. He was promptly admitted to a hospital to have a strained tendon examined. Later, Clarizo's countryman, Guisto Umek, limped into Seligman with a bad knee and indicated to doctors that he was considering quitting. That's the last thing he wanted to do, however, after hearing about

Clarizo. The definition of stress isn't letting down your country, it's letting down your country *and* your dictator—Benito Mussolini.

For the others, the race was ravaging their legs and lungs. They started at 1,000 feet in elevation but ended the day at 7,000 feet and gasping for air in the higher altitudes.

Approximately 100 men remained in the race; 5 days earlier, Pyle's referee had mentioned that he hoped 100 runners would reach Chicago.

That evening, after dinner, the runners huddled under their blankets in their tents. But soon they were afraid that if they fell asleep in the plunging temperatures, they wouldn't wake up.

Pyle found an empty one-room school and ushered his runners inside. Sleeping on the floor, under a dirty blanket, packed tight with sweaty men was not an ideal way to spend the night. Frank Von Flue recalled it as being 100 and possibly more men inside, which may mean the trainers were huddled with them, too, while the wind raged outside. It was uncomfortable, and no one really got what could be termed a restful sleep, but it was warmer than the tents.

And for a few hours, they were better off than one man coming in from the cold. Frank Johnson finally staggered past the finish line, 5 minutes before the midnight deadline.

March 16, Seligman to Williams, 43.9 Miles

The next morning, Umek with his bad knee was at the starting line. So was, improbably, Johnson.

But not Charles Hart. The day before, by the time he reached Seligman, he had run 38 miles plus the previous day's 10. He was exhausted, and the effect of the rising elevations was too much for him.

Pete Gavuzzi was taken aback, to say the least. Hart was an amazing physical specimen, to say nothing of being Gavuzzi's friend and running partner. Gavuzzi at least didn't have to say good-bye to his comrade. Hart was asked to stay with the caravan as a judge.

Not long after, Gavuzzi's sponsor sent him a telegram, saying, "Now everything's on your shoulders." Gavuzzi knew he would have to give up the idea of sprinting to win occasional races, an idea he was already quickly coming to realize wasn't helping his and Hart's cause anyway, since Pyle still hadn't come through on his promise of prizes for each day's winner.

"Feeling fine, no complaints," Andy Payne said when he was asked how he felt at the starting line. Shy and retiring, Payne was always brief when reporters spoke to him, but, in that elevation, with oxygen so scarce, he was probably better served by keeping his mouth shut and conserving his wind.

As always, the whistle blew.

As always, everyone took off.

This leg of the race led the men through pine forests and a rocky landscape. Occasionally, snow huddled in pockets of shade, and the air was increasingly thin. Even Newton was struggling. "While running up that 1,500-foot incline to Williams yesterday, I was on the verge of collapse," he said later. "I drove myself into a sprint stride to keep going. Whether that venture will be costly, time and miles will tell."

Nick Quamawahu, struggling ever since he cut his foot on the third day of the race, finally dropped out 20 miles into the day's run. The final insult came the night before, before everyone had made the switch to the schoolhouse. He had been shuffling around the dark camp and cut his shin on a tent stake.

Once the runners staggered into Williams, they were—as usual—famished. Only there was a problem. Pyle had had a disagreement with the man who ran his commissary, and not long after, the cook was packing up. Without a chef, that evening, Pyle was forced to treat his hundred runners to dinner at a small restaurant. The crew ate there as well.

The proprietors were naturally overwhelmed. Everyone was fed, but many runners had to wait up to 2 hours before they could eat.

At least the sleeping quarters were better this night. The runners slept in the roomier Williams Opera House, sheltered from the chilly wind.

Newton lay in his cot, wondering how much farther he could make it. He was suffering from an inflamed sinew in his right ankle, which had developed from his favoring his right leg after he hurt his left tendon some time ago. "As the thing had been foreseen from the start, I wasn't as much worried as I might have been," wrote Newton. "There was only one thing to do, of course; keep going on, in the hope that I could get over it before the other leg also caved in."

Hugo Quist, the physical director, attempted to treat Newton's right ankle before bed, but it had been determined to be too damaged and sunburned to treat or even touch. Newton described it as "raw flesh."

March 17, Williams to Flagstaff, 36.3 Miles

Even though the temperatures had plummeted the night before, it was still a little startling to find 4 inches of snow covering the region. Runners scrambled to find woolen socks and fleecy shirts before starting the race, and while today's mileage was significantly shorter than on the past few days, that pleasantry was offset by the mountainous terrain that climbed 7,000 feet.

Once again, the runners slogged on, some slogging their last. In a town called Maine, Rod Ellsworth succumbed to shin splints. Guisto Umek navigated the road with a severely sore leg, somehow placing 12th for the day. Newton was visibly struggling, too, with pain in his ankle and knee, but he arrived third to Flagstaff and was still comfortably in first place overall, 8 hours ahead of Payne, in second place.

"It was pretty much a holiday here," wrote the *Coconino Sun*. Hundreds of cars lined the roads, as revelers honked and waved at the army of athletes. Pyle finally outdid himself here, due to Bill Pickens, who used his aviation connections to bring in a flying circus—stunt pilots—as well as Eddie Stinson, the famed stunt pilot who never wore a parachute. Eddie may have been tempting fate, but he was a brilliant flier with reportedly the lowest insurance premiums of any airline pilot at the time. He was the first to fly nonstop from Chicago to New York, and he taught the army how to fly, at a time when its fleet had only three airplanes.

Also entertaining the crowd were the Dolly Sisters, Hungarian American twin sisters who danced and specialized in musical comedy. They were major stars in the 1920s, having performed everywhere from beer halls to the movies.

Despite the flash and abundance of cash, once again, there were no daily prizes for the runners. It depressed and discouraged the runners, especially when they saw former Bunion Derby runner Nick Quamawahu in the crowd. He was out of the race, but his financial backer, John Lorenzo Hubbell, brought him into Flagstaff and then on to Winslow, where several hundred Hopi Indians congregated to see him. Celebrating Quamawahu's effort, Hubbell awarded him $200.

William T. Elliott, an Atlanta transplant to Coronado, California, dropped out the day before the race came to Flagstaff and traveled ahead with the caravan. He was interviewed by the *Coconino Sun* and handicapped the race, predicting, among other things, that Andy Payne would come in first and Phillip Granville, second. He also spoke highly of Andrew Gemmell, of Oakland, California, and John Cronick, of Saskatchewan, Canada.

Pickens, Pyle's right-hand man, came to Flagstaff ahead of the others and seconded Elliott's vote for Payne, although he did qualify his remarks, saying, "If the Indian stays in shape, he'll make all of them work. He's the fastest in the bunch, and with good luck, if he's got the guts, he can win."

CHAPTER 9

Like so many of the runners attempting to cross the country, Norman Codeluppi was really just a kid. (Courtesy of Marguerite Brandgard.)

ARIZONA ANXIETY

DISTANCE SO FAR: 515 MILES; 93 RUNNERS

MARCH 18, FLAGSTAFF TO TWO GUNS CAMP, 35.8 MILES

Nobody missed the cook. "Nice, juicy steaks for supper tonight, boys," said the man who served up the slop. Every time John Pederson, the jeweler from Spokane, Washington, glanced into the pot, he was repulsed. Dinner always looked like really old meat.

If there was a bright side to dropping out of the race, it was that your diet immediately improved.

From the beginning, C. C. Pyle promised that he would feed his men from a rolling commissary, and the runners had visions of nutritious, replenishing meals, like steaks, bread, fresh vegetables, served by talented and skilled chefs. Instead, they got one man serving 199 runners and around as many employees for the race: a former army cook named Butch Bircher.

Pederson remembered Bircher's most recent position as a dietician, while Harry Sheare, a runner from San Francisco, recalled that the cook had worked at a carnival, and that he served hot dogs, sauerkraut, and hash. Whatever Bircher served, it was barely edible.

"The man in charge had every possible facility to serve good food," recalled Frank Johnson, "but he never varied from the menu, and he started with tough meat and continued to serve the same meat, same style."

Bircher was relieved of his duties the day before arriving in Flagstaff, though the circumstances of his firing are in some dispute. Some said later that Bircher asked for a raise, and Pyle promptly fired him. The Flagstaff paper reported that Pyle was dissatisfied with the runners' food, so he dispatched one of his colleagues—who used to run an ice palace Pyle owned in Los Angeles—to fire the army chef. And Johnson remembers that Pyle, who probably was dining in restaurants, wasn't particularly dissatisfied with the chef's performance, but so many runners complained that he felt forced to can Bircher, who took his mobile kitchen with him.

After Bircher disappeared, "A man who really knew how to cook a good stew and who knew how to mix up the menu, took over the work," according to Johnson. "But he had no equipment." Some runners remembered hearing that the new cook was an ex–baseball player.

As the miles added up, and Pyle's financial problems mounted, the runners' food portions were slowly reduced. The latecomers weren't served anything at all. Johnson recalled, "Of course, some of us were lucky enough to have a little money with us, and when we struck towns or lunch stands, we could buy our own food to add to what was doled out to us. But there were some runners who didn't have a cent, and I saw one man grab four slices of dry bread off the evening table and stick it in his pocket. I asked him why, and he said the meal wagon didn't ever reach him during the last few days for lunch, and that he was starving."

Eventually, the replacement cook also got the boot, and Pyle began issuing meal tickets that were good at restaurants. Each voucher was worth 35 cents.

Even in 1928 that wasn't much of a deal. Pederson asked a reporter rhetorically, "Did you ever try to run 60 miles a day on three 35-cent meals?" The runners' plight was such that townspeople frequently offered food to the undernourished plodders.

According to Sheare, the meal tickets were an inadequate solution, and Pyle eventually gave them $1.50 in cash a day to spend on food, which was hardly better than the $1.05 in meal tickets they had received.

A more nutritious diet probably wouldn't have helped Arthur Newton, but it couldn't have hurt either. He was finding that it was an effort just to get out of bed. "By now, both ankles were so swollen that the ends of my legs were mere shapeless chunks," wrote Newton. "And if I stopped only for a moment, at any time, I stiffened so badly that it took many minutes before I could get into proper action again."

Still, Newton was gamely trying on Day 15, an extremely competitive racing day—but only between the first two men. Ed Gardner and Earl Dilks, a runner from New Castle, Pennsylvania, were in the lead for most of the day, and by the end of 36 miles, they were running side by side. Neither could shake the other, and they ended up in a dead heat as they passed the finish line, crowded with hundreds of spectators. Eight minutes later, Newton came hurrying in, but he knew more than anyone that he couldn't last much longer.

March 19, Two Guns Camp to Winslow, 24.1 Miles

Newton dreaded what was about to come next. It was getting more and more difficult to get out of bed. But, as usual, he would make the attempt. Gingerly, Newton placed a foot on the ground and let it hang off his cot, until he could slowly bring around his other leg. He cursed, but not out loud, and then forced himself to stand. Sweating by now and grimacing, Newton hung on to the bed and took a step or two, and then he let go. He could walk.

Newton hobbled to the starting line—no time to sightsee and look at the restored cliff dwellings nearby, which tourists were paying 50 cents to visit. Once the whistle was blown, he ran with the rest. It took about a mile, but eventually he was his old self again. Over the next 5 miles, he began passing the others, as he always did.

"But this was only a flash in the pan," wrote Newton later. "Suddenly, the pain in my right ankle became acute, and, knowing what was bound to occur if I attempted to carry on for the rest of the day, I sat down . . . "

It was over.

He found a parked car, climbed onto its running board, and waited for a car with a race official to pass by.

Fifteen minutes later, Pyle's private motor home picked him up. Newton informed Pyle that he was through. Pyle was disappointed but ready for this. Newton was his star, basically the only star he had left, and Pyle respected his talent immensely. Pyle suggested that Newton lie down in the motor home for a few days until his legs healed, at which point he could serve as a technical advisor for the rest of the race.

Newton readily agreed, never mentioning in his autobiography if Pyle actually paid him for his new work. In any case, the legendary runner was given a berth in the top deck of the camper, where he wrapped himself in blankets and watched former rivals make their way through the desert.

March 20, Winslow to Holbrook, 34.3 Miles

Hardrock and Frank Johnson realized on the same day that they were each in serious trouble. They had shin splints.

Shin splints are the precursors to a stress fracture and intensely painful. Johnson was informed—probably by Dr. Baker and possibly by Hardrock—that it was possible to run with shin splints, although no reputable medical doctor today would ever recommend that. Johnson was told that shin splints often heal after 3 or 4 days, and so he kept shuffling along.

Hardrock did, too. As long as he could move, he would.

ANDY PAYNE was in agony. He was sweating far more than normal and was running a fever. He had tonsillitis.

Newton's withdrawal should have been his big chance. Payne began the morning as the front-runner, but by late afternoon he had lost his prized position. Pete Gavuzzi, Arne Suominen, and many others passed him up. By evening, everyone assumed Payne would go the way of Newton, Nick Quamawahu, and Willie Kolehmainen.

Today, tonsillitis is easily treated with antibiotics or with a simple operation. In 1928, a capable physician could safely remove tonsils, if he didn't kill the patient with the anesthetic. Of course, sometimes tonsillitis—a bacterial infection—faded after rest. But sometimes it didn't go away. Sometimes an afflicted person wound up like Samuel Grizen, a janitor in New York who in 1925 was found in his basement, barely breathing. He was carried out of his house to a waiting ambulance, where he died, surrounded by his family and a priest.

Payne reached Holbrook in 8 hours—almost 3 hours after Earl Dilks, that day's winner. Payne was so sick that the officials took him off the list of active runners. They didn't ask him if he had quit. They didn't need to.

Payne went to bed that night with a fever, a sore throat, probably a headache, and possibly a stomachache. Dr. Baker worried that he might have diphtheria, which often stems from tonsillitis and can be highly contagious. It isn't known, but it seems logical that Payne slept away from the other runners that night.

SOMETHING ELSE was going on that evening. While Holbrook's citizens embraced the Bunion Derby, turning out for Pyle's carnival in record numbers, some of the more unsavory elements of the town found something else to do with their time. Twenty-one houses were robbed while their residents sampled the carnival. The runners tried, as usual, to sleep, but it wasn't easy. If the carnival didn't keep you up, your bunkmates did.

"After we had been running for a while, the nights were terrible," recalled Johnson. "Each tent sounded like a hospital ward after a big train wreck. Men groaned and moaned, and many of them wept over their bruises and aches. Every time a man turned over during the night, it hurt so bad that his groans awoke everyone near who happened to be asleep."

Edwin D. Barry could have predicted it would be like this. He was Cleveland's safety director, a conscientious government official who about this time was griping to the media about dance marathons. His criticisms echoed the problem with all endurance competitions: "Maybe it wouldn't be so bad if they would dance them straight to death," griped Barry. "But they don't. They allow them to rest and revive them with massage and medical treatment. It is slow torture."

March 21, Holbrook to Navajo, 41.8 Miles

The next morning when the race began, to everyone's surprise, Payne was there. He was only moderately healthier than he was the evening before, but not suffering from diphtheria. Payne was healthy enough to climb to his feet—meaning, in the mind-set of many of the men: If you could stand, you could run. "The first three weeks of the race were characterized by almost every violation of the accepted principles of diet and hygiene, and disregard for physical injuries, infections, and human endurance," Dr. Baker lamented. But Payne had no intention of giving up.

Payne had always been a runner. When he was a young boy, his parents had given him a gentle but swift horse, whom he named Prince. But Andy really didn't have much use for the animal. His brothers and sisters all went to school in a saddle, but Andy preferred to run. It was a couple miles to the school, but often he made it to the one-room building before his siblings. One Friday, his parents insisted he take Prince, and so Andy did. But at the end of the day, he was so excited to have reached the weekend that he raced out of the school and sprinted home. It was only after he started his chores that someone asked him where his horse was. Andy ran back to get him.

When he was a teenager in high school, Payne still ran. It was a farther distance of 4½ miles, but he didn't care.

His tiny high school had a track team, and when there was a meet in Miami, Oklahoma, a fair distance from Foyil, Payne got a ride from one of his friends. On one occasion, the car broke down, and by the time they made it to the competition, Payne didn't have time to change clothes. Still in street clothes and farm boots, he sprinted to the starting line, seconds before the race began. Undaunted, Payne won.

He even ran alongside his family, when his parents took the buggy into the next town. Andy often outran them. Doc Payne was impressed by his son's speed and diligence, not that he thought anything would come of it.

Andy wasn't about to give up on winning the Bunion Derby, not as long as he could still run. After all, he had a girl to impress. But he couldn't ignore the fact that he was still sick, and when he finished the 41.8 miles to Navajo, Payne, once again, was not in the top 10.

Instead, he placed 11th.

FAR BACK in the middle of the pack, Norman Codeluppi marveled at the jumble of 225-million-year-old fossils strewn about the land, including a good bit of multicolored petrified wood. President Theodore Roosevelt had made the Petrified Forest a national monument more than 20 years earlier, and Codeluppi felt compelled to linger—and rest—and admire the otherworldly scenery.

And why not? Unlike everyone else, the 19-year-old Codeluppi wasn't in the race to win. He didn't even plan on running the entire distance. He had only one mission.

Her name was Mary.

Codeluppi had met her in Cleveland when the two were working at a mayonnaise factory. They had fallen for each other, but Norman's parents, George and Carmelia, didn't approve. Mary was Hungarian, and the Codeluppis, who were Italian, loathed Hungary, which had opposed Italy during

World War I. Understanding that Norman's flirtation with Mary was serious, they were determined to keep their teenage son away from her, and so George and Carmelia sent Norman to live and work with an uncle in Pasadena, California.

When Norman learned about the race, though, he realized that it offered him a ready-made excuse to get back to Mary. The route was mapped to go directly through Cleveland. He would run the race from California to Ohio, where he would drop out and wed Mary.

Norman didn't have much money, but he was able to scrape enough together for some good running shoes, the $100 travel deposit, and the $25 entry fee. He could have used that money to travel across the country to Ohio, but by the time he arrived he would be practically penniless. But if he could run to Ohio, Pyle would give him his $100 travel deposit back, ostensibly to travel back to Pasadena. Instead, he would arrive in Cleveland with a tiny nest egg to help him and Mary get started.

Codeluppi grabbed a few pieces of petrified wood for his 4-year-old sister, Gloria, and kept running.

STALEY COOK was still in his taxi when he saw Hardrock's silhouette on the horizon, about a mile away. The closer Cook got to Hardrock, the more alarmed the *Burlington Daily Times* reporter became. The 23-year-old looked like a caveman. He hadn't shaved in weeks, and his naturally bushy hair was out of control, each strand heading in a different direction. He was sunburned. His lips were dry and cracked.

Cook was dropped off near Hardrock, assigned to trail him for a few weeks and send dispatches from the road. According to Cook's editor, Burlington had more interest in Hardrock than they had in the Charles Lindbergh story the previous year.

In fact, as far as Burlington was concerned, Hardrock was in the pilot's same league. The mayor of Burlington, Earl B. Horner, described Hardrock in a letter to another mayor: "He is a Lindbergh type of man, always pleasant, meets conditions in a heroic manner, never complains, but pushes on to the front in his timidity, which is only surpassed by Lindbergh, if anyone."

Hardrock was pleased to see Cook, who in turn was distressed to see Hardrock. The once-great athlete appeared to run in slow motion, victim to shin splints and an extremely painful charley horse. When Cook asked about his odds of finishing the race, Hardrock had little doubt. "It has become mechanical with me," he said of the running. "I feel better, and I believe I am heavier than when I started this race. I really am enjoying it."

Cook must have felt somewhat relieved. Hardrock didn't look like himself, but there was no mistaking his trademark optimism.

Just a few minutes before midnight, after almost 15 hours of hobbling, Hardrock reached the night control point. Cook put Hardrock up in his hotel room, where the young runner was able to take a bath, and then the reporter produced a straight razor and spent an hour giving Burlington's hometown hero a shave. When Hardrock looked in the mirror at his once-familiar reflection, he hardly recognized himself.

March 22, Navajo to Lupton, 34.7 Miles

Cook couldn't help being impressed by Hardrock's commitment, and he soon noticed that Hardrock wasn't the only athlete struggling. Fifteen-year-old Tobie Cotton was far back in the rear. Frank Johnson was little more than a walking zombie. The other Frank, Von Flue, had a big bruise on one of his heels, and blisters covered his feet, and a bad molar was causing him a lot of pain, keeping him up nights, sapping his strength. Billy Busch's legs crumpled underneath him; the previous day, the Bostonian "ran his legs off," in his words, and he was paying for that. Masseurs worked on him for hours into the night, until he finally was able to walk again and continue the race the next day.

But even they seemed in fairly good shape compared to James Pollard, a 26-year-old from Reno, Nevada. He sprained a ligament in his knee on the third day of running, and it was still bothering him a little over 2 weeks later. So were the boils, seven of which had recently broken out on one of his legs. The balls of his feet were covered in blisters. And yet, he still ran.

Only John Salo seemed to be enjoying himself.

Salo was born in Finland in 1893 and came to America when he was 15. By 1917, Salo, now an American citizen, married Amalia Huovila, another Finn. Shortly after, Salo was drafted. Twenty-four and unemployed, Salo was probably glad to have the work.

The military made good use of Salo's nautical skills. He served as an officer of the Mercantile Marine, making 10 expeditions through the Atlantic, dodging submarines and other enemy vessels. After the war Salo captained riverboats on the Hudson River—for exercise, he ran around the deck. He had only begun running in 1925, and 3 years later Salo somehow felt ready to accept Pyle's outlandish challenge.

Arthur Newton remembered Salo as a really nice guy: "No man ever met Salo who did not at once instinctively like him, and continue to like him."

Man's best friend apparently felt the same way. That evening, Salo befriended a dog, and suddenly the animal wouldn't leave his side, traveling with the runners from town to town.

Pyle didn't mind this dog accompanying them. Besides, the crowds of spectators, particularly the young children, seemed to enjoy watching the dog. The Bunion Derby had found an unofficial mascot, and it didn't take long for Salo to think of an appropriate name for his new friend—Blisters.

CHAPTER 10

Andy Payne, shown here in a family portrait probably taken during his last year of high school, was one of the race's top runners from the beginning. (Courtesy of the Vivian S. Payne collection.)

New Horizons, New Mexico

Distance So Far: 685.7 Miles; 92 Runners

As grand and imposing as the *America* was, there was another vehicle in C. C. Pyle's motorcade that particularly stood out: the mobile radio station.

In 1927, 36-year-old Jay Peters built his station in a truck and traveled around Reno, Nevada, trying to find talent and interesting stories to broadcast. By 1928, Pyle and Peters found each other, and the Bunion Derby appeared to be a perfect marriage of their resources. Peters had the broadcast equipment; Pyle provided the show. The way Pyle saw it, anyone tuning in to a radio could listen to the runners come in, which would help draw in the public, building excitement about the race.

It was a daring move on Pyle's part. While radio grew increasingly popular throughout the 1920s, it was still a new medium. Although some drivers used battery-operated radios in their cars, the first factory-installed car radio was a year away, and the golden age of radio remained in the relatively distant future. But it was close. The day Arthur Newton dropped out, the long-running *Amos 'n' Andy* radio sitcom debuted.

The rolling studio was also quite expensive; Pyle shelled out $650 a week to pay for Peters's operation, which included the salaries of three young men who helped run the radio station. But what Pyle was paying was par for the course; he was spending a fortune to keep the race functioning. Some reports indicate that he spent as much as $100,000 just to keep the race afloat, but because he had cash-flow problems, it sometimes seemed as though it was a much more threadbare operation.

"Cash and Carry" Pyle had never been good at managing money. He had a shrewd intellect and a catchy nickname, and he dressed the part, but no one was going to mistake him for John D. Rockefeller or Henry Ford. As tennis promoter Bill O'Brien, yet another Bunion Derby staffer, once said of Pyle, "C. C. couldn't keep the dough, but, boy, he sure could make it."

It was a character flaw that plagued him for most of his adult life. In the waning years of his first marriage, when Pyle was in his early to mid-twenties, he tried to maintain a lifestyle he couldn't possibly keep up, and in May 1908, Pyle lost everything, which to his horror, everyone who knew him and read the paper could see.

An auction house put the following advertisement in the *Oakland Tribune*:

STORAGE AUCTION SALE

ON FRIDAY, MAY 29, 1908, AT 11 A.M., WE WILL SELL TO THE HIGHEST BIDDER FOR CASH WITHOUT PREFERENCE OR RESERVE, ALL THE FURNITURE BELONGING TO CHAS. C. PYLE. THIS IS A FINE LOT OF GOODS, CONSISTING OF BIRD'S-EYE MAPLE, MAHOGANY AND OAK FURNITURE, ALSO LACE CURTAINS AND CARPETS. THESE GOODS MUST BE SOLD TO PAY STORAGE CHARGES.

GUARANTEE AUCTION COMPANY,
CORNER EIGHTH AND CLAY.

Not long afterward, Pyle fled from his wife and daughter and headed east.

His financial management skills improved over the years, but his earning money seemed to almost be contingent on someone else losing it. During World War I, Pyle worked as a sales manager at the Bartola Musical Instrument Company, which specialized in making opulent piano organs for movie theatres, selling for as high as $7,000. Deluged with orders, Bartola began outsourcing to other organ makers. They made the organs, and Bartola slapped its name on the product, ensuring that they get the maximum dollar from their customers. Whether that was Pyle's doing or not, he was selling organs that he almost certainly knew were not Bartola organs. When the scandal was uncovered, once again, a taint of unsavoriness trailed Pyle.

From Bartola, he went to the Disco Security Company, becoming its vice president. As for what they did, aside from sell worthless stock in their company, it's not exactly clear, but afterward, Pyle went into business with an A. W. Stoolman, building a movie palace, the Virginia Theatre, which featured films and vaudeville. The Marx Brothers, Buster Keaton, Red Skelton, and W. C. Fields all passed through during Pyle's tenure. From the outside, Pyle finally seemed to be a pillar of respectability—but it wasn't long before Stoolman was suing Pyle for mismanaging the books.

Pyle's financial problems were usually akin to ingesting mercury: difficult to detect and slow to travel through the system, but ultimately lethal.

March 23, Lupton, Arizona, to Gallup, New Mexico, 22.8 Miles

As the Bunion Derby reached New Mexico, reporter Staley Cook spent some time in the *America*, talking to Pyle and Red Grange about Burlington's most famous resident.

Hardrock was struggling. With blisters covering his feet, he was the

91st runner to reach Gallup, troubling since there were 92 runners. "I am going to lead the boys into Albuquerque next Wednesday," Hardrock predicted, with reason for optimism: Upon entering Arizona, he had been in 95th place overall, but by Gallup he was in 71st.

After settling into the newest night control, Frank Von Flue found a dentist, Dr. Riley, willing to yank his tooth out. They naturally started discussing the race and learned that they had a mutual connection—Riley's wife was from Fresno, a proverbial hop, skip, and jump from where Von Flue lived. Dr. Riley refused to take money for his services, and Von Flue left the dentist, feeling better than he probably should have.

March 24, Gallup to Thoreau, 32.3 Miles

The next morning, Von Flue's dentist and his wife were at the starting line, with the morning crowd, to see the men off. The Rileys told Von Flue that they were going to drive along with him for the day and that they'd treat him to a chicken dinner at the end of the run.

Reenergized, Von Flue took off after the whistle blew, and whenever he stopped to rest, the Rileys gave him apples, oranges, and nuts. It was like having his own set of personal trainers with him. Von Flue, and all of the runners, needed extra rest and fuel. They were crossing the Continental Divide, 7,265 feet above sea level.

Pyle surveyed the land from his camper and gleefully exclaimed, "We're sitting on top of the world."

Sitting? Any sweat-stenched runner overhearing that must have summoned all the willpower in the world not to strangle the man right there and then. One athlete who didn't hear the comment was Hardrock, who wasn't fast enough to be anywhere near Pyle. In fact, some people were suggesting Hardrock's nickname be changed to Hard Luck. He was still plugging along, but in terrible pain. Pyle usually refrained from commenting specifically on the abilities of the runners, lest anyone think he was playing favorites, but he admitted to Staley Cook: "He's a speedy boy, a good boy, and will again be heard from when he works off his shin muscle soreness."

Days later, Pyle broke his rule again, marveling at how Hardrock kept going. "That boy has guts," he said, "plenty of guts."

March 25, Thoreau to Grants, 30.5 Miles

Forty-six years earlier, on March 25, 1882, C. C. Pyle was born Charles Cassius Pile, or Charles Clifton Pile, depending what resource one wants to believe. The spelling of his original last name, Pile, may explain why he always took pains to remain well-groomed. *Pile* is slang for hemorrhoids.

Pile has defined the condition since the Middle Ages, but by the 1880s, advertisers were becoming quite bold when promoting their cures to the public. During the 1880s, newspapers were filled with advertisements touting Dr. William's Indian Pile Ointment, which "supports the tumors and allays the intense itching at once." One has to think the Pile clan—a farming family in Van Wert, Ohio—grew weary of the comparisons. Around the time Charley's father, William, a farmer in poor health, moved his family to take a job as a minister, the spelling of Pile was changed to Pyle, lest parishioners start giggling every time he came to the pulpit.

By 1889, if not before, William O. Pyle moved his family to Delaware, Ohio. Like many of his peers who didn't have their own congregation, the Reverend Pyle traveled to churches near his family's home, filling in for various congregations. It may be helpful to note that during his most formative years, Charley saw that a man didn't have to plow a field and work himself to death. He could make a respected living by talking about something he believed in, and for much of Charley's childhood, his mother urged him to be a preacher. Like his late father.

William Pyle died in 1890 on a Sunday morning at 6:10. Even though tending to his flock was less demanding than tending to his fields, he had been wasting away for some time. He had tuberculosis, or as it was then called, consumption.

William must have suffered terribly. Among tuberculosis's symptoms are weakness, high fevers, night sweats, and severe coughing. The hallmark of this wretched disease was the coughing up of blood.

Now in 1928, Pyle hadn't just outlived his father by a dozen years; he had outdone him entirely. He wasn't influencing a few churches in a community. The entire country was his church. Fittingly, from his perspective, Pyle was in the midst of creating a miracle. His runners were crossing a state a week and racking up impressive times.

Pete Gavuzzi led the pack on the way to Grants, averaging 8 miles an hour over a rocky road made up of lava and taking him less than 4 hours to navigate the distance. Arne Suominen came in second. Andy Payne was third. Not too far behind was Von Flue, who for a while still had the Rileys driving alongside him, handing him fruit. He was sad when they left. He came in 11th for the day and discovered he was in 20th place overall.

He was still far behind, though. Suominen was in first place, having eclipsed Payne's overall time by 3 hours. Payne, meanwhile, was 17 hours ahead of William Kerr, in 10th place. Exactly what Von Flue's time was on that day isn't known, but he had a long way to go before dreaming of even reaching 10th place.

Those in the rear, stumbling over rock and lava, patiently hoped that one, two, or all three of the front-runners would crack. With more than two-thirds of the country to cross, it seemed more than likely. And yet no one had dropped out for several days.

As Frank Johnson listlessly stumbled along, the break that Pyle promised finally came. His trainer arrived, one of Granite City's finest—Walter Francis, a local basketball and football player. Francis fetched the suitcase and blankets and gave him his much-needed rubdown, which, though helpful, didn't prevent Johnson from writhing in agony.

March 26, Grants to Laguna, 33.9 Miles

The runners crossed 12 more miles of ancient lava beds and then had to run over sand and cobblestone, which was particularly cruel to the feet. Suominen was in the lead, determined to keep it, and those within reach of him were doing everything they could to make him lose it.

Gavuzzi rocketed past Suominen, and the physician never caught up. Payne was somewhere behind Suominen. Constantly on the horizon, threatening to catch up to Payne, was Seth Gonzales, from Denver. Otherwise, everyone was quite spread out, with runners able to go a mile or two before catching up with another, or being passed.

One hour after the whistle blew, Hardrock and his blistered feet took off at a slow jog along the lava beds. He was moving at 5 miles an hour—but the lead athletes covered as many as 8 miles an hour and had a 60-minute head start.

Hardrock had recently taken to starting his race an hour or two later than the others so that Hugo Quist, the race's physical director, could perform therapy on his ravaged body. Hardrock and some other badly injured runners had begun calling Quist "The Physical Magic Man." To his surprise, Hardrock was feeling better than he had in days, and before long, he was able to pass some of the stragglers.

Hardrock sometimes ran with George Rehayn, the runner who, especially near the finish line, had a tendency to break into song, usually in his native German. Rehayn generally finished just before or just after August Scherrer, from Uster, Switzerland. The two men often accompanied each other, lobbing good-natured insults in German at every turn in the bend.

Those near last place had no reason to sing. If anyone had a reason to croon a tune, it was the race leaders, who because of finishing earlier, sometimes spent as much as half a day relaxing. By comparison, Johnson most often spent his evenings running or, if he was lucky, recuperating in his bunk.

On this night, however, Johnson caught some live entertainment on an

Indian reservation in Laguna. "The Indians would sing and do their war dances for us, after we took up a collection for them," recalled Johnson.

Between the entertainment and sleep, Hardrock found some rare time to write a letter to his mother, who sent it to their hometown paper, which printed excerpts:

> I am improving every day. I walked 34 miles in less than eight hours and placed about 50th today. . . .
>
> This race is doing more for me than anything I ever did. . . .
>
> The only thing that keeps me here is realizing how much I can do for you all, if I go through with this. . . .
>
> I am getting so I love every man in the race. I am getting so no task looks too large for me. Physically, I get stronger every day, and the miles seem to click off in no time, and I always finish fresh.

All was true, except for finishing fresh. Hardrock wanted to spare his mother some of the gory details, like the toenail missing on his left foot. It was so tender and raw that he had stopped wearing that shoe.

For at least 4 days in New Mexico, his right shoe on, his left shoe off, Hardrock covered ground at a miniscule 3 miles an hour.

C. C. PYLE unwittingly swallowed some of his mercury poisoning in Holbrook, Arizona, and he was now feeling the aftereffects.

Albuquerque's mayor, Clyde Tingley, a future governor of New Mexico, sent word that he wouldn't allow the Bunion Derby to pass through his city. Days earlier, he read about the robberies in Holbrook and, from there, formed a devastating opinion of Pyle's character.

Fearful that could happen in Albuquerque—and against the wishes of the chamber of commerce—Tingley refused to pay the $2,000 that Pyle requested to bring the race into the city. (The bigger the community, the bigger the payoff Pyle expected.) Instead, he barred Albuquerque's door to the Bunion Derby.

Having spent a lifetime in politics, Tingley believed he knew a swindler when he saw one. Still, he tried to accommodate Pyle. "I'm perfectly willing to let them detour around Albuquerque," Tingley said. "I will show them some good roads they can follow and will mark the detour with a flag."

Pyle was incensed. He drove ahead to meet the mayor, in hopes of changing his mind, but things didn't go well. What was said was apparently never recorded, possibly because some of the words weren't fit to print in a family newspaper. Grange once remarked that Pyle "couldn't get over the habit of arguing." He also gave out too many orders, according to Elmer Wilson, the driver of Pyle's luxury camper. It was about this time that Wilson handed in his notice, leaving Pyle to find another crew member to take over the driving duties.

PYLE RETURNED to the runners and informed them that they would not run anywhere near Albuquerque. ("Some people," observed a sardonic *New York Times*, "were heartless enough to refer to that incident as a local improvement.")

Why take the race to the edge of the city, where out-of-towners would still end up visiting Tingley's kingdom? Better to teach a lesson and make it nearly impossible for the city to profit from his event.

It's easy to see why Pyle was angry. Several days earlier in Gallup, Pyle shed some of his excess trucks, saying good-bye to Charles C. Orr, an executive who owned the vehicles and ran some of the services. It was probably at this point that Pyle, if it hadn't happened sooner, lost his mobile barbershop and laundry facilities.

The $2,000 that Pyle was supposed to receive from Albuquerque was gone, and some of that money was meant for Jay Peters, who was strapped for cash. Distressed, Peters drove into the city and sold his radio station to a wealthy radio enthusiast. Peters kept control of the station until the end of the race, but he was no longer the owner; as a result, Peters's station,

KGGM, remains in Albuquerque, although it morphed into a television station long ago.

For their part, the runners were miffed by Pyle's decision to pass an oasis of civilization in the great American desert. "Everybody got sore when Pyle ducked Albuquerque," recalled Johnson.

If he hadn't, the following day might have gone quite differently.

March 27, Laguna to Los Lunas, 48 Miles

Arthur Newton began the day with his customary 12-mile run, following the runners, discussing their troubles and offering what advice and help he could. Then he drove to the night control, a tiny town called Los Lunas, far from Albuquerque. There, he had a leisurely lunch and then started running down the gravelly highway, knowing he would eventually meet up with someone. He figured that Gavuzzi or Suominen would be in the lead.

But this was rocky, mountainous terrain that the Rio Grande helped create, with an elevation of 4,000 feet, and after 4 miles Newton had enough and flagged down a car in Pyle's caravan. They drove 10 more miles, passing Gavuzzi, Suominen, Payne, Ed Gardner, and many others. The wind was at their backs, fortunately—but sand and gravel nevertheless pelted their faces, and minute by minute, the airstream was getting more aggressive.

When Newton got out of the car near the last of the runners, he shielded his eyes from a blast of sand and kept his head low. The sandstorm was now in full fury, but pushing *toward* Los Lunas.

Had the wind barreled toward the runners, instead of somewhat carrying them to their destination, they never would have made it, Newton concluded. As it was, not everyone did. Billy Endrizzi, 32, from Hurley, Wisconsin, immediately stopped running when the arches in his feet broke. He was taken to a hospital in Albuquerque. He remained a lifelong runner, however, and even brought out his Bunion Derby number when participating in some races as a senior citizen.

Newton checked with those in the back—Mike Kelly, Tobie Cotton, and Frank Johnson—and made his way up to the middle where Hardrock and Norman Codeluppi were plodding along. But Newton, unable to see individuals until he was practically falling over them, couldn't check on everyone.

Von Flue later said, "The sand was so dense, as the wind swept it into the faces of all the runners, that you couldn't see." Von Flue and many of the others periodically sought shelter in the rocks and waited for the storm to quit, but it never did. So they'd return to pushing their way through the blinding sand.

The only good thing about the sandstorm was that it forced everyone to try to run faster, just to get out of it. Not that everyone could. Von Flue developed another shin splint and limped toward the night control.

March 28, Los Lunas to Seven Springs, 38 Miles

Ed Gardner and Harry Rea were in the lead, covering the distance in about 5½ hours, with the others close behind but far enough away that it wasn't a photo finish. Olli Wantinnen, suffering from shin splints, nevertheless was next—22 minutes later. Suominen came in sixth but was still managing to hold on to first place overall. Not far behind him were Gavuzzi and Payne, each running briskly, each crossing the finish line at the same time, after 6 hours, 22 minutes, and 20 seconds. James Pollard, from Reno, Nevada, felt good about being 10th for the day, but he was 46 hours behind Suominen.

The run had been the usual miserable grind, traveling through another type of Jungle Run. While the cars in the caravan found another route, for a time the runners had no highway to follow. They followed cardboard arrows, crossing sand and sagebrush until they once again reached an actual road. As usual, Pyle didn't seem to care that they had left Highway 66, just as long as they returned eventually.

It got worse. The runners landed in what Newton called "a wild and desolate pass in the mountains known as Seven Springs. When we got there, we found a narrow gully with a torrent rushing down it, and not an inch of level ground anywhere."

Wherever Pyle chose to camp on Day 25, it wasn't in Seven Springs's business district. He had them in a place where there were no restaurants and no shelter where food could easily be prepared and served. Late into the night, the runners were given some mulligan stew, cooked over a fire, although the mountain chill blowing up from the creek and cliffs rendered the meal moot. The runners sat on rocks and shivered, trying to wolf down cold stew.

Pyle's crew, meanwhile, could not manage to stake down the tents, as the wind kept yanking up the canvas walls. Eventually, all of them except one were pitched into the ground, and all the runners crammed inside, nursing their wounds and shivering.

The wind howled all night, and the temperature kept plunging. Newton remembers the experience as "easily the worst night of the whole trip."

March 29, Seven Springs to Moriarty, 29.5 Miles

The next morning, on lonely Highway 470, Frank Johnson asked himself again why he was still in the race. They were running almost 30 miles up a mountain road leading to a desolate and uninspiring piece of land, which was just as well. Everyone was too numb with cold to fully appreciate the scenery.

Moriarty had a hotel and a few stores, and the adobe garages and warehouses Pyle found for the runners to sleep in were like four-star hotels in comparison to their shelter the night before. Still, when Johnson read a telegram from his wife, he decided he had had enough. Clara urged her husband to come home, certain her husband was on a fool's errand. Johnson concurred.

"These are my wife's orders to hurry home, and I don't dare refuse,"

Johnson quipped, showing a referee the telegram. It seemed a pragmatic decision: He was in 77th place.

Days after his homecoming in Granite City, Illinois, Johnson sat down for a lengthy interview with J. Roy Stockton of the *St. Louis Post-Dispatch*. When Stockton remarked that Johnson appeared remarkably well, looking 10 years younger than *before* the race, Clara Johnson spoke up:

"You may think he looks younger, but you should have seen him when he arrived here Monday. His left ankle was swollen to twice its natural size. His lips were cracked so badly that they bled when he tried to chew his food. His nose was blistered and peeling from sunburn, and he hobbled like a cripple. That's just the sunburn that makes him look healthy. And he's hollow from head to heel. I know, because I've been cooking for him and feeding him, and I can't fill him up. You never saw a man eat so much in your life. He could eat six meals a day, and then do a lot of eating between meals, and be ravenous every time he sat down at the table."

Mrs. Johnson also blamed Pyle for the ribbing her husband received upon arriving home. "I wish you'd correct the impression that Pyle has given the public about my telegram to Frank," she told Stockton. "All Frank's friends have been joshing him, because Pyle made it appear that I ordered him to quit, and that he had to accept orders. He's never learned to take orders from me yet. Of course, I was worried about him, especially when he wrote that he wasn't getting enough to eat. But I merely asked him if he hadn't had enough. If he had been a man to take orders from his wife, he never would have entered the race. I certainly tried to talk him out of it."

March 30, Moriarty to Palma, 37.2 Miles

Clara wasn't the only one annoyed at Pyle. Alex Finn, trainer for Nestor Erickson, August Fager, and Olli Wantinnen, started griping about the conditions on behalf of his clients. At one point Finn asked, "What year will we reach the Mississippi?"

"You're fired," Pyle replied.

Finn wasn't employed by Pyle, but he didn't argue. Instead, on his way back to Los Angeles, Finn stopped in Albuquerque to do a little venting.

Finn told the press that the runners were threatening to hold an "indignation meeting" and issue demands to Pyle, insisting that he provide better accommodations and food. Finn said that the food wasn't "fit for a dog to eat."

On the morning of the journey to Palma, Erickson and Fager promptly dropped out after their trainer's firing, but thinking the better of it, they opted back in and resumed running. Wantinnen had no such qualms, taking off as the whistle blew and coming in third for the day; Erickson and Fager were still running well into the night.

There were now 90 runners, less than half of the starting field, and they were only at the first of three 1,000-mile marks. The *New York Times* sneered, "The C. C. Pyle caravan covered one-third of the transcontinental course with a loss of two-thirds of the starters in the race. A mathematician has figured out that this sort of thing can't go on indefinitely."

Critics enjoyed pointing out to Pyle that what he was attempting wasn't even groundbreaking. It had been done before, relatively recently—and by an old man at that. In 1909, when Edward Payson Weston was 70, he walked from New York to San Francisco in 104 days.

The origins of Weston's long walks date back to the 1860 presidential election. Weston made an election year bet with a friend, stipulating that the person whose candidate lost had to walk from Boston to Washington, D.C., where he would receive a ticket to the inaugural ball and (for some unknown reason) a bag of peanuts. Since Stephen Douglas lost to Abraham Lincoln, Weston began walking. He covered the distance in 10 days.

When word got out, the nation embraced Weston's quest; Lincoln had no hard feelings and shook Weston's hand after he reached the capital. (Some believe that the expression "for peanuts"—as in, "He did it for peanuts"—was born with Weston's walk.)

It was Weston's 1909 nationwide walking expedition, however, that made him a superstar. He wrote almost-daily reports for the *New York Times* and truly captivated the country. As late as 1922, when he was 83, he walked from Buffalo to New York City. In 1924, four youths attacked Weston, and though he was injured, he was able to fight them off. Weston, though, was not invulnerable: He experienced the pedestrian's worst nightmare when he was hit by a taxicab in 1927, after which he remained in poor health. He would die in 1929 at the age of 90.

March 31, Palma to Santa Rosa, 45.4 Miles

It was a quiet day but a quick one for some of the runners. Payne and Gavuzzi did their best to chip away at Suominen's lead by coming in first after about 6 hours. Predictably, Suominen wasn't far behind. He was the next man to pass the finish line, 19 minutes later, still well over 4 hours ahead in elapsed time.

April 1, Santa Rosa to Newkirk, 32.2 Miles

Depending on how badly a runner wanted to quit or stay in the race, Newton could be their best friend or worst enemy, as Dick LeSage discovered. Twenty-one miles after leaving Santa Rosa, LeSage petered out and quit, and afterward, the race officials brought him to Newton. By design or accident, Pyle had installed another bulwark against runners dropping out. Newton loved to run, and as the official trainer for the race he now felt a personal responsibility to keep everyone in the competition. Newton, a pleasant and caring man, could easily persuade runners to stay in the race—even if they didn't want to.

"A little chat soon convinced us that there was really nothing seriously wrong," wrote Newton in his autobiography, of his conference with LeSage. "To be quite plain, the man was just tired and homesick. So I suggested that he and I should get into a car and go back to the place where he had been picked up, after which I would run with him all the way to the control."

LeSage agreed, learning that it was easier to enter the race than to exit it. As Newton and LeSage ran, the veteran suggested to the younger man that his style of running was causing him to get tired and bored, and that if he alternated his gait he might do better. LeSage agreed, and before they knew it, they passed seven men and arrived at the next night control before dark.

IT WAS ABOUT DARK when Morris Munitz, the official shoemaker, began working at full speed. It was a thankless job, in which he frequently toiled until dawn, when he then needed to drive with the caravan. He vowed he would never do anything like this again. Munitz, who used to own some shoe-repair shops in New York City, was getting on in years and living in a California village when he read about Pyle's race and concluded that men pounding their feet into the pavement every day could be a tremendous way to earn some income.

His entrepreneurial mind-set whirling, Munitz contacted Pyle, telling the impresario that he would need a shoeman to repair all of the runners' footwear, which was sure to disintegrate. Pyle invited Munitz along, provided he bring his own truck. If any runner needed assistance with his shoes, they—not Pyle—would pay Munitz's expenses.

All the same, if a runner couldn't afford Munitz's services, the shoemaker was still obligated to fix the offending footwear. "Whether I get paid or not, Pyle makes me repair every shoe," Munitz told one reporter midway through the Bunion Derby.

Many times, there were pairs of shoes that he simply couldn't resuscitate. On April Fools' Day, Mike Kelly, trudging along in last place, sent his mother in Goshen, Indiana, a telegram, but his request was no joke: "My shoes are about gone," he informed her. "Send dad's old ones."

Two days after Kelly's telegram, and 24 hours after Clarence H. Jensen, a runner from California, withdrew on account of infected feet, Charles Miller Gallena, 60, ended his gallant bid for the $25,000 prize in New

Mexico. Somewhere among the desert willows and ponderosa pines, he gave up and out.

Gallena, of West Palm Beach, Florida, was an accomplished athlete who held the world record for jumping rope, clearing the rope 11,000 times. He had run from New Jersey to Florida in 26 days. Later in life, in 1934, he was featured in a *Ripley's Believe It Or Not!* cartoon celebrating the fact that the 66-year-old had run 376,000 miles during his lifetime, most of it well before he had ever heard the name C. C. Pyle. Indeed, long after Pyle's race, Gallena would keep at his pastime and remain in excellent health, living into his nineties. But for all of Gallena's vast talent and training, even he couldn't hack the daily onslaught of the Bunion Derby. In the end, it wasn't only his body threatening to deteriorate but his mind as well. The doctors described his collapse as a general breakdown.

CHAPTER 11

Missouri's finest, John A. Gober (left), sweats along with Seattle's Ed Gardner (right), nicknamed The Sheik by sportswriters. Gardner welcomed the nickname. Look closely: The word Sheik *is imprinted on his shirt. (Courtesy of the El Reno Carnegie Library.)*

WEATHERING THE STORM

DISTANCE SO FAR: 1,035.5 MILES; 88 RUNNERS

APRIL 2, NEWKIRK TO TUCUMCARI, 34.3 MILES

The reporters, after pounding out hastily written stories on portable typewriters, were traveling untold miles to find the nearest telegraph station along desolate stretches of road.

Ominously, given that the runners were always parched, once in Tucumcari, the runners were warned not to drink the water. It was unsafe. There was some happy news, though; the runners were told at the outset that they would be treated to a chicken dinner with the trimmings once they reached the town, and that knowledge, and the relatively short distance of 34.3 miles ignited everyone. No one dropped out, at least, and it appears that C. C. Pyle's promise of good food actually came true on this day.

The town of Tucumcari was only 27 years old, with scattered farms and businesses. The railroad had fueled its development, but the 2-year-old

Highway 66 was truly bringing new life to the community. The top-flight athletes reached Tucumcari in the early afternoon, which meant that they had the rest of the day for recharging. In their third week of the race, the runners and crew had adjusted to their new, sometimes mind-numbing, routine, and a certain normalcy settled over the race.

Every morning, someone from Pyle's camp—generally Bill Pickens—traveled ahead to visit an upcoming town and prepare them for what and who was coming. Pyle, too, would make his way toward the town in the *America*, always arriving well ahead of the runners. Another automobile lagged behind the athletes. Dubbed "the dead wagon," it followed the runners, searching for those in trouble and picking up those waving the proverbial white flag. Yet another car would shuttle back and forth along the route, stocked with observers on the lookout for anyone who might try to gain an advantage by hitchhiking. Frequently, Harry Gunn's millionaire father drove up and down the route in his own car, thoroughly enjoying playing detective.

Most runners busied themselves with getting from Point A to Point B, sometimes focusing more on finishing for the day than beating anyone else to the finish line. Sometimes, it was easy to forget that they were competing against one another.

The race especially had become an exercise of monotony for the crew, many of whom killed time and tedium by drinking too much while they waited for the runners to cross the finish line. Even C. C. Pyle grew weary. Early on in the race, he suggested to sportswriter Russ Newland that they guess the make of every seventh automobile that passed their camper from the opposite direction. Then to make it more exciting, they began putting bets on the make. Newland usually won, because he stuck with small and cheap makes, while Pyle would always guess a more expensive model. Newland figured he won $940 million from Pyle, though they settled the bet by having the showman buy the reporter a ham sandwich.

The runners were no different when it came to struggling with ways to pass the time. There were three main causes for dropping out, observed Dr.

Baker in his study on the Bunion Derby runners: foot problems, financial difficulties back home, and boredom. But for those who could survive all three, the race became a way of life.

Cleveland's Mike Joyce once described his typical day: "I always take it easy the first 5 miles after breakfast. Then I speed up."

Even breakfast was mind-numbingly the same: eggs and bacon, or eggs and ham. Every single morning—that is, until the cook was let go and the men were left to fend for themselves at breakfast time.

The two vegetarians of the bunch, Roy Sandsberry and Karl Larsen, both from California, spent a good deal of their spare time making sure they were getting the proper fuel to run. "We both have a pint of orange juice mixed with honey for breakfast," explained Larsen to a reporter. "Then each hour on the road we have more orange juice. At night, we eat our one meal of the day, milk, whole wheat bread, cottage cheese, a head of lettuce. Some may scoff, but we are carrying on without meat or eggs and pulling ahead daily."

Some did scoff, accusing Sandsberry and Larsen of occasionally sneaking a steak into their diet, but they vehemently insisted that wasn't the case.

Ted Buckley, a former Idaho University football star and the man who literally checked every runner in as he ran past the finish line, saw the men every day and said, "Most of the runners spend their time in the evenings eating and sleeping. Practically all of 'em stay in bed until it is time for breakfast. They need lots of sleep and straight through, they take it."

But not always. Ed Gardner was constantly embraced by members of each town's black community, and he was often treated to dinner and drinks, sometimes to his detriment the next day. William Kerr had his American Legion friends to see that he was rarely bored. If a Tom Mix cowboy flick was in the theatres, so was Harry Abramowitz. Andy Payne was a regular at the movies, too, 10 cents for a ho-hum film, or a quarter for something a little racy, like a movie starring Joan Crawford. He also wrote daily letters to Vivian and, at least once, did some fishing.

APRIL 3, TUCUMCARI TO GLENRIO, 44.1 MILES

Arne Suominen continued to have the best cumulative score, although Gardner and Olli Wantinnen led the 88 runners, sprinting past the finish line at the same precise moment. Soon after, Suominen rocketed past the finish line, and not long after came Payne, running at his usual conservative pace. Payne was excited, though. They were nearing the Texas border, which meant Oklahoma was up next. "I'm nearing the home country, and naturally the folks will expect me to do my stuff," he told reporters.

APRIL 4, GLENRIO, NEW MEXICO, TO VEGA, TEXAS, 37.3 MILES

As the men ran into their latest night control, a tiny farming community, everyone lost one precious hour of rest and relaxation by entering the Central time zone. That was unsettling; however, one man received an *un*welcome like none other.

Gardner had been making some spectacular runs, winning several stages to put him in fifth place overall as he raced into Texas. And this bothered the Ku Klux Klan.

Specific details are sketchy, but the *Afro-American*, a Baltimore-based newspaper, later reported that the Klansmen were enraged that there were blacks running alongside whites. Worse, from their point of view, Gardner outpaced most of the white athletes. Somewhere between the border of Texas and the town of Vega, a mob tried to set fire to a car full of people shouting encouraging words to Gardner.

History, so far, doesn't have a record of where Pyle was during this time, but he was likely somewhere at the carnival.

For all of Pyle's faults, he wasn't a racist. The facts of his life indicate that he appreciated and maybe even was sympathetic to ethnic groups that weren't welcomed into the rest of society. Pyle spent much of his career in vaudeville, where many actors had eccentricities and were regarded as curiosities by the general public. His carnival freak show, he felt, offered odd people employment in a world that otherwise had no use for them. Pyle was also exposed to a diverse range of ethnic groups in the three cities he called home during the 1920s: New York, Los Angeles, and Chicago. In short, he seems to have had a healthy sense of diversity for someone in 1928.

Maybe the best evidence for how Pyle thought would occur several weeks later, at a Chicago lunch counter. After the Bunion Derby reached the city, several runners lined up to get a meal, and Pyle was standing behind Gardner. The man serving the food blatantly ignored Gardner, giving Pyle his food first. Pyle refused, snarling, "Serve the men as they come."

Whatever happened as Gardner raced into Texas, he and his supporters eluded the Klan. But they sent Gardner a message, which he took seriously. He was not about to drop out, but he kept a low profile throughout Texas. During the Lone Star State, his overall standing fell two spots to seventh place. He didn't finish among the top 10 runners in any of the four Texas stages, until the fifth afternoon, when he crossed into Oklahoma and came in sixth place for the day.

Phillip Granville, another black runner who had received death threats from the Klan in New Mexico, recorded several impressive performances in Texas; either Granville wasn't harassed by the Klan, or he managed to pay their threats no mind. By the end of the run through the Panhandle, Granville was in fifth place overall, switching places with Gardner.

At least one white runner commented on the racism. Frank Von Flue, a few months later, told his hometown newspaper, the *Fresno Bee*, "When we hit Texas, it was rumored among the runners that the natives of Oklahoma were going gunning for the four colored boys in the race. Race prejudice, that's all. Well, it wasn't that bad, but the quartet did not dare enter restaurants. They had to have their food carried to them in the camps." That routine carried on through Oklahoma.

Whether or not Von Flue was naïve to what the four men were going through, and whatever their strategies and however they coped, Gardner, Granville, and the two other African American runners, Sammy Robinson and Tobie Cotton, fully understood that the Klan would gladly lynch them if given the opportunity. They knew they couldn't prevent men covered in white sheets from stalking them, but the four men's resolve deepened in Texas. One way or another, they were all going to reach New York City. The marathon had become a deeply personal quest.

April 5, Vega to Amarillo, 37 Miles

"If the people don't get you, the weather will," a Spanish explorer reputedly said about Texas centuries ago. The Panhandle wasn't populated until the early 20th century, when modern farming techniques allowed hardscrabble men and women to grow crops in a land of cracked dirt and trees that have grown sideways because of the wind. When the morning began with some rain, and then a little sleet, the runners had no reason to be too concerned with the skies above them.

Instead, they were frustrated with the ground beneath them. The dense clay clung to their shoes like microbes on a dish towel. John Salo had worn through six pairs of shoes before hitting Texas, but now that he was in the Panhandle, he had changed his shoes already and would have to replace them every 2 to 3 days. Blisters, his faithful canine companion, had paws that were caked with clay.

Salo and Blisters were in good company. Paul A. Smith, a 43-year-old athlete from Oregon, was wearing out two or three pairs of shoes each week and destroying an average of two pairs of socks every day, even before the Panhandle. Harry Gunn started the race with 10 pairs of $21 walking moccasins and changed the shoes often, but that still didn't prevent him from obliterating a heel every 2 days and having to restock his footwear. Von Flue began the race in baseball shoes with the spikes removed, but those wore out after 3 days. Then he tried patent leather shoes, which ground off his toenails. After that, he sampled basketball shoes but quickly wore out two pairs. From there, Von Flue attempted boxing shoes but hated them. Finally, when one runner with similarly sized feet dropped out, Von

Flue convinced the guy to let him wear his custom-made shoes. From then on, his daily runs were almost enjoyable.

That was about to change. It was cold, and the trainers, in cars and on motorcycles, trailed after their runners, ready to hand them a coat or hat if they were needed. But it wasn't common knowledge that the temperatures were dropping or that the flurries were just the beginning. Hardrock, for one, without a trainer, was running in a simple track suit, pleasant for cool temperatures but hardly formidable protection from inclement weather.

The sleet turned into snow.

A storm was coming. This blizzard was part of a tempest sweeping across New Mexico, Texas, Oklahoma, Kansas, Missouri, and Arkansas. In most of the states, there was an onslaught of rain, wind, hail, and tornadoes. Shawnee, Oklahoma, saw the worst of it when a usually docile creek flooded the town, sending more than 1,000 residents racing for their lives. Seven inches of rain and 2 hours later, six people were dead, including a woman and her adopted 18-year-old son. Near Topeka, Kansas, a 25-year-old woman made the tragic mistake of hiding in a chicken house. In Chelsea, a 17-year-old farm boy was crushed underneath a tree. Across the state, 125 oil rigs and derricks were overturned. As a tornado mowed down 20 houses in Duncan, Oklahoma, teachers led students into an underground shelter, just before their school building was smashed into splinters. And many miles south of the Bunion Derby runners, a tornado hit Coleman, Texas, leveling 35 buildings and leaving approximately 75 people homeless.

Oblivious, the runners pushed on through the falling snow.

Arthur Newton remembers the race as a cruel affair, saying: "It began with a cold head wind, developed into rain, worked gradually into sleet, and finally blanketed the country with a real snowstorm."

At least one runner was eventually waylaid. Anton Toste, 25, found that one of his legs was, in his words, "completely frozen. I tried hopping on one foot—but, well, you can't do that."

It seems astounding that spectators braved the blizzard to watch the runners, until one considers that there were no television forecasts, and KGGM, the race's radio station, wouldn't have discouraged people from coming out to watch Pyle's spectacle. In any event, thousands of spectators sat in their cars parked on the road between Vega and Amarillo, hoping to get a glimpse of the runners through the white blur.

Patrick De Marr, a boxer, was the first to trudge into Amarillo. It was a remarkable comeback, considering that in the first few days of the race his feet had been blistered and bleeding, enough that Dr. Baker suggested he bow out. De Marr, however, refused, securing two walking canes. He hobbled on those for days, until both his feet grew giant calluses tougher than any shoe.

He told sportswriter Leland Lewis: "I'm not a derby horse. The going is all the same to me whether it be wet or dry. Just keep plodding along, singing a song, that's my motto."

Suominen came in next, followed by Payne, third for the day but in second place overall. Although Payne later told a cousin that the Cajon Pass was possibly the worst day of the race, he informed at least two reporters that the trek to Amarillo was worse. "We got caught in cold rain and hail," he said. "I mean, I was really stiff. I just barely made it."

Then Payne saw what must have made him forget about the blizzard, if only for a second. As he reached Amarillo, a surge of relief and happiness overcame him when he spotted the man who at one point saw no reason for him to enter the race. But there he was, in the crowd, dressed in his Sunday suit and tie, "all dolled up," as Doc liked to say.

Andrew "Doc" Payne Sr. arrived in Amarillo, intending to trail his son into Oklahoma and possibly for the rest of the race. Whatever misgivings Doc Payne had about his son not following in his farm boots were long forgotten. Days earlier, Doc announced his plan to join the Bunion Derby "an' stick by that boy o' mine, until he trots in New York as the winner of the whole outfit."

When reporters asked about his decision to look after his son instead of his land, Doc said, "I've got more invested in that boy than in my farm." Then the proud father boarded a bus.

Andy, as usual, stayed away from the press in Amarillo, but Doc was always eager to talk. He told the sportswriters that his sage advice to his son had been "Keep your head and feet timed together, Andy." Some additional wisdom that day might well have been "and get inside."

The Bunion Derby brigade had been poised to sleep in a ballpark, but Pyle abandoned that idea and put everyone up in a hotel. He sort of had little choice but to be magnanimous for one day. The official bus with the tents had skidded off the highway and was stuck in the thick Texas clay, and now a thin blanket of snow draped over the vehicle. The tents weren't coming to the runners any time soon.

In the evening, as most of the runners crawled into cozy hotel beds, Frank Chavez inexplicably decided to do something else with his free time, something most people might not do after trudging 37 miles in the snow. He went dancing. And there were other runners who were still fighting their way through the elements, hoping to reach Amarillo by midnight. Hardrock was among those hapless few, still running even after 12 hours, still shivering in his thin track suit.

April 6, Amarillo to Groom, 40.6 Miles

The next morning, snow and ice covered the plains and the road ahead. However, the skies were bright, and the day was looking better. The wheat farmers and laborers picking fruit were pleased. Because temperatures had hovered around the freezing mark, a killing frost had been avoided, and remarkably the blizzard produced less than an inch of snow. Meanwhile, Pyle was glad to know that the cars could travel relatively easily, and all of the runners were delighted about the day's weather. But there was one snag.

It's a mystery as to exactly what happened—though plenty of runners indirectly referred to it later—but somewhere around Amarillo the tents were no longer used. What seems possible is that the tents were jettisoned to lighten the bus's weight and help get it out of the thick mud and snow that it had lodged itself into the previous night. No matter. While Pyle still had his carnival tents, those of the sleeping variety were no more, now just a part of Bunion Derby history.

PICKED UP the day before "half frozen," Nick Anthony, a 16-year-old runner from Long Beach, California, was driven 12 miles west from Amarillo to start the race anew. There were also five others picked up by the police, who had been dispatched to search for them. The men—Mike Kelly, Sam Richman, Andrew Gemmell, Billy Busch, and Anton Toste—all vowed that they would make up the mileage on the next day, and indeed, they made a valiant attempt.

But a few hours into the day's lap, Gemmell dropped out, claiming that a wrenched ankle had done him in. Busch gave up the next day; and 2 days later, Toste, the one who had been reduced to hopping in the race, gave up. His leg had thawed, but it hadn't recovered.

As Toste took the train back to his home in Berkeley, California, his thoughts surely turned back to the surreal events of the past month. Even beyond the snowstorm, the race had some rough moments. When one woman saw Toste run by her house in what she thought was his underwear, she sent her dog chasing after him. On another occasion, after a long run in the mountains, the soles in Toste's shoes disintegrated, and he arrived at the finish line barefoot. From then on, he stuffed cotton in his spare pair of shoes.

Toste comforted himself knowing that his financial backer, who was also his uncle, had a plan for his future. Toste's uncle was a sports promoter and promised to get his nephew into a new line of work, though it looked to be no less challenging than what he had been doing. Anton Toste was going to become a matador.

ASIDE FROM HIS SHOE, four wool socks padded Hardrock's sore right foot. His left foot had the socks and a plaster cast.

Staley Cook left that morning to return to Burlington, his newspaper budget for the assignment depleted. He hated to go, but Hardrock tried to make it easier for him by being stoic. "A man may be down, but he is never out," said Hardrock, quoting a well-known Salvation Army slogan.

Cook offered some parting hope: He would attempt to get the money being raised back home and funnel it into hiring a trainer for Hardrock. It was painfully obvious he needed one; Hardrock was constantly falling behind. That day was no different. Before the day ended, he quit 20 miles away from the finish line and was driven to the night control. He had been through this enough to know that he would make up the distance on the following day.

Of all the aches and soreness that day, however, Chavez was a candidate for being in the worst shape. His ankle was no longer working the way it once had, and all because after running 1,189 miles, he went dancing. He made his way tenuously back to his hotel room, likely cursing his judgment the whole way. Chavez navigated the next 40 miles to Groom, but just barely.

He bowed out the next day without making much of an impression, save for one incident.

One or two states back, when running through the desert, Chavez insisted on wearing a pair of red swimming trunks. At first his choice paid off; the trunks were comfortable. One day, though, a roaming bull spotted the flash of red ambling down the highway, and the animal started chasing him. Chavez broke into a horrified run, and, according to one sportswriter, "for a few minutes that day, made the best time that has been made during the race."

Sadly, aspiring bullfighter Anton Toste wasn't in the position to help him.

April 7, Groom to McLean, 38.8 Miles

Almost a week after being personally tutored by the great Arthur Newton, Dick LeSage quit. Homesickness having finally gotten the better of him and claiming a heart ailment, LeSage handed in his resignation and took the train back to Montreal. Newton felt a pang of regret; he had failed the boy. Pyle took it even more personally; he had to shell out another hundred bucks.

The roads were still icy, causing more trouble. James White, of Duluth, Minnesota, who already had an aggravated hernia, quit after he kept slipping on the road.

Hardrock kept hobbling along on his 58-mile trip through the slush, trying to make up mileage from the previous day. People clearly were inspired by his willingness to keep at it, though. Someone brought Hardrock a pair of dry shoes shortly before nightfall, helping his progress immensely, and that evening, several states away in Burlington, Simpson's townsfolk held a fund-raiser. Thirty of the most beautiful coeds were on the streets of Burlington, playing tag; anyone touched by the ladies had the opportunity to donate some money to Elon College's favorite son.

STAYING IN MCLEAN was something of a nightmare.

The town wasn't unpleasant, but the sleeping arrangements were less than ideal: a vacant storefront. And that wouldn't have been such a disappointment had the baggage truck been there.

Instead, all of the bedding and baggage were still on the road, with the driver navigating the ice and snow. Many of the runners earlier that day jogged along the roadside ditch, which offered better traction than the highway. The truck, obligated to stick with the roads, didn't. While waiting for the truck to dislodge itself once again, the runners made do with eight chairs and an electric heater that someone had installed for them. Everyone without chairs sat or lay down on the concrete floor.

The truck arrived at 5:00 in the morning. Everyone was given a cot and blankets and was allowed to sleep in—until 9:00.

April 8, McLean, Texas, to Texola, Oklahoma, 35 Miles

Suominen had every reason to feel optimistic. He had survived the blizzard and was still in excellent condition, with only Pete Gavuzzi and Payne threatening his hold on the race—and they were several hours behind him. The day's hail and sleet were unfortunate, but they were no blizzard. Suominen was feeling few effects from running halfway across the country. If anything, his body was getting stronger every—

Then his heel cord snapped.

It's also known as the Achilles tendon, which connects the gastrocnemius and soleus muscles in the calf to the heel bone. Suffice it to say, when it goes, it hurts, and suddenly he was no longer vertical. After Suominen was driven to the finish line, Dr. Baker declared that his new patient had a pulled tendon. Even though his injury was similar to Newton's, Suominen felt he could try to finish the day's lap and stay in the race, and so Baker did what he could for his new patient, and then the wounded doctor was driven back to where he had fallen. Suominen gingerly started to run again, but he couldn't. He wasn't going to kid himself any longer. He was out.

It was also a bad day for Harry Sheare. The 49-year-old had endured his share of misery and misfortune and was accustomed to exposure to the frigid elements. He used to live in Alaska, digging gold out of hills, steering dog teams through the snow, hauling freight and supplies from Nome to far-flung areas of the state. He later became a longshoreman in San Francisco.

But after 35 miles of running through some truly lousy weather on Day 36 of the race, Sheare had had it.

He stirred up trouble shortly after arriving at the Texola night control point. Exactly what he said may never be known, but he was in a foul mood, and he wanted to rally support before he confronted Pyle. Most runners wanted nothing to do with Sheare's gripes. They remembered the trainer who was booted off the Bunion Derby for complaining, and race leaders like Payne and Gavuzzi didn't see an advantage in antagonizing

Pyle. Sheare had some shot at winning prize money, being in the top third of runners, but he had less to lose in prodding Pyle.

Sheare recruited several runners to voice their displeasure. He may have brought William Kerr, who despite help from the American Legion was disgusted with the way the race was run. John Pederson, the jeweler from Spokane, was also vocal about the runners' pitiful conditions.

Whatever Sheare and his fellows said, Pyle didn't like it.

The general director of C. C. Pyle's First Annual International Transcontinental Foot Race from Los Angeles to New York was suddenly inspired to have a heart-to-heart talk with all of the men, but without any heart. Very little is known about that evening, but trainer Nicky Fisher told a reporter several months later: "Pyle made a ding-dong speech and bawled them out plenty." Fisher implied that the stressed showman then ordered the runners into the rain and mud outside. Pyle dared the men to keep challenging him and threatened to pack everything up and make them run to another town or two down the highway.

Sheare and his allies backed down. If Pyle had been a judge, a gavel would have come crashing down. His verdict was in. Only one man was in charge, and it was none of them.

CHAPTER 12

April 17, 1928: As Andy Payne ran into Chelsea, Oklahoma, the people of his home state made it clear they were thrilled to see him. (Courtesy of Gerry Payne.)

Home Sweet Home

Distance So Far: 1,302.6 Miles; 81 Runners

April 9, Texola to Sayre, 32.2 Miles

At least one spectator appreciated the Bunion Derby: Will Rogers, easily America's most beloved and influential humorist in 1928.

Rogers was keenly aware that a kid from Foyil was leading the affair. He also fondly remembered his tight friendship with Doc Payne when they were kids. Rogers wrote a spirited defense of the Bunion Derby that was published the following year in *American Magazine*. He noted that the race didn't get much respect because it was put on by "this fellow Pyle, that the sporting Writers had always taken much pleasure in rawhiding. Had Tex Rickard put it on an the men run half as fast, and took twice as long, it would have gone down in Sporting annals as 'the greatest test of stamina and grit that had ever been performed by man.' But Pyle put it on, so it must be funny, or a fake.

"A sporting writer will rave his head off over some football player making an 80-yard run," Rogers continued, in a folksy style that loved capital letters and eschewed a dictionary. "What would he do if he had to run 80 miles, and do it again the next day, sick, sore feet, bad colds, bum feet, cramps, blisters, no time to lay up and cure 'em, always had to get out in the morning, rain, snow, sleet, desert heat, always be there, ready to go? A Marathon that they train for years for is a little over 26 miles. Then they come in and faint, and crowds carry them off. You coulden't faint in this race, nobody to carry you off. If you did, you just layed there, maby some car run over you, but that was about all you could expect."

Hardrock would have appreciated Rogers's sentiment. He was having more trouble than usual—his feet were a mess, his legs were stiff, his body was faltering. At midnight, Hardrock again allowed himself to be driven to the control point, which was at least 10 miles away. It was a pattern he couldn't break, but soon he would have to. That morning, he and the others were told that once they arrived in Tulsa, everyone had to reach the finish line by midnight, or they would be disqualified.

Hardrock vowed that he wouldn't let that happen. He likely was no longer deluding himself with the idea that he had any realistic shot at winning. That no longer mattered. He had come this far. If he could help it, he was going to cross the finish line in New York City.

April 10, Sayre to Clinton, 50 Miles

Two miles after Sayre, C. C. Pyle's motor home came to a halt. Several feet ahead was a wooden bridge that stretched over a wide gully.

Pyle and his driver agreed that the bridge looked too flimsy to handle the motor home's 12 tons. They had been through this before, at least a dozen times, and as in the past, the lighter vehicles following the camper traveled over the bridge, making it safely across. After the last car made it, Pyle, Red Grange, Arthur Duffy, and several newspaper reporters exited the motor home. Only the driver remained on board. (Rumor has it, though, that Grange was at the wheel.)

Pyle gave the order, and the driver pressed the gas, inching the camper onto the bridge to test its strength. After about a third of the way, however, "the floorboards sank ominously," according to Arthur Newton, and the iron side rail tilted inward.

Pyle shouted to step on the gas and get across *now*.

The camper lurched forward, but it never had a chance. It crashed through the bridge, setting off an explosion of dust. When the hazy cloud cleared, the camper was in the gully. The rear end was smashed, two windows were broken, and a gaping hole was in one of the sides. Incredibly, the engine worked.

They managed to drive the camper out of the gully, but its passengers boarded the bus reserved for the press and guests. The driver, and possibly Pyle, drove the battered *America* to Oklahoma City in search of a mechanic.

Ed Gardner was the first to arrive at the missing bridge. At first perplexed, he soon discovered a trail through the gully that many of the other runners followed. Hardrock, 10 miles behind the nearest runner, was likely the last to come to the destroyed overpass. He was still hoofing his way toward Clinton late into the night.

April 11, Clinton to Bridgeport, 35.4 Miles

Bill Witt, a young reporter for the National Enterprise Association, had no idea what he was getting himself into when he was assigned to write a story about running a lap with the athletes of the Bunion Derby. For starters, he couldn't have known that he'd be running on not just a chilly, windy day, but one that offered the runners yet another sandstorm.

He began his article by admitting, "I have just finished one lap with C. C. Pyle's iron-footed derby racers, and I am old now, and my feet are petrified."

According to Witt's story, Arthur Newton took the young reporter aside before he began his run, and gave him some pointers: Short strides up the hills, lope down the hills, trot on the flatlands, and when you're training, keep training and don't quit. Cold water, said Newton, can harden your feet, making them more durable for a long race.

Witt started his run in good form, managing to stay for a while close to the most scrutinized of the race, Andy Payne and Pete Gavuzzi. Witt quickly came to admire the men, explaining, "You who run perhaps for your street cars some days, may know what running is like. You reach the car out of breath, ready to sit right down and puff your head off after only a block or two of intensive effort.

"Think of these men!" Witt continued. "After we had gone two miles on our run, I began to think my chest was bursting, my feet were on fire, my muscles like red-hot wires, drawing tighter at every bounce. Yet these runners have gone through California, Arizona, New Mexico, Texas, Oklahoma!"

After 10 miles, Witt wondered if he should just drop to his knees and try rolling himself the rest of the way to the finish line.

Witt eventually completed the 35.4-mile haul in 5 hours, 28 minutes, and 30 seconds but hardly felt that he had missed his calling as a marathon runner. Witt ruminated, "As I sat nursing the swollen appendages that once I was able to put shoes on, I realized that this isn't a race at all—it's a miracle."

Witt's ordeal, though, was whimsical compared to what Gardner experienced on his way to Bridgeport. Much of his run through Oklahoma had been relatively trouble free, and with each step Gardner was inspired by the black community's support. African Americans were raising money for him so that he could pay to get his shoes fixed and eat something other than the slop Pyle arranged. In one town, a group of black students held up a sign that read, "Gardner Must Win!" As if to oblige, Gardner ran faster.

But on that day, somewhere on a lonely stretch of Highway 66, an Oklahoma farmer riding a mule shadowed Gardner for miles. He aimed a shotgun at Gardner's back, daring him to pass a white runner.

Once the farmer finally gave up, Gardner took his revenge the only logical way he could—he ran faster. He passed nearly every white runner, except Payne and Gavuzzi, tying with both of them.

APRIL 12, BRIDGEPORT TO EL RENO, 37 MILES

Payne arrived in El Reno in 10th place, edging Gavuzzi and increasing his lead by about 5 minutes.

The local press was everywhere, and public interest was high, so the men of the Bunion Derby brigade were given a treat in the evening. Since the ever-generous Pyle expected a crowd of about 30,000 people in Oklahoma City, for the first time on the route he made sure that the runners' clothes were washed so that they would arrive in style.

Henry Swabey wouldn't be joining them. He quit because of the lack of rest and poor food, which, he said, exacerbated a foot problem. "You can't live on ham and eggs while running across the continent," Swabey declared in his parting shot before returning to Toronto. "And you can't sleep alongside a circus ballyhoo and get sufficient rest for a 28-mile trek across the Arizona desert."

APRIL 13, EL RENO TO OKLAHOMA CITY, 33.5 MILES

Among the reasons that the Oklahoma City Chamber of Commerce initially agreed to pay Pyle the hefty fee of $5,000 to steer the race through their city was that they thought the public would come out for their hometown boy, Leroy Freeman, known to his friends as "Doc." But one month before the runners arrived in Oklahoma City, Freeman dropped out in Williams, Arizona. So the chamber adopted Payne as their city's champion, and Oklahoma City was ready to give him a hero's welcome.

The chamber, forgetting they rebuffed Payne when he first requested sponsorship, wrote in their official newsletter, "An Oklahoma youth, Andrew Payne of near Claremore, and unheard of a few weeks ago outside his own community, is at present leading the field of runners. Since leaving Los Angeles, Payne has been either first or second for practically the entire distance, and there is an excellent chance for him to win this transcontinental race and win the $25,000.00 first prize."

One week before the runners were due, Walter C. Dean, the colorful and charismatic mayor of Oklahoma City, set the tone when he declared a 4-hour festival on April 13, 1928, honoring Pyle's foot race. His wordy proclamation ended with: " . . . Now, therefore, I, Walter C. Dean, mayor of the city of Oklahoma City, of a sound if eccentric mind, realizing the official dignity of my office and not giving a damn, do urge all citizens turn out to make this shindig an affair that will put the barbecue of my predecessor in the shade, and do proclaim Friday, the 13th day of April, from 2:00 to 6:00 p.m., a fitting vacation to celebrate a bunion derby holiday in Oklahoma City . . . "

Crowds craned their necks and gathered to cheer for their boy, Andy. That support was a mixed blessing, however. The cheering kept him going, but his newfound celebrity threatened to trip him up. Farmers and housewives and other ordinary folks were walking into the road to try to start a conversation with Payne.

He tried to focus on running, not running his mouth, but his father never passed up an opportunity to talk about his son. "Andy is hard as nails," the senior Payne told a reporter from Oklahoma City as his son checked into Bridgeport, 2 days from the state capital. "He weighed 180 when he started the race. He weighs 157 now. He's just running easy," Doc said proudly. "He's got some sense, and he won't try to run away with it all the way."

Just beyond the morning's starting line was Meredith Williams, one of the reporters at the *Oklahoman*. He was waiting for Payne and figured he'd run alongside the young man and do an interview. Just how far Williams thought he'd make it was uncertain, but surely he didn't think he'd run the entire lap with the state's newest hero. Williams, a middle-aged man with a receding hairline, was thin and fit, but he was wearing a suit and tie. He hardly looked like the sort who could jog over 33 miles.

Williams found some shade next to a giant sign reading, "Welcome to El Reno." He had some time to kill. The runners were supposed to leave at 7:00, but Pyle delayed the start of the race by 3 hours, looking to send the race through Oklahoma City in midafternoon. Arriving around noon seemed too early; dusk would be too late. The belated beginning would give the crowd time to assemble before the runners cascaded through town and would allow Pyle's outfit plenty of time to cater to the city afterward.

All in all, Pyle thought Payne was a rather boring kid, but he knew Andy was both well-liked and profitable in Oklahoma, and he was going to do everything he could to capitalize on that.

According to Williams's article, the Oklahoma crowds were in fine form: "They brought their luncheons, and their children ran about, bawling for the race, smearing the landscape with peanut butter and bread crusts and decaying bananas. That the race was started three hours later made little or no difference. They waited. The thing had been advertised as a holiday of no less importance than the Battle of Bull Run or a visit by the Rev. Billy Sunday, and they were determined to make the most of it. The men whittled or talked politics, the women knitted or spread gossip, the children alternately laughed or howled."

After an eternity, "Pyle's pedal pioneers" began showing up. When Payne trotted into view, Williams casually tried getting his attention. "'Lo, Andrew," said Williams.

Williams wrote that Payne "just stared at me like a flight of steps."

Williams tried again. "I'm a newspaperman."

"I knew you were," said Payne matter-of-factly.

Williams, hurrying alongside him, asked how Payne knew he was a journalist.

"They all look alike, kinda worm-eaten," Payne said, grinning.

Williams smiled, too. The ice was breaking. He might even get some sort of scoop. And so Williams offered Payne what seemed to him to be a no-lose proposition for the youth. "Andrew, how would you like to come to my office, tonight, and we'll go out and get a highball somewhere? You look like a party man to me."

Payne wasn't even tempted. "Never touch it," he said.

Even if Prohibition hadn't been in effect, Payne still wouldn't have drunk with Williams. He wasn't a drinker, and if he had been, after a month on the road with C. C. Pyle, Payne was media savvy enough to know that drinking with a reporter was inviting trouble.

There was a palpable pall between the two men. Williams knew he was losing Payne's trust—and his own stamina.

"Well, anyway, Andy, you don't mind if I run along with you awhile, do you?"

Not at all, Payne replied.

Williams tried prying a little information from Oklahoma's second most famous celebrity, but Payne didn't say much that Williams didn't already know, that he was in the race to the end and that he planned to nab first prize.

"There are a lot of fellows running here, who don't take the race seriously," said Payne. "Personally, I'm out for the money, and I expect to go into New York a winner by a great big margin."

Williams recalled in his article that growing up in Columbia, Missouri, he was pretty fast at getting from the third floor to the favorite seat at the dinner table, but it wasn't doing him any good here.

"I've had all I can stand," gasped Williams. "Too much is too much."

"Well, so long," said Payne, before dropping a popular 1920s catchphrase: "I'll see you in the funny papers." And then he was gone.

PYLE'S CARAVAN was already in Oklahoma City, preparing for the day's events. The governor was expected to appear, and Pyle instructed his men to wear clean underwear that morning.

The crowds were by far the most yet. The city estimated that 100,000 spectators came out to see the Bunion Derby, putting a notion into Pyle's head that he couldn't resist. He had long hated the idea that many people could watch the race and leave without paying a cent. So instead of coming down 66 and into Oklahoma City, Pyle changed the route near the end, steering the runners onto a nondescript dirt road that led directly into the fairgrounds, but *away* from massive cheering crowds.

Pyle believed that the people gathered on Highway 66 would be more willing to come to the fairgrounds and pay to enter if they didn't see the runners go by. He had top-notch celebrities to show them, like Red Grange and Andy Payne, and this was one day when he wasn't going to give his product away for free.

The chamber officials went along with the idea, because they desperately wanted to recoup the $5,000 that they gave away for the privilege of hosting the Bunion Derby.

Ralph Goodwin and his assistants sat at the racetrack, with time clocks and card indexes. Behind them was a crowd of workers, stretching ropes and laying the groundwork for sideshow tents and the rest of the carnival. Several marching bands, including a military brass band in the grandstands, were tuning their instruments as the public slowly made their way to seats.

The first wave of athletes was expected to jog past the finish line at the fairgrounds around 2:30 p.m. But, roughly half an hour earlier, Finnish runner Nestor Erickson crossed the finish line. Hardly anyone noticed. Several minutes later, Missouri's John A. Gober trotted into view, followed by Olli Wantinnen in fifth place overall. Each runner received a smattering of applause.

Allen D. Currier came next, followed by James Pollard. They were usually near last place but were doing quite nicely.

Payne was nowhere to be seen, nor was his rival, Gavuzzi.

Gardner came next. The African Americans broke into a raucous cheer. A reporter for the *Oklahoma Tribune* was impressed: "The sweat stood out on his black skin as he jogged in, but he didn't breathe as deeply as the average citizen who has just run a block to catch a car."

Still, no Payne. The disappointment among the crowd was obvious.

Next were John Salo and his dog, Blisters. Then along came Mike Baze, Harry Rea, August Fager, and Juri Lossman, none of whom caused a stir in the crowd—in fact, days later all four would be out of the race.

Finally, the crowd noticed a runner wearing the number 43, and they exploded with cheers and applause. Moments later, several chamber of commerce representatives and Payne's father joined the boy and hustled him to the speakers' stand. After a few speeches from local politicians, Payne was given a chance to speak. Not one for the limelight, Payne made his speech extremely short.

"Hello, home folks," said Payne. "I'm glad to be back. Hope to see you in New York." With that, he climbed off the stand and walked toward one of Pyle's buses. If anyone in the crowd wasn't paying attention, they would have missed Payne's speech completely.

Before Payne was able to hide from the crowd, two girls stopped him. "May we shake hands with you, Andy?"

"Sure," said Payne, sticking out his hand, which one of the girls grabbed enthusiastically.

"How do you like the race?" the other girl asked.

"All right, I guess," said Payne, hardly knowing what to say. The two girls tried to make small talk as Payne uncomfortably shifted from one foot to another, until his trainer, Tom Young, grabbed him by the arm and hurried him away.

At least the two girls had something to talk about when they went home. Most of the public felt cheated. Payne's disappearing act and the runners not coming through on Highway 66 were bad enough, but the post-show festivities seemed to be mediocre, unlike how they had been in Flagstaff, when Pyle invited Eddie Stinson and the Dolly Sisters.

The Oklahoma City show should have been a triumph. These were some of the largest crowds that the Bunion Derby had seen. While Pyle didn't receive a cut from ticket sales at the fairgrounds, he stood to make a mint from the carnival and concessions. Not only that, but positive word of mouth about the carnival in Oklahoma City could have spread to surrounding communities, enticing hundreds to visit the menagerie at other stops down the highway.

But maybe Pyle was too distracted to concentrate on putting on a good show. At 11:55 a.m. on Friday, April 13, just 2 hours before the first runner crossed the finish line, a sheriff and a deputy approached C. C. Pyle and handed him a garnishment summons. Pyle was being sued for $4,397.50, at a time when he was expecting a $5,000 check.

Once again, Pyle's own form of mercury poisoning—his inattention to pesky financial detail—was catching him, wounding him, paralyzing him.

The plaintiff was Ralph V. Scott, a giant of a man who a little over a year earlier had been having a pleasant interview with Pyle and *Los Angeles Times* scribe Braven Dyer before a big football game. Scott was coaching the football team that Pyle and Grange co-owned, the New York Yankees. He had gotten the job after being an all-American at the University of Wisconsin.

What Scott probably hadn't known when he accepted the position was that Ed Healy, an all-NFL tackle with the Chicago Bears, turned down the job offer first, precisely because he had sensed that he might end up in the situation Scott was currently in. In a meeting at the Morrison Hotel, attended by Grange and tennis pro Suzanne Lenglen, Pyle had offered Ed Healy a then-staggering sum of $10,000 to coach and play for the Yankees. Healy was in shock but decided Pyle was a man he couldn't trust. For him, the red flag was that another woman was in the adjoining hotel room—and as he put it later, she "did not answer to the name Mrs. Pyle."

And now Scott insisted that Pyle owed him $4,397.50—basically half of what Ed Healy had been promised—mostly for work he had done with the team in 1926. According to the suit, Scott should have been paid $4,160 for his work as a coach and player and $237.50 for securing other players for the team.

Scott may have read that Oklahoma City was paying Pyle $5,000. But judging from the summons's perfect timing, it seems plausible that one of the football players whom Pyle hired tipped off Scott that a $5,000 check was coming. However, the chamber hadn't given Pyle the money yet, and now they couldn't without interference from the court. Pyle's legal trouble may explain why chamber president Edward Overholser was nowhere to be seen on the day of the race, arguably the biggest, most exciting day of 1928 for Oklahoma City.

Maybe it was just as well. Overholser would have been disappointed at what he saw. The crowd at the fairgrounds was around 4,500 spectators strong, an impressive number, but 25 percent less than what the chamber had hoped.

Lon Scott, publicity man for Highway 66, was discouraged. The whole point of having the race on 66 was to publicize it. The road wasn't mentioned in the title of the race on the programs, and it had been abandoned several times, whenever Pyle found it convenient, including that day. Scott was not amused, nor was the local press.

As "a goodwill builder," pulling a switch on the crowd, leaving them to wait on the roads for nothing, "the move wasn't much of a success," concluded *Oklahoman* reporter C. M. McMillen.

IN THE EVENING, crowds of people milled about sampling Pyle's carnival; admiring Kah-Ko, the police dog; and taking a peek at "the Oklahoma outlaw." Most of the paying public would have been unaware that the stars of the attraction, the Bunion Derby runners, were just underneath the grandstands in a bunkhouse.

At least one reporter from the *Oklahoman* was allowed inside, where he found runners grumbling and cursing. The sportswriter didn't get a byline or mention the names of the athletes moaning and complaining. But he did give an interesting account of the mood of the runners, and it was clear that no one was happy.

"Many of the men who have been forced out of the race have stayed with the caravan as trainers or in some capacity. They swear at the race, but they stay," noted the reporter, not realizing that some of them likely followed the troupe because they were waiting to receive their deposit money. "Those who finish at all have been promised jobs by Pyle, the men said. What kind of job didn't seem very clear. They thought it would be a running job. If it is, they don't want it. One runner said if he ever got to New York, he never intended to run again, not even to catch a street car. His fondest hope is to have someone push him around in a wheelchair for the rest of his life, if he gets the $25,000.

"Hot toes are common. Some of the men even sleep with their feet sticking out from under the covers," added the reporter, probably referring to all of the men whose toes were scraped raw of either toenail or flesh and the burning sensation that they must have felt. "Every man has a different method of caring for his feet and legs. Blister derby might be a more fitting title, some of the men said. Pavement running is going to make the race worse, they fear."

EVEN IF PYLE felt that he could fight Ralph Scott's lawsuit, he didn't have time. He wouldn't be able to stay in Oklahoma City for a trial without irreparable harm to the race. Pyle wanted to come up with a plan that would solve his legal issues and keep him in the money.

Pyle had been unpainting himself out of corners for years now. Two years earlier, when he was helping to produce Red Grange's movie *One Minute to Play*, Sam Wood, the director, told Pyle that they needed 5,000 extras, wearing winter clothing, to fill the stands for several football scenes. It was going to cost Pyle $5 per person.

Pyle couldn't quite stomach the thought of parting with $25,000, and so he invited football star Red Flaherty and several other players down to a stadium and advertised to the public that Grange was going to be playing, stressing that anyone who came wearing a fedora or an overcoat would be admitted for free. In the middle of July, 10,000 winter-clad spectators showed up, giving the movie twice as many people as needed. Pyle didn't spend a nickel.

One year earlier, after Grange's team was clobbered in a football game in Los Angeles, Pyle worried that the public wouldn't want to attend the upcoming matches over the next few weeks in the city, and so he lured the masses to the Biltmore Hotel. Grange stood on the roof, while Pyle promised $50 to anyone who caught one of Red's footballs. People milled about in the street, creating a traffic jam for blocks, while Grange hurled footballs down to the crowd. Even the most physically fit men fumbled, and at the end of the stunt, Pyle still had his $50, and he got what he wanted: Instead of discussing Grange's recent lousy game, everyone was talking about the quarterback's powerful throwing ability.

Pyle had a complicated relationship with money, noted Grange, who once said that Pyle was the type of man who would argue with someone over a nickel and then later that evening take that same person to a nightclub and spend $500.

But how could Pyle get out of this corner? Eventually, it came to him. He proposed to the chamber that he sign a release, stating that the chamber didn't owe him $5,000 because the race hadn't arrived by April 2, the original date planned for Oklahoma City. With no $5,000 check coming, it couldn't be garnished. Pyle would avoid court costs and a lengthy trial.

After Edward Overholser, the president and general manager of the chamber, swore on a Bible and told a judge that the chamber no longer owed Pyle the money, Pyle put Plan B into action. He made the friendly suggestion to Overholser that now that the legal issues were behind them, the chamber could pay him his money under the table.

Overholser reminded Pyle that he had testified in court that the money wasn't owed to him. If the chamber paid him in any shape or form, Overholser would perjure himself. Overholser was as rigorously ethical as Pyle was crafty. Pyle, in a way, had met his match.

And Ralph Scott had, too. Pyle's dodge was another blow for Scott, whose life had already peaked. By the 1930s, Scott's football career was finished, and for some time he suffered a painful sinus infection. In August 1936, Scott, who had survived the sinking of his troop ship in World War I, drove to an out-of-the-way spot, closed the windows, kept the motor running, and parked somewhere enclosed. His body was found a few hours later.

Not that Pyle knew what was to come for Scott, and avoiding his lawsuit wasn't personal. For Pyle, keeping money in his pockets was as much a sport as a means of survival.

But Pyle lost this round, out $5,000 from the chamber, which itself was disappointed in only bringing in $1,000 in gate receipts. He had dozens of people on payroll and spent approximately $120 a day on meal tickets. He paid to fuel a fleet of vehicles, and gas prices had been creeping up a penny during the last few months, rising to 18 cents a gallon. At that rate, $5,000 would have bought him 27,778 gallons of fuel.

Several hours later, Pyle's newly repaired *America* drove off the premises of the American Body Company—slipping away without making payment on the $288 bill.

April 14, Oklahoma City to Chandler, 51.9 Miles

As Newton remembered it, that day was "one of the coldest runs we had. Fortunately, there was no rain or snow, but the wind, dead in our faces for half the day, was bitter."

Phillip Granville, who had quit the previous day because of a leg injury, returned to the race, but in utter pain. Mike Baze was in the worst shape, however, having been hit by a car. His leg broken, Baze quit permanently, and now Payne was even more valuable to his trainer, as Baze was one of Young's clients. Ironically, Baze's wife joined the caravan in Oklahoma City because she had been worried about her husband's health.

After reaching the finish line, three runners took a stand. Nestor Erickson, August Fager, and Juri Lossman, the latter two of whom made it to Oklahoma City just ahead of Payne, had become tight friends and were collectively fed up: They refused to run another inch unless Pyle started providing daily prize money as he had promised long before the race and during the early days of the event.

Erickson and Fager had made this kind of threat before. When their trainer, Alex Finn, had been sacked in New Mexico, the two had temporarily quit. This time, when Pyle didn't blink, Erickson, Fager, and Lossman stuck to their word and dropped out.

Pyle could not have been pleased by their departures. All three men were fine runners who had been or would be in the Olympics.

Pyle should have taken the dissent as a warning. Cliques and lifelong friendships were forming. The runners were bonding and establishing alliances. It explains why three elite runners would decide to drop out together, and it explains why, when Von Flue caught up with Wynn Roberts, from Wallace, Idaho, he slowed down to jog with him, instead of running by him. As they caught up to George Rehayn, singing a German song with lots of spirit but absolutely no melody, both Roberts and Von Flue knew they could easily sprint past him, but they figured it would do him some good to lead them to the finish, and so they let him. Rehayn, incidentally, looked a sight: He hadn't shaved or cut his hair since the start of the race.

Payne did not discuss much with Gavuzzi, other than small talk. Their rivalry kept them from striking up much of a friendship, but otherwise, Payne and Gavuzzi made a number of other friends. If nothing else, each of the 75 runners left in the race found that they had something in common, aside from wanting to win the prize money: They were all collectively coming to despise C. C. Pyle.

April 15, Chandler to Bristow, 34.8 Miles

Payne and Gavuzzi were running into Davenport when the crowds watching the race got to see an example of how fast these two could run. A train was coming down the tracks, and Payne and Gavuzzi both broke into a fever-pitched dash, trying to cross the railroad tracks before the engine and cars passed. Moments before it rushed by, Payne and Gavuzzi ran across, and the runners following them, many of whom were limping and had bandages on their feet, were forced to stop and wait for it to pass.

Payne and Gavuzzi, of course, kept running.

Once in Bristow, Payne was made an honorary chief of police, though town officials gave the impression that he had a job on the force if he wanted it. Everyone in Oklahoma wanted to be associated with their hero, though their enthusiasm was marred by one salient problem: Gavuzzi was now in first place by 23 minutes.

WHAT NO ONE involved in the Bunion Derby knew was that someone else had just joined the race, in a fashion. Earlier in the day, Asa Hall set off from Kansas City, Missouri, in pursuit of the Bunion Derby runners—on roller skates.

Hall had been roller-skating since he was 9. Two years earlier, to win a $500 bet, the 37-year-old roller-skated from Los Angeles to Milwaukee. Now he was chasing after the Bunion Derby runners, which he would do for over a month, making it from Kansas City to Ashtabula, Ohio, before his skates and will gave out.

Hall did reach New York City—though a couple of months later.

The following year, he had a job with a roller-skating company, for which he was to skate every day for 50 miles, according to his contract, and promote the pastime. By 1939, living in Mexico, Missouri, Hall skated from his home to the New York City World's Fair. That year, he swore it was his last cross-country roller-skating trip. But in 1940, *Ripley's Believe It or Not!* featured Hall in its newspaper cartoon, which only served to encourage him. During World War II, Hall, by then in his midfifties, roller-skated around the country, taking odd jobs that were often available because of the worker shortage created when men left their jobs to serve overseas.

Hall's mania may help explain why many of the runners who dropped out of the race stayed with the caravan, selling programs for Pyle and helping out however they could. True, Pyle encouraged that, especially if it meant holding off returning their travel deposit, but the race was difficult for some runners to get out of their system. Once someone began a cause like running or skating across the country, or sitting on a flagpole for 12 days straight, it became something of an addiction.

More accurately, those who were successful at the endurance contests found that these competitions defined their personality so much that it became a difficult lifestyle to give up. When the applause died down and the spotlight moved on, it was hard for them to accept that they were returning to their life as average citizens. After George Young finished his triumphant swim from Catalina, a family rift developed between him and his mother and aunt; he had a falling out with his best friend, Bill Hastings; and his manager made the idiotic decision to turn down a movie offer for Young of $250,000 and a $5,000-a-week personal appearance tour, because he thought he could get the lad more money. He couldn't and didn't.

Young won a 21-mile marathon in 1931, but otherwise, he never recaptured the glorious few weeks he had after the Catalina swim. By 1949, he was profiled in the Canadian magazine *Maclean's* and shown to be down-and-out, overweight, and graying. He admitted to being depressed and that fame had been difficult. "The trouble is, you've got to win all the time," he said. "It's funny how people can be."

Shipwreck Kelly, the flagpole sitter, also had a rough time. He kept up his flagpole sitting during the 1920s and 1930s, but when World War II broke out, people had other matters on their minds. He died on October 11, 1952, suffering a heart attack just across the street from Madison Square Garden, where he once performed. Kelly collapsed, rolling off the sidewalk and into the gutter. A small crowd of people, including two policemen, gathered around Kelly, just like in the good old days, only this time their heads weren't craned up to the sky.

Inside Shipwreck Kelly's coat was a relief check, and underneath his arm, a scrapbook of fading newspaper articles.

April 16, Bristow to Tulsa, 41.7 Miles

Hardrock was 214 hours behind Gavuzzi, but his hometown newspaper pointed out that there were still 2,000 miles to go, optimistically proclaiming, "It's anybody's race."

If so, Hardrock's trainer arrived just in time. His classmate and best friend, Wesley Williams, turned up in Tulsa in a Ford coupe paid for with the money that Burlington's townspeople had raised through "The Faith in Hardrock Fund."

Wesley had his work cut out for him. Gavuzzi made it to Tulsa in just under 5 hours; Hardrock, in just over 10. Still, Wesley was simply glad to see his friend. He wired the newspaper with the message, "Found Paul in good shape. Everything going fine."

Wesley was fortunate to be catching Hardrock in Tulsa, as opposed to a desolate town like Mojave Wells. Tulsa was an oil town, built over the last 2 decades by firms like Independent Oil and Gas Company and Prairie Oil and Gas Company. Skyscrapers filled Tulsa's downtown, and Art Deco buildings were cropping up everywhere. This was a city that had the funds and resources to throw a celebratory bash, and they did just that.

Pyle loved the response; the runners didn't. Reporters tried to slow the runners down, asking them for interviews; autograph seekers waved pens and notebooks; motorists with cars leaking overpowering gas fumes drove next to the athletes and tried to strike up conversations. Trying to make his way through the well-wishers, Payne fell an hour behind Gavuzzi.

In Sapulpa, an assemblage of Creek Indians gave a rousing welcome to Payne. The Bunion Derby's passing through was the second wave of excitement in Sapulpa within a few weeks. Frances Anderson, the nationally famous champion female billiard player, had recently committed suicide in a nearby hotel. She had crushed opponents for 30 years but ended everything with a razor. That would have been shocking enough, but when they prepared her for burial, it was discovered that she was a he. When a woman arrived from Newton, Kansas, and viewed the body, she was pretty certain the man was the brother she hadn't seen in 38 years.

Not far from Sapulpa was the Tulsa finish line, where the runners were each given a pint of ice cream by city officials. Over at the carnival, a happy mob descended on the games, food, and curiosities on display. This time, the runners were required to stick around long enough for Pyle to introduce each man to the public. It's a wonder Pyle didn't think of this sooner. It was such a successful way of incorporating the race with the carnival that the introductions became a mandatory part of the evening.

Much as the multitude seemed to relish Pyle's carnival, one oddity was off-limits. As Pyle's convoy of cars and buses entered Oklahoma, he and Elmer McCurdy's guardian, Edward Sonney, removed the outlaw from the show. McCurdy was from Oklahoma, and Sonney had worried that a relative might drop by to claim one of his family's most profitable assets. Pyle, who didn't want to lose McCurdy either, agreed that it was best for the bandit to lay low in the state. It seemed prudent; many newspaper reporters had mentioned the Oklahoma outlaw in their stories.

Sonney's and Pyle's fears turned out to be unfounded, but one old acquaintance did show up: Bob Fenton, the deputy whose bullet felled the thief in 1911. He had heard about his old nemesis having a part in the Bunion Derby, and curiosity got the better of him. He quietly showed up in Tulsa at the carnival and spoke to Sonney, and the two slipped into the tent. The lawman stared at McCurdy for a few reflective and maybe uncomfortable moments. Then Fenton went outside and wandered off into the sunset.

C. C. Pyle's idyllic experience in Tulsa was marred by one piece of unfortunate, if inevitable, luck. The police informed Pyle that he was being sued by the American Body Company, and for good measure they were naming Red Grange in their lawsuit. The authorities took possession of the *America*, telling Pyle he could have it back when he paid his $288 bill. Pyle hastily assured them that he could do so and settled his bill on the spot.

April 17, Tulsa to Chelsea, 49.7 Miles

The new rule was now put on the dockets, ensuring that for the time being anyway the Bunion Derby would truly be a race again. From now on, anyone who didn't make it to the finish line by *midnight* was finished, through, gone, dumped, outta there. It looked like bad news for Hardrock. Predicted one journalist snidely, "The weak sisters that are bringing up the rear will soon be out of the race."

The strongest runners were faring well, as usual. Payne took the lead over Gavuzzi, breaking his wonted measured pace and running as fast as he dared to without destroying himself. Foyil, his hometown, was right in the path of Highway 66, and there was no way he wasn't going to be the first one there. But he still had several miles to run and towns to pass through before reaching Foyil.

Payne was the first to flash through Claremore, Will Rogers's hometown, and the community sponsoring him.

Earlier in the day, from New York City, Will Rogers sent word by telegraph that he was going to award prize money of $500 for the first four runners to reach Claremore, with the top runner receiving $250. Rogers hoped Payne would win the first prize, saying he wanted to "keep the money in Claremore."

Not so fast, C. C. Pyle said in effect. He stressed that the offer couldn't be accepted because all the runners hadn't been notified in time.

You didn't say no to Will Rogers. The cowboy comedian sent another telegram saying that he would just give $250 to Payne.

The entire week spent in Oklahoma had belonged to Payne, but this especially was his day. When he ran into Claremore, a chamber official pressed a $100 bill in his hand, and children from the area were excused from school, so they could crane their necks and climb trees to watch and cheer for their new hometown hero.

Farmers, ranchers, and oil fielders left their stations to see the young Oklahoman run. Payne was given a military salute from the Oklahoma

Military Academy, which fired 22 shots—one more than it gave the president of the United States—and Mayor Flynn's military band played "The Thunderer," by John Philip Sousa.

Once in Foyil, a banner stretching over the street welcomed the hometown hero, and children clung from tree branches to get a better view of the race. Meanwhile, Payne's family was getting the royal treatment. Doc and his wife, Zona, and their kids, Hensel, 19; Mary, 16; Faye, 13; Pauline, 10; Charles, 8; and Will Rogers Payne, 5, all trooped into Pyle's motor home and were given a ride to Chelsea, the next night control, as the runners, of course, made their way on foot.

And the long-feared rule of being eliminated for not making it to the finish line by midnight? That didn't even stay in place for a full day.

John Salo, who was in third place, had to drop out at some point when he was nearing the end of the route. Pyle apparently realized what a devastating financial blow it would be near the end of the race to not have Salo, if that didn't have to be the case. Salo's home of Passaic, New Jersey, was the second-to-last stop in the race. Pyle could see what having Payne around was doing for his bottom line in Oklahoma. It's a good guess that when Salo's stomach brought him down, Pyle may have thought that perhaps the new rule had been made a little impulsively. Things had been going fine. Why remake the wheel?

ABOUT A THOUSAND AUTOMOBILES followed Payne, and behind him were some very annoyed competitors, including Gavuzzi.

Though Gavuzzi probably didn't begrudge Payne his moment of glory, he wasn't about to let him take away the race. As the cars dwindled, Gavuzzi picked up the pace, but he was too far behind to do any good. Several others had better luck, like John Cronick and Harry Rea. Cronick and Rea tore up the road, trying desperately to catch up to Payne, who did everything he could to stay ahead, though he was having trouble himself, dodging crowds of cars and well-wishers.

Eventually, Cronick and Rea appeared in view of the hometown hero, and the crowd broke into raucous cheers, alerting Payne, if he wasn't already aware, that runners were on his trail. Payne sped up, but so did Cronick and Rea. Payne won, by 20 seconds. It was one of those rare moments when the race actually resembled a race.

Gavuzzi hurried into Chelsea 3 hours later.

He was now 1 hour, 56 minutes, and 20 seconds behind Payne's elapsed time. He was exhausted and more than irritated at how the townspeople had inadvertently conspired to slow him down. He was a good sport, though, and not one to despair easily. Payne had his day, and now, if he could help it, Gavuzzi would have his.

April 18, Chelsea to Miami, 52 Miles

Sure enough, Gavuzzi won the lap. Salo was back, recovered from his stomach problems. Doc Payne left the caravan and returned to Foyil, while Andy reverted to his 6½-mile-an-hour pace and, as it turned out, ran over half of the day's race alongside Ed Gardner.

As the sun reached its height, Payne and Gardner stripped off their shirts, tying them around their waists. They tied for fifth that day. Payne spent the night at the home of a cousin, but that was the last hint that he was still in his home state. The parade of fans was already thinning. The gaggle of news reporters, angling for quotes and photos, returned to covering chamber of commerce meetings and baseball games. It was back to business as usual.

CHAPTER 13

Andy Payne and Pete Gavuzzi became intense rivals during the course of the race. (Courtesy of the El Reno Carnegie Library.)

SLOW GOING

DISTANCE SO FAR: 1,720.8 MILES; 75 RUNNERS

The endurance craze was still flourishing.

While the majority of the world's population was obviously concerned with making money, raising children, shopping, planting a garden, taking a vacation, watching a sporting event, and a whole host of activities, there were an awful lot of endurance competitions going on, especially throughout the United States, and there were many that were conceived but never carried out. For instance, as Andy Payne ran through Oklahoma, he would have been interested, if embarrassed, to know that one of his state's residents, Luther Slayton, was trying to organize a race in which people would *crawl* from Oklahoma City to Dallas. Shockingly, no one in their right mind or with money would back the venture.

The month before, on March 30, as C. C. Pyle's circus headed to

Palma, New Mexico, pilots George Haldeman and Eddie Stinson, who had entertained the Bunion Derby in Flagstaff, landed their plane at Jackson Beach, Florida, after remaining in the air for 53 hours, 36 minutes, and 30 seconds.

Two days later, Mrs. Lottie Moore Schoemmel, who attempted the Catalina Island contest the year before, swam in a pool for 32 hours, beating the old record by an hour, a record by a woman in England that had stood for 47 years.

And as the month of April aged, Dare Devil Warner, a stunt driver, plotted out the details of a road trip in which he would soon handcuff himself to the wheel of his car—and drive around the country for an entire year. It was a successful stunt, all to promote the Auburn 8-88, made by the White Auto Company. Looking back on it all now, between the advertising and the live-action drama unfolding across the country, who needed television?

April 19, Miami, Oklahoma, to Joplin, Missouri, 40 Miles

Pete Gavuzzi had been running well until he came to a well. Shortly after reaching Missouri, he sampled some of its water and, for the next 6 hours, felt like he was being tortured. He ended up coming in 26th place for the day and for the rest of his time in the state, he would drink hot tea.

Despite the rainy weather, spectators showed up. The crowds always gave the runners a lift; it beat running on a deserted road alone. That day's race, however, would have been comforting regardless: The runners left Oklahoma, ran about 12 miles in Kansas, and then entered Missouri, all in 40 miles. Traveling through three states at least gave them a sense of movement, and simultaneously, there was another sign of progress.

The southeastern tip of Kansas that the runners cut through was in the Ozark Mountains. Cascading down the hills were newly made streams from the rain. The mountains had their first signs of vegetation, and the trees were starting to show hints of turning green. It was Day 47, and spring was coming.

THE PUBLIC had all heard about the "derby of the century" and weren't about to let a little weather stop them from seeing it. The merchants of Joplin did their part to stir up some race-inspired frenzy and made sure they were in line to benefit. One such store, Mitchell's, advertised directly to fans of the derby, albeit misstating the number of runners left, easy to do when one considers how many men were dropping out then changing their minds the next morning: "When You Come to Joplin Today to See 'Red' Grange, C. C. Pyle and the 70 'Bunion Derby' Runners, DON'T FORGET that we cordially invite you to visit this store and make it your headquarters for the day."

From Miami to Joplin, the highway was lined with cars, full of spectators waving and cheering. In Joplin, the crowds were so thick that they blocked the runners as they tried to make their way down Main Street. The runners had to push their way through the masses to reach the finish line.

There was a lot of incentive to complete the day's tour as fast as possible. That morning, as he had before, Pyle promised all 75 runners a chicken dinner in Joplin. The practically emaciated runners began cheering. Still, in a 40-mile race, there were going to be people who were going to rest, no matter what rewards were being dangled at the end of the line; thus, many of the runners chose an establishment in Baxter Springs, Kansas, to sit for a spell, drying off from the rain and eating what they could afford.

Payne came in seventh that day, still in the lead in overall time, 90 minutes ahead of Gavuzzi. But the winner for the day's lap was an ecstatic John Gober, who hadn't won any of the previous legs of the race. As was becoming the custom, the runners—who were generally getting more fond of each other as a group every day—would dial their performance back a bit and let hometown boys race through their community first. Considering how tired everyone was, holding back was not difficult.

A native of Greece, Gober had lived in Missouri for some time and weeks ago vowed he would be the first runner through the Show Me State. "When we hit Missouri, watch my smoke," he promised.

Sure enough, the 34-year-old showed everyone, charging into Missouri ahead of the other runners and finishing first for the day. He traveled the 40-mile stretch at 8 miles an hour, no doubt thrilling his wife, who was on hand to see him arrive in Joplin. Gober finished 30 minutes ahead of the second runner of the day, Sam Richman of New York. Several hours later, Hardrock crept in with his trainer of several days following in his car.

That night, trainer and friend Wesley Williams, whose nickname was for reasons unknown "Chop Suey," wrote the student newspaper at Elon College:

> I am getting along fine, and Hardrock is improving fast. Ran through sleet and rain all day but did well. I like the country pretty well but prefer the East. I will be glad when I strike Eastern soil again. We have great crowds waiting for us in every town and all along the road, so we have plenty of company. I have just attended to Hardrock, and he is now reading the *Maroon and Gold*. He seems to be getting quite a kick out of it. Will write more soon, as I am tired and must "hit the hay."
>
> Best regards to all,
> Chop Suey

Several runners didn't take up Pyle on his chicken dinner. That night, Gober celebrated in a cafeteria with his wife and some friends, devouring every morsel of food he could find. Meanwhile, Payne ordered a substantial meal at a restaurant.

"Watch that boy eat," said an admirer.

Payne looked uncomfortable. He couldn't get used to the idea that he was a celebrity.

His trainer rescued him from having to engage in a lengthy dialogue. "You ain't seen nothing yet," promised Tom Young. "He'll eat two or three servings like that before he gets done."

A reporter interrupted Payne's dinner by asking about his running performance throughout Oklahoma. Payne gave him a quick quote before returning to focus on his food: "It was pretty hard to keep up the pace in the home state when everybody wants to stop and take your picture while you're running."

"Andy's a better runner in the hills than on level ground," Young told the reporter and the crowd gathered around his protégé's table. "I guess we'll have to change his stride a little, now that we're on leveler ground. His average time is 7 miles an hour, and we plan to keep up that pace, all the time—rather than increase it," said Young, who either automatically rounded up the 6.5-mile plan in conversation or modified the plan a bit. "Gavuzzi runs 8 miles an hour some days and then has to slow down. We figure that it's the steady grind that gets them there."

"How did you find it today?" asked someone in the crowd.

"Well, I had to change socks twice," said Payne, probably referring to the rain, although the sweat made sock changing important.

As Payne finished his meal, another patron asked if he was going to rest. "No, I think I'll go to a show," he replied. As usual, he was polite but taciturn. Payne had no interest in being a celebrity, and his indifference may have been just as well. The farther away he got from Oklahoma City, the less well-known he was. The next morning, when Payne showed up in running trunks and a white sweater with blue trim, several people broke into applause, clearly thinking the rest of the crowd would join them. No one did, and the group of people stopped in mid-clap, embarrassed.

Because of the day's weather ("drenching rain," according to Joplin's paper), Young paid $2 for a room at the Hotel Conner for Payne, protecting the health of his best runner and his chance to earn 10 percent of $25,000.

Gober slept indoors that night as well, finally able to commune with his wife and get a shower. Gober had renewed energy, a vigorous appetite, and one great advantage over everyone else: He was a shoemaker by trade. That said, he didn't cause Payne to lose any sleep or prompt Gavuzzi to rethink his running strategy, which had so far kept him at the front of the pack after 1,760.8 miles.

Both Payne's and Gavuzzi's elapsed time hovered around 295 hours. Gober had run the same distance in 445 hours.

April 20, Joplin to Miller, 46.7 Miles

Frank Von Flue went to the starting line, more lethargic than normal. The day before, he had also been sluggish in the morning and missed the start of the race. Although he had been the second-to-last person to take off running, he at least gained mileage, coming past the finish line in 45th place for the day. Now, as they prepared for another run, he didn't feel very well, like he had picked up a cold or something fairly innocuous. He had no pep.

People noticed. In the crowd, some guy said to another: "There's a fellow who isn't going to finish the day out."

Von Flue tensed up, knowing the man meant him. He vowed that he *would* finish, and after the whistle blew, he took off in a hurry. He wasn't the only one. Recovered from his stomach pain, Gavuzzi flew down the road. There was no chance of Von Flue, or anyone else, catching him; everyone was going to have to quickly get used to the idea of coming in no better than second on that day.

Running like mad, Gavuzzi was attempting to recover all of the time he lost over the last few days, from being stuck behind cars in Oklahoma to being sick in Missouri. He barreled through the town of Carthage a full 15 minutes before the next runner, Gober. Payne, still the front-runner in elapsed time, was the sixth man to pass by; heeding his trainer's advice, he kept to moving at approximately 7 miles an hour. Many of the runners going through Carthage didn't notice anything amiss, though Gavuzzi received a hint of what was to come.

"We don't want you foreigners on our roads," shouted a man, leaning out of his car window and driving a little too close for Gavuzzi's comfort. "Clear out, or we'll run you down."

Otherwise, Gavuzzi and the runners were given a hearty welcome.

Mothers holding their babies waved; businessmen stood on the sidewalk, smoked, and watched the proceedings; students from Ozark Wesleyan College and schoolchildren cheered the runners, as both groups took advantage of the partial holiday, which allowed them the opportunity to catch part of the national event. It looked like a typical crowd, and yet—

"PYLE AND JOPLIN DOUBLE-CROSS CARTHAGE," one local newspaper headline bellowed. The Bunion Derby was slated to come to Carthage the night before, but at the last minute, Joplin offered Pyle more money to make it the stopping point. Pyle, in usual form, accepted its generous offer. But now, 8 miles into the daily lap, Pyle learned the consequences of that decision.

When Pyle's caravan passed through, there were jeers and boos from some in the audience, and several youths began hurling their chicken's finest. Eggs coated at least two cars and covered Frankie Sullivan, a disabled war veteran selling Pyle's programs. There were shouts at Sullivan as the police came for him, with people overheard saying, "He's one of that crowd," "The jail for him," and "Give him a long sentence."

Indeed, instead of the chief of police asking Sullivan if he needed assistance, he arrested him and, soon after, fined him $8 for selling without a license.

The fury that some Carthage residents had for Pyle can't be overstated. Around the same time, Morton Harrison, a staff member for Oklahoma governor Henry S. Johnston, was in the town, promoting the Sooner State, talking up Andy Payne, and lauding their staple product, radium water. One large man grabbed Harrison, thinking he was part of Pyle's crew, and prepared to beat him to a pulp. Harrison hollered that he was only representing Payne and radium water. After the man released him, he quickly explained that he had nothing to do with C. C. Pyle and was allowed to return to his Packard with his limbs still intact.

The Bunion Derby passed through Carthage without any additional problems, but if it hadn't been before, it was now clear to anyone following the event that C. C. Pyle was making up this race as it went along. He was laying railroad track as fast as he could, hoping the train wouldn't catch up with him. Organizing such a massive, complex event was a terrible ordeal, and Pyle would have been well-served to draw the route and make arrangements with the cities his troops would stop in long before the race began. Contracts could have been drawn up with every town—not just some of the bigger cities—which would have protected Pyle's interests as well as the towns' that he was working with.

The 12 months that he allotted to plan the race may not have been enough time, given that he worked with a small team apparently consisting of only himself, Bill Pickens, and one secretary. Communication was also a difficult matter, as the telephone system was still working through its growing pains. Calling across town required hooking up with an operator; connecting across the country required the assistance of several. Doing business on the telephone also required a good deal of patience, a virtue Pyle didn't have. Wrong numbers were a common occurrence, and if no one was around to answer the telephone, there was no way to leave a message.

Given these inconveniences, it's very likely that Pyle rarely used the telephone for his Bunion Derby business and instead depended heavily on the U.S. Postal Service along with the occasional telegram. The mail, however, could be slow going. While airmail had taken off during the 1920s and made transporting letters very efficient, plane crashes were frighteningly routine, which could slow down the speed of a letter's journey.

Given the primitive methods of communication available to him, it is easy to understand why Pyle didn't have every detail in place when the starter bomb went off. But it's also true that the impresario wasn't organized. In the spring of 1924, Pyle was sued by A. W. Stoolman, his former partner in the Rialto Theatre and the Virginia Theatre, both in Champaign, Illinois. In his complaint to the Circuit Court of Champaign, Stoolman made it clear that Pyle was careless with his paperwork. Box-office receipts were supposed to be completed daily, but Stoolman asserted that "no complete and intelligent record has ever been made of the receipts and disbursements of the partnership . . . by the said Charles C. Pyle."

Of course, that may be in part because, according to Stoolman, Pyle was using the business account as his own personal piggy bank. Stoolman claimed that Pyle "drew out large sums of money from the receipts taken in by said partnership, for his purely personal and private needs, such as the purchase of an automobile, payment of life insurance premiums for his own life insurance, and in which the said partnership was in no way whatever interested, personal telephone bills and large and numerous withdrawals of cash from the said partnership funds for his own private and personal uses, all without the consent or knowledge of his partner . . . "

Innocent or guilty—the judge later said guilty—Pyle was a mess when it came to managing details. Pyle's inefficiency was clear to anyone who listened to him first explain how the Bunion Derby would work. Although Pyle had specific, cost-effective plans in mind for the race, they were impossible to pull off.

"Every town through which this unparalleled race will be run must agree to furnish one judge for each contestant," Pyle told reporters in 1927. "These civic referees must meet the racer at the town hall and follow him in a car until he reaches the next town. Every contestant will be numbered and each judge will be responsible for the ethics of the contestant whose number he has been assigned. At each town, the contestant must get his judge's okay on a card and these cards will be checked at the end of the race. Every mile that is walked or run must be vouched for."

IT WASN'T JUST SOME JERK in Carthage. Gavuzzi was treated badly as he neared Miller as well. He told race officials that some unsportsmanlike motorists had threatened to run him down, hurting his race time that day. The officials, sympathetic or not, couldn't help. They didn't know how much time Gavuzzi had lost because of the threats, and aiding Gavuzzi with extra time would only inflame the anger among the rest of the runners, who were irate enough. Arriving in Miller was certainly unpleasant—it was a mile off the highway, and the road leading to the community was a muddy mess. At least they got to sleep out of the mess, in the high school gymnasium.

Like so many elements along the route, fan harassment was beyond Pyle's control. He could only hope that the police would provide protection whenever possible.

April 21, Miller to Springfield, 33.6 Miles

Mike Kelly was in last place, but he kept running, despite being drenched by persistent rain showers, his feet stumbling along the puddle-laced gravel road. He looked for the little things to buoy his confidence, as when someone sent him a new pair of trunks. "Those pants I put on Thursday were red," he reported in a letter to his hometown paper, "and even through the rain, felt warm, so I just opened up and jogged along."

He also kept running because a small group of businessmen in Goshen, Indiana, was helping to fund his race, and he didn't want to disappoint his hometown. Workers at the I-XL furniture factory were so inspired by his involvement in the race that they scraped up $28.10 to help with incidental expenses, and a group from Goshen, including the chief of police, even came to see him. They spent 3 days in Missouri with Kelly, who wasn't exactly honest about his chances of winning. He was extremely optimistic when talking to the committee from Goshen, so much so that they told Goshen's newspaper that "Mike is expected to make up much of the time he is behind by the time the runners reach Chicago."

Yeah, right.

He was still in the race, though, and Kelly could be pleased with himself for that. Four other men couldn't say the same. Before the day ended, two men were disqualified for not reaching the control point by midnight, and another man willingly quit. Harold McNutt, from Alberta, Canada, stopped on the advice of Dr. Baker, who felt the young man's body simply couldn't take any more. McNutt agreed, telling reporters, "The going was too rough. I could not stand up under it."

And Patrick De Marr of Los Angeles was ejected from the race. He was caught hitching a ride.

April 22, Springfield to Conway, 43.1 Miles

De Marr had hurt his feet early on and hobbled across the California desert with two canes until he healed, inspiring everyone in the race, and he had emerged from a Texas blizzard in first place. He was sick at the thought of crossing 5½ states only to have his role in the race end in this humiliating way. And so De Marr stayed in the race, running in the pouring rain to Springfield and coming in third, hoping to change the referee's mind. No such luck; Arthur Duffy would have none of that. The disgraced boxer returned to Los Angeles.

John Gober won again, as Missouri continued to do wonders for his morale and performance. Unfortunately for Gober, after Missouri morphed into Illinois, he again became an obscure middle-of-the-pack plodder.

April 23, Conway to Waynesville, 51.9 Miles

John Salo's faithful companion followed him all the way from Navajo, Arizona, until the animal finally earned his name, developing blisters on his paws. Pyle then agreed to let the dog recuperate in one of his buses—but on this particular morning, Blisters was nowhere to be found. There was a quick search, but the Bunion Derby had to move on. Everyone hoped that, wherever the dog had wandered off to, he would find a good home.

The human runners continued crossing rolling green hills and mountainous terrain. Ed Gardner and Phillip Granville led the race that day, clocking in at 7 hours, 42 minutes, and a few spare seconds. Farther back, about 30 minutes after Von Flue, were Payne and Gavuzzi, each tying with William Kerr, all coming in 11th place, in around 9 hours and 23 minutes.

Hardrock came in 2 hours later.

As usual, Kelly was one of the last in, and reporters knew why. Earlier in the day, some of them came across the boxer in his bathrobe, sleeping alongside the road. "It's the first warm sun I've seen for a week," he explained after they woke him. "I'll be in before midnight, and don't worry about that."

APRIL 24, WAYNESVILLE TO ROLLA, 32.4 MILES

The next day, Kelly took another nap. "Those Goshen folks that were with me last week encouraged me, but when they left, I went to lagging behind," he admitted. But there was a bright spot. The Goshen delegation left behind a gift: a trainer. His name was Burt Snyder, a 55-year-old factory laborer.

It may have been fortunate for Kelly that Snyder came along when he did. Even though the rules were sketchy, Pyle's men could have still made a good case for kicking Kelly out. Earlier, in El Reno, Oklahoma, runner Alex Joachim, who had been in last place, was kicked out of the race by referee Duffy for showcasing an "indifferent attitude." Duffy explained that Joachim had loitered along the highway past 12 o'clock "with nothing apparently wrong with him."

Snyder could only do so much to keep Kelly in line, though. When the coast was clear, Kelly still found time to nap underneath bridge overpasses and railroad trestles. In fact, of all the runners, Kelly was one of the more curious, colorful, and even enterprising. At this point in the race, he was often stopping at gas stations and country stores, handing out his business card—and wearing a bathrobe. He was never exactly in a hurry.

Kelly had reason to want to take it easy that day. The road to Rolla was a hard-packed gravel highway, easy to slip on and painful on everyone's tender feet. That made it all the more sweet when Von Flue arrived in Rolla and learned that $35 had been wired to him from business leaders in his hometown of Kerman, California. He immediately went downtown and bought himself a pair of special running shoes. They had a cork cushion in between the inner and outer soles, and he couldn't help feeling proud and confident that his running would improve even more.

With the money he had left over, he bought food. Like all of the runners, he was perpetually starving.

But after Von Flue returned in his new shoes, there was a moment when it looked as if he might have wasted his money. Rolla's health department and the sheriff had stepped in. The health department officials insisted that they would find a way to shut down the race if Pyle's crew didn't gather up all of the filthy blankets and sheets and burn them. Pyle wasn't going to get any help or sympathy from the sheriff, who himself shut down the carnival for operating games of chance.

Lon Scott, publicity man for Highway 66, read the newspapers' account and considered what the public's opinion of Highway 66 would be if the public began equating it with con games. Scott fumed.

The runners lay on cots, with only spare clothes to pull over them, and shivered and groaned throughout the night.

April 25, Rolla to Sullivan, 42.9 Miles

Because he had learned that the road surface would change near the end of the day's run, Arthur Newton gave a brief speech before Duffy blew the whistle. "Watch out for shin splints," he said. "The return to pavement after desert sand and graveled roads will bring back a recurrence of foot complaints. Surfaced roads and with the continual pounding of the feet upon them will, in even a single day, wipe out the bulk of any leader's edge. The pace is naturally getting hotter, and men who were stragglers a few weeks ago move up in menacing fashion daily."

WHEN THE ASSOCIATED PRESS missed a day in sending Bunion Derby updates to the U.S. territory of Hawaii, a reporter from Honolulu cabled a message back: "Continue daily reports of bunion derby; schools using it to teach geography lessons."

On the mainland, the excitement was more tempered. It's not that people across the country didn't appreciate what was being accomplished, but a race with high excitement it was not. As reporter Bill Witt wrote: "The trouble with Pyle's race is that it's too long to be taken seriously." Witt, having run the distance from Clinton to Bridgeport, Oklahoma, knew of what he spoke. "There is drama in a 100-yard-dash and even a short cross-country sprint, but a race that goes on for months and months becomes, to the people in general, a thing of humor and the butt of many jokes."

It was exciting to be in any town through which the race passed, to watch the men run by and to cheer and shout and marvel and point at their gaunt, weary frames. But if you were states away, in Florida or Montana, and not much of a sports enthusiast, you could easily live your life and be absolutely unaware that a cross-country race was going on.

Some people who lived along Highway 66 were equally oblivious. Runner Arthur Killingsworth observed later, "Many people in the country, especially in Illinois, would ask us what race we were training for. They wouldn't know what race was in progress and think that some local fellows were training for exhibition."

Pyle was born 100 years too early. If the Bunion Derby had been organized in modern times, either a television network or a sports-specific channel like ESPN would have aired a reality series on the race. Cable news networks would have cut in throughout the day and night to cover it. There would have been a Web site with a daily Bunion Derby blog, a *People* magazine cover, and interviews with *Entertainment Tonight*. But instead, with only daily news reports in the sports page and the occasional newsreel to pique the public's interest, political enthusiasts could instead wonder if candidates Herbert Hoover or Alfred E. Smith would be the next president, sports buffs lapped up stories on Babe Ruth's home run streak, and some concerned citizens were monitoring the progress of First Lady Coolidge's mother, who had been battling influenza for months.

And anyone with a pulse was following the ongoing adventures of Charles Lindbergh, almost a year after his famous flight. His latest exploit involved flying 500 miles from New York to Quebec to bring serum to

Floyd Bennett, a pilot suffering from pneumonia. Tragically, Lindbergh was given the wrong medicine, and Bennett died. The *Los Angeles Times* sympathetically editorialized, "He did all a mortal man could do."

The Bunion Derby might have been covered more frequently in front-page stories and in editorials of the *Los Angeles Times* if the race was somewhat close between the athletes, but when the runners reached Sullivan, Missouri, they ended Day 53 in what was believed to be a 90-day race. With Payne and Gavuzzi *30 hours ahead* of the third-place foot soldier, Salo, it soon became glaringly obvious not only who was certain to win, barring an unforeseen dilemma, but also who didn't stand a chance—men like Mike Kelly and more and more, Hardrock. The race was hardly riveting theatre, with action unfolding minute by minute. Not for the spectators, anyway.

The drama was behind the scenes. For instance, how much longer could Pyle keep the race functioning before it imploded? And the runners felt the suspense acutely. On April 25, Gavuzzi finally sped past Payne on the way to Sullivan, Missouri, putting him 32 minutes and 51 seconds ahead in cumulative time. On April 26, Gavuzzi expanded his lead to an hour, 49 minutes, and 35 seconds. He and Payne tied the following day, running through St. Louis and dodging its heavy city traffic, but the next day, the Englishman pulled ahead to lead by 3 hours, 32 minutes, and 7 seconds. On April 29, Gavuzzi pulled ahead by 4 hours, 5 minutes, and 36 seconds. The drama was unfurling slowly, too slowly for a nationwide audience to care, but Gavuzzi cared and Payne particularly cared, since his chance for the first-prize money, which he wanted for a multitude of both worthy and materialistic reasons, was slipping away.

Pyle silently rooted for Gavuzzi. From Pyle's perspective, the bearded Englishman was far more compelling than the quiet country boy. Visually, Gavuzzi was interesting. He hadn't shaved since the race began and looked like a wiry mountain man. Pyle encouraged that, knowing the sportswriters were having fun writing about Gavuzzi's unkempt, shaggy look. They kept describing Gavuzzi with phrases like "the bearded Britisher."

There were other reasons Gavuzzi was a better fit as the winner of the race. Unlike Payne, he was more wholly committed to the sport with a longer history of running, something Pyle could exploit once the race was over. Gavuzzi was also more marketable than Payne. Once the derby concluded, figured Pyle, Gavuzzi would be a celebrity in America and a household name in England. Thanks to Gavuzzi's French mother and Italian father, a running tour through France and Italy might prove profitable as well. Payne, meanwhile, had spent his entire life growing up in the tiny rural burg of Foyil, Oklahoma.

Most important, Pete Gavuzzi would actually give the audience something. He'd give a speech in that rich Cockney accent, or he'd sing a song. About the most Pyle could hope for from Payne was that he'd say, "Howdy."

Pyle wouldn't have even cared if Payne had been unpleasant, as long as he had been a more colorful character, or at least talkative. In fact, he might have preferred he be disagreeable. When Pyle was creating the concept of professional tennis, soon after taking on Grange, the fact that some people were repelled by superstar diva athlete Suzanne Lenglen made him eager to line her up as a client. Happily for Pyle, after much convincing, Lenglen signed up.

Pyle explained it this way to the *New Yorker*: "The fact that people hated her was enough for me. When she walked out and left the crowd flat, and when she refused to meet the king and queen because she was taking a hot bath, she made herself with me. People will pay to see anybody they hate, and the whole problem was to keep them hating her. Suzanne is charming when she wants to be, and we had to repress that side of her nature."

Pyle made around $100,000 from representing her, and he was still collecting royalties on the Suzanne Lenglen tennis racquet and Suzanne Lenglen perfume.

Although Payne was no Lenglen, Pyle recognized that the wholesome young man had some compelling points. Although neither Andy nor Doc likely shared their financial woes with Pyle, the showman was able to detect enough details to paint a grim picture of the Payne family's finances. The articles started appearing as early as 3 weeks into the race and kept gaining momentum as the event continued.

One columnist early on said, "It's funny that this one hasn't come to light long ago. There's a runner . . . who is there for no other purpose than to win the race; rush back to Claremore, Okl., and pay off the mortgage on the old hill farm just before the walrus-mustached sheriff evicts pa and ma."

Another article noted that the Payne family's shack resembled Abraham Lincoln's log cabin. Yet another writer aimed for the older generation's sympathies, making Doc's boy out to be the most Norman Rockwellian of characters: "Andy has no sweetheart and does not seem to care anything for the girls. He does not write any of them and has seldom been seen with one. He is a great home boy and enjoys his own sisters. Andy has been a healthy boy all his life and has never had any severe sickness. Always had plenty of out-door exercise. He does not use tobacco in any form. However, it is said that he has smoked a few times in his life, but not now. He does not use any bad language and is a fine type of boy, with no bad habits and no bad associates."

Pyle may not have started the rumor of the Payne family's dire condition, but he didn't do anything to dissuade anybody of the idea that they were destitute. And make no mistake: The Payne family was not well off. The shack they lived in was built after their house burned to the ground. They still had a mortgage to pay off, but Doc later insisted that all he had left on it was a significant but manageable $2,800.

Second, third, or fourth prize money from the Bunion Derby could have taken care of that. It was a better story, however, for Pyle and the press if Andy was the nicest kid on earth who only wanted to run across the country to save the family farm—instead of being a well-adjusted, intelligent, pleasant young man who wanted to pay off the mortgage, impress the girl of his dreams, and maybe buy a nice car.

April 26, Sullivan to Hillside View, 45.6 Miles

The reporters along for the ride were occasionally discreet about reporting negative news during the race. One has to conclude that by having the reporters embedded with the Bunion Derby, ground rules were easier to establish on what could be reported and what couldn't—no sportswriter likely relished the thought of being left behind at some dusty two-room-shack town in the middle of nowhere.

Only after the race did runners, trainers, and sportswriters make oblique references to mysterious goings-on in the race. For instance, on one particular day in the Show Me State, Pyle didn't have enough money to pay the ferry fees to transport all of the vehicles and runners, so he made his athletes take a 20-mile detour, again branching off of Highway 66.

Payne caught a cold as he traversed Missouri, the third runner to fall ill recently. Salo had stomach problems a few days earlier, and before that Gavuzzi, from drinking the well water. But Payne's cold didn't set him back the way the tonsillitis had; still firmly in second place, he dashed into the tiny town of Hillside View in fifth place, tying with Gardner.

April 27, Hillside View, Missouri, to East St. Louis, Illinois, 28.4 Miles

In St. Louis, the runners jogged carefully across the cobblestone streets that threatened to wrench an ankle or wreak havoc on a toe. As they neared the edge of the city, closing in on the bridge across the Mississippi, Frank Von Flue, Roy McMurtry, Phillip Granville, and Mike Joyce were traveling together—until they met a baker and his wife handing out bags of doughnuts. Von Flue and McMurtry gratefully accepted, and though they only had a few more miles to go and were far ahead of most of the runners, they sat on the curb to eat and take a rest. Granville and Joyce happily took their bags but kept moving. They were, after all, top 10 runners, and they never felt they could afford to lose much time.

When Von Flue and McMurtry resumed running a few minutes later, Von Flue was struck by how small the river looked, but later he took another glance and decided it was impressive, after all. Either way, it was a morale boost. The Bunion Derby runners were now into the eastern half of the country.

Gardner was the most east, winning for the day. Shortly behind him was Gavuzzi, continually advancing his lead for first place. By the time he crossed over the Mississippi River and edged into East St. Louis, he was an hour and 40 minutes ahead of Payne, who was still a threat to his overall first-place standing but a rapidly diminishing one. Gavuzzi had a nagging toothache, but other than that, the road ahead of him looked like the pavement he was running on—smooth and without bumps.

JUST AS ALBUQUERQUE balked at paying Pyle's rates, so, too, did St. Louis, which is how Pyle's people wound up across the Mississippi in East St. Louis, Illinois. It was obvious that these last-minute negotiations with cities were hurting the race. As a result, Pyle sent Bill Pickens ahead to Chicago, to lay the groundwork for hammering out the financials and to generate excitement. But Pickens, at his press conference, met with skeptical reporters who pressed to know if the race was as much of a financial disaster as it seemed.

Rumors, Pickens assured them: "I am delighted to be at liberty to announce that Mr. Pyle and Mr. Grange are doing so well that they occupy twin beds opposite to one another that they may each keep an eye on the carpet under which the profits are hidden."

Pickens didn't stop there. "Some folks don't appreciate the magnitude and scope of this unprecedented competition. Two hundred and forty runners began the grueling grind, but stone bruises, desert hardships, and physical collapses have taken their pitiless toll until Chicagoans will see only 70."

Pickens continued his oratory: "The first recorded feat of great pedal effort is found in biblical records. An unnamed messenger ran from the scene of battle to David at Jerusalem with the news that Saul had been slain. Later, an Athenian youth carried the message from the Marathon to his home city telling the citizenry that the Greeks had won. But with all the available records and all hearsay of marvelous foot racing duly considered, none compares with the magnitude of the race now being staged across the United States. The winner of the $25,000 grand prize, and those who finish close up with, have established for themselves a niche in history comparable to that now occupied by the unnamed Hebrew and Athenian," promised Pickens, wiping the sweat off his forehead.

"And what about Pyle?" a reporter asked. "How is he standing the rigors of the long march?"

"Ah, he's great. Incomparable," replied Pickens without hesitation. "What courage! What fortitude! Such an inspiration to his men! Day after day, he rides back and forth over the line of the march, lolling back in a highly cushioned seat, sipping fragrant liqueurs, ever smiling and shouting words of encouragement to his footsore champions. What a leader!"

NICK ANTHONY was called into a tent where Hugo Quist, Dr. Baker, and perhaps Duffy and Pyle were present. They were about to do what they almost never did, unless a runner had broken a rule. They informed the young runner—he was only 16—that he needed to drop out voluntarily, or they would eject him.

Anthony was surprised, then incensed.

Sympathetic but firm, the officials explained that Anthony's feet were in terrible condition. They were afraid he would develop blood poisoning.

Anthony couldn't believe what he was hearing. He had entered the race, despite pleading from his mother and friends not to do it. He had come extremely close to quitting on his way to Needles, California, and so it had been a triumph when he actually reached the desert city. Near Albuquerque, when his expensive shoes finally deteriorated, he took the advice of his trainer, who insisted that cheap shoes were as durable as the expensive ones. Then the heel blisters came. Soon after, Anthony ran with blood pouring out of his shoes.

His trainer was a joke. The guy liked to party and was rarely around. Anthony would wake up mornings, freezing. And while other runners warmed up with a massage from their trainers, he didn't. It usually took him 2 hours before he had limbered up.

But he had run nonetheless and survived, not only through the desert but also over mountains and in rain and a blizzard and the punishing Missouri hills. Now after 2,000 miles, with his mind and even his body still willing, he was being told he was out.

Anthony pleaded with them. "I'll assume full responsibility for myself," he insisted to deaf ears.

Dejected, rejected, and ejected, Nick Anthony accepted his travel money and returned to Long Beach, California, wondering what he was going to do with the rest of his life. It didn't take him much time to find his lifelong calling. He took a job as a shoe salesman.

CHAPTER 14

It was a daily ritual among all the men. Alongside the road, apparently taking a rest from running, Frank Von Flue studies the blisters on his left foot. (Courtesy of Scott Von Flue.)

Rough Going

Distance So Far: 2,085.4 Miles; 70 Runners

April 28, East St. Louis to Staunton, 42.5 Miles

Frank Von Flue finally had his own trainer. In St. Louis, he met Red Workman, an ex-prizefighter. Von Flue had been considering getting help, and Workman agreed for the shot of earning 10 percent of any possible winnings. In a car or possibly on a motorbike, Workman trailed after Von Flue, offering encouragement, massages, and anything else the running wounded tended to need.

Andy Payne kept following his own trainer's dictum, even if it didn't seem to be panning out. He finished the day's race in eighth place, tying with William Kerr, Roy McMurtry, John Cronick, and Louis Perrella. Payne still ranked second overall, more than 30 hours ahead of John Salo, but first place looked increasingly unlikely. Pete Gavuzzi was $3\frac{1}{2}$ hours ahead.

And another runner was kicked out, but it was nowhere near as painful for the officials as it had been with Nick Anthony. Dick Frost, the bearded Hollywood extra, was caught hiding in the trunk of a woman's sedan. Someone apparently saw his highly identifiable whiskers poking out. There had been suspicion for some time that the cult member was occasionally pulling a fast one. Several weeks earlier, someone noticed that he had "run" several miles in 17 minutes, quicker than anyone had ever seen him travel. The party line from race officials was that no one could prove anything.

Later that week, in a *Chicago Tribune* editorial cartoon, Frost was called a cheater and shown wearing roller skates and clinging to the rear bumper of a car. In hindsight, Frost hinted days earlier that his downfall was coming: "I feel like hell," he told a reporter. "I'll be tickled to death if I ever get to New York."

Frost wasn't tickled now. He begged Arthur Duffy to let him back in the race. "Let me make up my mileage," pleaded Frost. "Add plenty of time penalty, too. My foolishness means curtains for my movie career." Then he began to cry.

Unmoved, Duffy handed Frost his travel deposit. The aspiring movie star was left abandoned on the road.

April 29, Staunton to Virden, 44.4 Miles

Going through Carlinville, quite likely some of the runners knew that this had originally been their destination, but as often happened, the leaders and C. C. Pyle couldn't work out a deal. Pyle instead went with Virden, almost 20 miles down the road, where he secured room and board for the runners. Similar to the experience in Rolla, the runners were cheered, and Pyle's luxury camper was egged.

One woman was on her way to a dance marathon in the town. But, as she told the *Decatur Review,* she saw the traveling castaways, who "were a sorry sight." Her stomach turned at the idea of seeing another endurance competition, so she canceled her plans.

Meanwhile, Gavuzzi again led the field, distancing himself from Payne even more, and was now 4 hours ahead.

Pyle was about the same amount of hours ahead of his creditors.

That evening, Ray Henderson, a Virden police officer, was handed the unenviable assignment to search for C. C. Pyle. Three years earlier, Pyle had taken out two bank loans that he hadn't yet paid a dime on—one worth $21,500 and the other, $21,502. Plenty of publicity alerted the good people of Illinois that Pyle was coming through, inspiring the Illinois Trust and Savings Bank of Champaign, which had gone out of business not long ago, to try to get their money back. They decided one way would be to take the *America,* which bank officials understood Pyle paid $25,000 for.

Henderson had a writ of attachment, a document that would allow him to seize the luxury camper. But the mammoth vehicle and Pyle were nowhere to be found. Henderson looked all night.

The Illinois state police, escorting the runners, also couldn't find him. Pyle had disappeared, along with the most famous football star in the world and a very large camper. Now he wasn't just running a race, he was running from the law.

April 30, Virden to Springfield, 26 Miles

Gavuzzi saw the speeding car and leapt off the road just in time. Paul Baldwin, the driver, told the county justice of the peace that he was in a rush, on his way to visit his ailing mother in Springfield, and he was subsequently released.

Gavuzzi's car dodging was his first lucky break in ages. He was far ahead of Payne and an average of 36 hours ahead of the rest of the pack, but his toothache was getting increasingly worse.

Several months earlier in England, Gavuzzi had seen his dentist, who suggested extracting several aching teeth. But Gavuzzi learned that he wouldn't be able to eat solid foods for some time, which wouldn't do when training for or running in a big race. So he decided to visit his dentist when he returned.

But with his teeth in so much pain, Gavuzzi was choosing soup instead of steak, and bread over beef. Still, despite his misery, Gavuzzi came in first, tying with Seth Gonzales.

After the race, someone offered runner George Jussick a bottle of Southern Illinois moonshine, which he gratefully accepted. Then Jussick proceeded to get stinking drunk.

For a while, he strolled into the countryside and then got the idea to start pushing cars into a ditch. In an era before parking brakes and heavier cars, this wasn't so difficult. Jussick had pushed a seventh sedan into a ditch when race officials found him. He didn't agree to return to the camp; they brought him back, tied up with rope. It was reported that 20 to 50 penalty hours were added to Jussick's time, effectively killing any chance he had of landing among the top 10 runners—not that he'd had much hope.

In Springfield, the runners were hosted by the Elks Club and given a good meal and a swimming pool to soak their aching muscles in. Some men had enough energy to attend a cabaret dance on the roof garden of the Elks building, where Red Grange played the host. Several runners later said it was the nicest time that they had had on the entire trip.

Not Hardrock. He missed all the festivities, taking over 18 hours to complete the latest lap.

Meanwhile, as the carnival drew in crowds from Sangamon County and beyond, Chief Deputy Sheriff Jean Saner and his deputies looked for pickpockets and the man they considered the biggest thief—C. C. Pyle. Deputy Saner had a writ for Pyle's arrest. Few runners were surprised to see the police inquiring about Pyle, who no one could remember seeing after they crossed the state line. From the moment they came over the Mississippi, recalled Von Flue, they would hear comments like "Go over to Champaign, Illinois, if you want to find out what kind of bird Pyle is."

But no runner knew where Pyle was. Some helpful soul—possibly trying not to laugh—suggested that the sheriff seek out the assistant director of the race, who could be found in his room at the Elks Club.

Shortly after midnight, just as Grange was preparing to get some shut-eye, Saner and his deputies ambled into the room. Grange brightened, assuming the law officers wanted him to sign autographs. Instead, they told him of their intentions and asked for Pyle's whereabouts. When Grange came up blank, Deputy Saner informed him that he also was empowered to arrest Grange for the bank's second debt—$21,502.

Saner produced his legal document that demanded payment. Grange grabbed and hurriedly studied it.

"I don't owe the bank anything, or I would have paid it a long time ago," protested Grange.

Pyle's name came up again, and Grange told the deputies that the bank debts were the showman's concern, not his.

The deputies asked where Pyle might be.

Grange launched into a monologue about where Pyle probably was and where he should be, but in the end, Grange insisted that he just didn't know.

The deputies threatened to seize Grange's property, but after searching his room, they realized the football star didn't have anything except his toothbrush and a change of clothes. The police chewed over arresting a football hero, who had been born and raised near here, and decided to leave Grange alone for the time being.

"These writs mean nothing," said Grange later to reporters. "I have nothing here which they can attach and hold. I do not owe the money, or I should have paid it." Grange added that, contrary to popular belief, he was just a client of Pyle's and not his business partner. What's more, he knew nothing of Pyle's business affairs. If Red had kept talking to the reporters, the way he was going, it wouldn't have been long until he insisted that he had never met the man.

May 1, Springfield to Lincoln, 31.6 Miles

Shortly before 9:00 a.m., in Joliet, Illinois, Pyle stepped out of his $25,000 camper, with the mobile radio station traveling with him. Once the day started, Pyle went to work, immediately seeking out Arthur Hedquist, man ager of the Joliet Chamber of Commerce.

Hedquist was friendly but unwilling to upset his schedule for Pyle. Unruffled, the showman arranged a meeting later in the day and then had a breakfast of wheat cakes in the Woodruff Hotel with a sportswriter from the *Joliet Evening Herald-News*.

Referring to his upcoming meeting with Hedquist, "I will come back again," Pyle said, "because I don't want to tell my story in two pieces. In that, I am something like a book agent that called at my office in Chicago. He started in with his canvass and after he had talked a few minutes, I interrupted him to see how the books were bound."

The book agent, said Pyle, became flustered. "'Now, see here, Mr. Pyle,' he said. 'It took me 7 weeks to learn this story, and if you are going to interrupt me in the middle of it, what am I going to do?'"

Pyle felt the same way. His pitch to chamber of commerce executives had been honed for almost 2 months. "My story runs about 20 minutes, and when I start, I want to finish. Then anyone can ask all the questions he likes. The race is the greatest show, the greatest free show on Earth. When the runners arrive in a city, there are thousands of people to watch them. People come from miles around. They line the highways, they line the streets," said Pyle, his voice full of regret, almost sounding as if he were talking to himself rather than the reporter. "They are everywhere, and you can't charge them anything."

THAT AFTERNOON, Pyle was almost maniacally cheerful. "Ah, ah," smiled Pyle, rubbing his hands. "Joliet's a good-sized town. It should bring in $1,000 to have my runners stop here Friday night. Yes, $1,000, please."

"What?" said an astonished Hedquist. "Try and get it."

Pyle wasn't dissuaded. "Yes, but you see, you will get it all back. We will put on a show that night, get a tent, and let the good people of Joliet view the derby runners at two-bits a peep."

"Yes," echoed Hedquist, running the numbers through his head. "That would take 4,000 persons. How are you going to get that many in a tent?"

"Never mind," said Pyle, realizing he was getting nowhere.

Hedquist made it clear that the Bunion Derby was welcome, but he did not want the chamber to part with $1,000 for the privilege. Pyle pointed out that he needed the money to help organize the infrastructure to bring the race into town. He said that it also helped protect him against rain and cut down his losses. "If I did not have these funds, the race would cost me about $225,000," said Pyle.

"But it does not affect me or the Chamber of Commerce how much you lose," Hedquist said, undercutting Pyle's argument with unsympathetic logic.

Pyle reminded Hedquist that his streets would be packed, that folks from miles around would want to see the men who had run all this way from Los Angeles, that for 24 hours Joliet would be the center of international attention—and that all the city's businesses would benefit from the influx of traffic into the community.

Hedquist asked another logical question: Could Pyle promise the retailers that the race would be profitable for everyone? Pyle released an audible sigh and replied: "Of course, you cannot guarantee a merchant that he will sell $1,000 worth of goods."

"Nor can you guarantee him that he will sell a pocket handkerchief," snapped Hedquist. "The chief beneficiaries will be the soda fountains, the gas stations, hotels, and restaurants—and I would like to see you get money out of *them*."

Taking the challenge, Pyle looked animated. "Jump in the bus," said Pyle, referring to his camper, "and we shall canvass the business district for contributions."

Hedquist couldn't think of a reason to say no and was probably, like everyone, curious to see the inside of the *America*. The camper started through Joliet, first stopping at a gas station, where Pyle made his pitch. Minutes later, no richer than they had been before, he and Hedquist climbed back into the bus. Then they went to a grocery, returning with no sale. Then they visited a pharmacy, where a druggist offered $10. Pyle's camper pulled up to a restaurant, where again, no luck. Finally, they went into a Chinese restaurant. Thirty minutes later, Pyle, Hedquist, and the owner of the eatery emerged, meeting the gaggle of journalists waiting outside for them.

"It's all fixed," said Pyle.

Hedquist nodded.

"Did you get the $1,000?" a reporter asked.

"It's all fixed," was all Pyle would say.

The sportswriters pressed for more information. What, they asked, was the secret to getting the race to come through Joliet?

"Chop suey," said Pyle, and again, Hedquist nodded.

The Chinese restaurant owner was then asked if he could clear up this little mystery. Echoing Pyle, he said, "Chop suey."

"Never mind," interjected Pyle. "The runners will stop at Joliet, and there will be one of the biggest surprises Friday when they arrive."

Pyle was bluffing. Hedquist wouldn't budge, except to offer to introduce Bill Pickens to local merchants, to see if he had better luck persuading them to pitch in.

Full of bravado, Pyle promised reporters that he would be back at the end of the week, and then he headed south, ambling toward the runners. But Pyle made it only a handful of miles. Several deputy sheriffs spotted the camper near Elwood, a little village outside of Joliet.

They stopped the vehicle, handed Pyle a writ of attachment from the Illinois Trust and Savings Bank of Champaign, and impounded it behind the jail. Pyle could have his luxury camper back immediately, authorities told him, if he paid the bank $21,502.04.

The timing couldn't have been worse. Pyle's funds were very low and would remain that way until the Highway 66 Association could bail him out with the $60,000 that they had promised. Even so, Pyle couldn't give a third of that money to this bank, not without destroying the infrastructure keeping the race going. If he was going to make serious money, it would be this week in Chicago, the second most populous city on the route, and having to deal with a legal migraine was the last distraction he needed.

Pyle's humiliation must have been worse for personal reasons as well. Grange understood Pyle's financial situation, and for Pyle to lose face in front of him was nothing new. The remainder of his employees, too, understood that Pyle had some income issues. As did the sportswriters, certainly the Bunion Derby runners, and many sports fans.

Someone new, however, had joined him for the ride, and the indignity of being escorted off his luxury vehicle must have dredged up some painful memories that he hadn't had to consider for almost 20 years. The authorities handled C. C. Pyle as if he were a common criminal, right in front of his wife of 14 years, Mrs. Effie Pyle.

EFFIE WAS Pyle's third wife. Martha Russell was his second. When Pyle moved to Chicago in 1910, divorce papers followed him. Dot, aware of Pyle's financial acumen, wanted assistance for herself and their daughter. Pyle argued that he wasn't as well off as his wife thought and that she wasn't living badly either. Pyle told the judge that he had left behind a wife who was impossible to live with and who was making a good living and could support their daughter.

A year after the divorce, Pyle married again. He wed Martha Lindsay Russell on April 14, 1911, in Indiana's Lake County. Pyle was back in familiar territory—like Dot, Martha was an actress on the vaudeville circuit. She had long brown hair that fell past her shoulders, full lips, and large, expressive eyes. If the photos can be believed, there was an aura of kindness and freshness about her that Pyle must have found irresistible.

Pyle didn't waste time making Martha not just his wife, but his livelihood. He became her business manager, as well as a film producer. Pyle was working for the Essanay Film Company, which had studios in Chicago and Los Angeles, and put his industry connections to good use. In 1912,

Martha starred in a series of 10 movie shorts, mostly crime films or melodramas, and reportedly was receiving $1,250 a week, the highest salary of any actress of her day. That same year, Pyle and Russell traveled to Austin, Texas, where he hooked up with an enterprising filmmaker named Hope Tilley, who owned a small studio. Pyle and Tilley shot footage of cities throughout Texas and Missouri and then sent the films to the movie palaces in the same cities, figuring civic-minded people would love seeing their communities captured on celluloid. They did, and they cleaned up; meanwhile, Martha did well in the same cities on a lecture circuit, talking about her experiences in the movies.

Naturally, Pyle's success led him to try something that would bring him even more money. He talked a group of investors into forking over $25,000 to him and Tilley. It wasn't long, however, until Pyle had spent $12,000, and he wasn't able to account to his stockholders, to their satisfaction, where the money had gone. Moreover, during his first film, Pyle and his crew crossed over the Mexico border to shoot some scenes and were promptly thrown into a jail, by guerilla leader Pancho Villa no less. About half a dozen more films followed, many shot in dramatic locations, like on top of the 60-foot Austin dam, with dangerous stunts that went awry. Pyle's films made money, but in the process, Tilley's studio went bankrupt, their distributor took a bath, and all of the stockholders lost their money.

Maybe it was the stress of the business falling apart that led to the marriage disintegrating. In any case, Pyle and Martha's marriage was annulled on December 5, 1914. On December 23, Pyle quickly rebounded—or already had a backup—and he married Effie.

SHE WAS BORN Euphemia Rebou. Of all his wives, he may have known her the least, or felt the least connected to her.

When Pyle met Effie, she was Effie B. Arnold, a lovely woman, according to one of her distant relatives. But it's difficult to understand what first attracted him to her. When Effie married Pyle in 1914, she was a 27-year-old with an ex-husband who had deserted her and their two young children, Donald and Florence. Seeing how Pyle treated his baby daughter, it seems odd that he decided to marry into a family. By becoming the head of a ready-made clan, perhaps the then-32-year-old Pyle felt that he was filling a void or making up for past mistakes.

Or maybe Effie was wealthy. In the 1910 census records, at a time when she had recently been deserted by her first husband, her occupation is listed as "own income." That she wasn't listed as having some sort of job, with two children to provide for, seems to suggest that she may have had some measure of wealth.

Pyle was doing his own part, though, to bring money into his new household. He adopted the role of businessman, eventually becoming a sales manager at the Bartola Musical Instrument Company, which specialized in making opulent piano organs. They were so pricey and well-regarded that the movie theatre advertisements often mentioned the Bartola organ as a selling point, even going so far as to tell the customers how much they had paid for the instrument.

By 1920, when Pyle was 38 years old, he was successful enough that the family had their own live-in maid and cook, a 24-year-old Swedish American named Hazel Anderson. Financially, he was nowhere near where he would be in 5 years, when he would begin representing Grange, but he was in good shape.

C. C. PYLE was not in good shape on May 1, 1928. There's no evidence that he spent the night behind bars, but the *America* did. And as Pyle contacted his lawyer, he had to get new wheels until he could figure out a way to get back his luxury-home-on-wheels. He ended up hiring a car.

ON THE ROAD, Edward Burns of the *Chicago Tribune* stared at the runners in wonder. He wasn't shocked that Dick Frost had recently tried to bamboozle race officials by hitching a ride, but he was amazed that a week after he was disqualified, Frost was *still* running.

Frost had remained in the race "for the fun of it, which is one of the reasons we say this is an assignment for a psychologist," Burns quipped.

Burns was impressed with some of the runners, many of whom he felt were "intelligent appearing youngsters." Burns was less impressed with most of the others, though. "Several have that wild cuckoo look in their eyes," he remarked. Others, he noted, "are shameless in soiled, white pants and ragged undershirts."

Prompted perhaps by the comments they were getting from people like Burns, the incredibly shaggy Gavuzzi decided to visit a barbershop for "a trimmer."

"Make it look a little better than it does," Gavuzzi told the barber, gesturing to his whiskers. "It looks a bit rough there."

"Sure, buddy, I'll trim it up," the barber said.

Gavuzzi settled into his chair—a little too comfortably. When he awoke, Gavuzzi hardly recognized himself—and didn't like what he saw, or what he didn't see. He was clean shaven, save for a small mustache. *Well, nothing I can do about that now*, thought Gavuzzi, who paid the man and went on his way.

THAT EVENING, Red Grange broke the news gently to the runners about the lost luxury camper. Grange sincerely seemed worried that the runners would crumble, knowing that their ringleader faced such problems. His goal was to seem stoic and unyielding in front of the handful of reporters who were gathered and to pull off a speech in a manner that would make the showman Pyle proud.

Grange entered the hall that would serve as the runners' dormitory and asked for silence. Then he added, shouting over the noise, "Champions of the long trail, I have an announcement to make."

"Make it after we eat," someone suggested.

"Tell it to Oscar," shouted another runner, referring to the Oklahoma mummy.

"No, my news cannot wait," said Grange. "Our leader, Charles C. Pyle, has sustained a loss."

Seventy runners broke into cheers.

"Hold, hold, hold everything," stammered Grange, baffled by their reaction. "A deputy constable working for railroad magnates seized his $25,000 bus this afternoon at Joliet, and it is now parked behind the jailhouse."

Pete Gavuzzi perked up, wondering if the showman was behind bars: "Is Charley in or out?" he asked.

"He's out," answered Grange.

"Too bad," the runners shouted—in unison, according to Edward Burns.

Grange ignored this and continued to make the case for his business partner: "Our great leader's equipage has been taken from him, but he will not be stopped. You'll all be thrilled to learn that Mr. Pyle now proposes to lead you into Chicago on foot. Tired as he is, what with riding all the way from Los Angeles, disappointed though he is at losing the magnificent bus, he is not discouraged. He wants you to know that from now on, he'll be at your head."

The runners snickered.

According to another sportswriter on the scene, several runners led a gray mare into the room at that point, suggesting that the horse would be a fitting method of travel for their great leader. Grange stopped speaking, perhaps resigned to what should have been obvious: Whatever faith and respect the runners had for Pyle had been lost long ago.

Grange somehow missed the fact that the athletes were like refugees, always forced to run, always hungry, and always resentful of the regime. If they had been the crew of a ship, there would have already been a mutiny.

That night, the Bunion Derby foot soldiers fretted. They knew that Pyle's bus was worth $25,000, the same amount as the first-place prize money. If he couldn't get his bus back—or even if he could—would that mean somehow that once everyone reached New York City, the money might not be there? There were whispers that the race might end in Chicago, and officials had already told the members of the carnival that their services would no longer be needed after the Windy City. Some of the athletes noticed that over the last several days the fat lady, snake girl, fortune teller, and tattoo artist were all looking a little glum.

The rumors among the runners and sportwriters—at least one reporter changed Pyle's nickname to "Cashless Charley"—reached the ears of Bill Pickens. Hoping to settle some nerves before the next morning's 7:00 a.m.–sharp departure, Pickens issued a terse statement to the media in defense of his boss: "Believing that his runners need his personal leadership, Mr. Pyle has decided to leave his $25,000 bus temporarily in Joliet and accompany the runners on foot. Reports that Mr. Pyle is planning to walk out on the rest of the walkers are libelous and untrue."

Small wonder that Edward Burns shook his head at this mess. From his typewriter in Lincoln, Burns informed readers, "This author will ride to Normal with the troupe tomorrow. Maybe we can think of something clever about these fellows being bound for a place called Normal."

May 2, Lincoln to Normal, 34.6 Miles

Of the legal problems swirling around them, Grange told reporters, "Lots of smoke and little fire. But we are going to keep faith with the runners who have braved the elements for 2,300 miles."

Oklahoma composer Al J. Palmer had just announced his completion of a song titled "The Bunion Derby Blues." Somehow, that seemed fitting, given the gloomy day that fell over the race, but it wasn't a hit, nor was his previous song, "Oh Marathon Forevermore."

The skies were dumping rain, cheating Pyle out of thousands of paying spectators. Instead, dozens of people showed up, feebly cheering as Ed Gardner crossed the finish line at 1:45 p.m. Still, a line of automobiles, packed with excited fans urging him on, trailed him.

The disappointing turnout may have been Pyle's own doing—at the last minute he decided that his runners wouldn't pass through the business district. "Owing to the fact that the mercantile interests have failed to make heavy the coffers of Mr. Pyle," wrote the paper, "it is believed that 'Cash and Carry' tore up his routing in a spirit of revenge."

True enough, but Pyle also felt that he had to show that a town could suffer if its officials crossed him. After all, there were many more towns and chambers of commerce left on the road to New York to negotiate with, and Pyle didn't need them all following Joliet's lead. Chicago had already made it clear that they weren't going to pay anything either.

On top of it all, when Pyle saw Gavuzzi, clean shaven, he was infuriated. "What in the hell has come over you?"

Rattled, Gavuzzi offered to wear a fake beard.

Pyle refused, citing the integrity of the race and his desire to not fool the public. "All you're asked to do is run and grow whiskers," he growled, "and now you shirked half of the responsibility. That's gratitude for you."

But Gavuzzi decided to grow the beard again. It had little to do with Pyle, or the editorial cartoon in the *Chicago Tribune* showing a man getting his beard shorn with scissors and a caption reading, "Pete Gavuzzi spoils the ballyhoo." Rather, it was that the gallop to Normal was one of his worst races in weeks, with Payne trimming Gavuzzi's lead by 35 minutes and 1 second. Declaring it a bad omen, he announced that he wouldn't shave again until reaching New York.

That evening in the Woodruff Hotel, after driving around in a Model T with the top down, Pyle reassured everyone that all was still under control and going as planned. "We will arrive in New York June 3," promised Pyle.

May 3, Normal to Pontiac, 34.7 Miles

Teodocio Rivera woke up, relieved that he felt healthy enough to run. It had been another story the evening before when he came down with food poisoning. Rivera, a dentist from the Philippines, had lost a lot of time the previous day after consuming $3 worth of asparagus tips smothered in Roquefort salad dressing. He was sidelined in the evening with stomach cramps and nausea, but this morning, with the rest of his competitors, he managed to stagger to his feet and run, avoiding what would have been one of the more bizarre reasons to have dropped out of the race: too much asparagus.

Then again, nothing was going the way anybody predicted. Pyle was flummoxed by the news: The Highway 66 Association would not be paying him $60,000, the remainder of his $110,000 fee. They had already paid him $50,000 up front and were still feeling robbed.

Highway 66 and Lon Scott had plenty of reasons for withholding the second payment. Pyle never put Highway 66 in the race's promotional material. His runners left the thoroughfare several times, entering Arizona by boat, circumventing Albuquerque, and taking convenient shortcuts when it suited him, which tacitly suggested to the public that sections of the road weren't fit for foot travel, let alone car traffic—not a message that Scott wanted sent about their *national* highway. And Pyle besmirched the good name of Highway 66 by inviting a barrage of negative publicity associated with the race, such as being egged and operating games of chance.

Once it was clear that Pyle wouldn't receive his $60,000, it became painfully evident that the race couldn't continue.

That day, in scattered newspapers around the country, a short article indicated that friends of Pyle, not quoting anyone in particular, "would carry on to its scheduled finish at Yankee Stadium here, in spite of the financial difficulties it is encountering, en route." The friends pointed out that recently Pyle and Grange received $38,000 in royalties from a candy company that used the football star's name.

Even if that was true, the money hadn't made much of a difference. Pyle had runners to feed, vehicles to fuel, and his extensive staff to pay. He was desperate. When a Red Cross nurse working at a government hospital in Chicago asked Pyle if he could direct the race past the building's windows so that the hundreds of disabled soldiers from the World War could watch the race, the showman sent a reply through his de facto spokesman, Grange, that they'd be happy to—if the hospital paid them. Grange was enjoying his job more every day. Maybe next, Pyle would ask him to beat up some orphans.

Arthur Duffy, meanwhile, was out of a job. He told the press that he needed to get back to his regular gig as a sportswriter at a Boston newspaper, implying that he had been away longer than intended, although so far the race had roughly conformed to the original schedule. Whether Pyle had to lay off Duffy, or Duffy did quit, the Bunion Derby was imploding.

And just as Pyle was in the process of shutting everything down, in stepped F. F. Gunn.

Gunn hadn't traveled 2,300 miles—albeit alternating between his own luxury camper and sports car—through desert heat, blizzards, and torrential rain, while his son walked through it all, only to have the race abruptly end midway. There was talk that Gunn was a gambler who bet money on his son winning or perhaps finishing the race, but even if that was true, that wasn't his motivation. F. F. Gunn loved this race. As disgusted as he was with Pyle's financial management, he believed the promoter was putting on an incredible show. And he would be damned if his son lost his chance to achieve his record to walk across the country *now*.

F. F. Gunn lent Pyle $50,000 in order to fund the rest of the race to New York City. It was $10,000 short of what Pyle had been expecting, of course, but it would be enough.

Gunn made two stipulations: First, Pyle would say nothing to the press of Gunn's involvement. One can only conclude that Gunn didn't want his friends, family, and business associates thinking he had lost his mind. And Pyle was happy to oblige.

The second was that Gunn would now make the day-to-day financial decisions. The reasons were obvious. It was his money Pyle was playing with—and as Gunn observed to sports columnist Westbrook Pegler a few weeks later, even while denying involvement in the race, "From the start, it was easy to see that Mr. Pyle's business methods were a bit loose."

Gunn's first financial decision was that the race needed to end quicker than June 3. The men would have to run more miles every day to get everyone across the country faster. That would save food and lodging costs as well other expenditures, some of which were indefensible, according to Gunn, such as shelling out $650 a week to run the mobile broadcasting station.

There was another pragmatic benefit: Making the race more difficult would weed out the stragglers, and fewer runners to feed would help lower upkeep costs. Too many men were clinging to false hopes of winning, or they just wanted to say that they had run across the country.

Gunn had control, but it was still Pyle's race. He remained the face of the Bunion Derby, and he would continue to cajole chamber of commerce members and steer the runners to New York City. But there was another trade-off that had to make Pyle queasy. If he wasn't able to pay back Gunn, Pyle would have to give up some of his assets, like his luxury camper. In effect, if the race was to finish, for the time being, Pyle would work for F. F. Gunn.

It must have killed him, but Pyle agreed.

MAY 4, PONTIAC TO JOLIET, 59.1 MILES

The next morning, Pyle was still getting hounded by reporters.

"Have you obtained possession of your home-on-wheels?" asked one.

"Yes, in a little bit," said Pyle, choosing his words carefully.

"Then you have not obtained it?"

"No," said Pyle, "but I will have it in a little while."

For once, Pyle wasn't bluffing. Within a few hours, Pyle reclaimed his camper, returning to the good life in a most familiar way—by taking a financial hit. His hardworking attorney, James A. Bray, convinced authorities to release the camper for a partial payment of what Pyle owed: $5,000. They arrived at the figure by determining that, given all the abuse the camper had suffered during the Bunion Derby so far, $5,000 was all it could be sold for.

After securing Pyle's written assurances that the rest of their money would be forthcoming, George R. McComb, receiver of the defunct Illinois Trust and Savings Bank of Champaign, released the *America*.

Reporters immediately bestowed new nicknames on Pyle: "Cash No Credit" and "Catch as Catch Can."

THE RUNNERS kept doing their thing. Gavuzzi wiped out Payne's gains with a blazing run to Joliet, increasing his lead by 2 hours, even though he came in third for the day. Gavuzzi was now 6 hours ahead of Payne, who came in seventh that day. Ed Gardner, who finished first, moved up from fifth place to fourth overall.

THE VERY DAY Pyle took possession of the keys to the *America,* he was informed that he was named in another lawsuit. This time, Pyle was served with papers notifying him that Valeska Suratt, fading film siren, was suing him and demanding that he pay her $2,000 for "securities" that he owed her. Pyle assured the public that it was much ado about nothing.

Unlike the runners in his care, Pyle appeared to have a leg to stand on. Miss Suratt, now 46 years old, looked to be starting a habit of suing luminaries. The year before, she brought legal action against legendary film director Cecil B. DeMille, suing him for $1 million and claiming that *King of Kings*, one of his masterpieces and a classic of the silent era, was based on a script that she wrote. She claimed that DeMille acquired it by way of a studio executive.

"It's just another one of those things," Pyle told a group of reporters in dismissing Suratt's frivolous lawsuit. "I guess I am the most attached man in the world. Ever since we started out on this race from Los Angeles last March, I have been sued and threatened. But all have come to naught, and the race goes on, and will go on."

A few weeks later, Suratt's attorney presented a letter to the court, dated February 28, 1920, and with the name and address of one C. C. Pyle.

> My darling:
>
> Your check for $1,100 received. Am enclosing receipts. Also paper for you to sign and send same to me at Kansas City. This stock will make you money. You can always have you [sic] money back anytime you want it. Always remember that. Yours was a sweet letter. I am in the office. Cant [sic] write much but honey I am thinking of you.
>
> Send my letter to Muelbach Hotel instead of Baltimore Hotel. I gave you the wrong name. Your [sic] a sweet girl. I love you very much.
>
> Yours always,
>
> Chas.

The judge sided with Miss Suratt.

May 5, Joliet to Chicago, 43.2 Miles

The Windy City was a distressing place to live. In the month before, the slaying of "Diamond Joe" Esposito made headlines; 3 days later, the discovery of a 50-year-old man's corpse in a deserted prairie near Chicago made the papers. Shortly after, Toledo police officer George Zientara was killed with a machine gun that authorities suspected must have come from Chicago. Will Rogers visited the city about that time, and in a column joked that Chicago was quiet and peaceful because the paper had "only one big murder headline today."

In recent days someone looking to have fun at the runners' expense told the Bunion Derby participants that before they crossed through the city, odds were they would be shot. Some of the runners were terrified and ran faster; at least one weary runner reportedly said he hoped he would be so lucky.

Pyle, however, seemed delighted to be in Chicago and would not miss the sight of his runners charging through his home city. The sidewalks were teeming with men, women, and children, cheering and applauding as John Salo came running in first, dodging Michigan Avenue traffic and waving to well-wishers—although one young lady in a bright red dress stood out. Concerned by the runners' gaunt appearances, she was trying to pin buttons with ribbons attached to every male passerby's coat, pleading with them to "give the poor runners something, mister."

In the background, in front of city hall, a band known as the City Machine Gun Corps played a rousing overture appropriately called "The Bunion Bearer."

Fifteen minutes after Salo, Phillip Granville hurried into the city, followed shortly afterward by Olli Wantinnen. But the crowd's cheers turned into shouts and gasps as a car smashed into Wantinnen, sending the 96-pound Finnish man crashing to the pavement.

It looked like the final indignity had been heaped on Wantinnen. He had suffered shin splints in New Mexico; dragged himself through Oklahoma City with a "bad foot," as one reporter called it; and then the next day, a bruised toe prevented him from going 15 more miles to Chandler, and so he had to make up the lost distance the following day. Now this. But as Wantinnen climbed to his feet, Pyle ran to his side and crossed the finish line with him. It was the first time he accompanied a runner—without wheels.

That turned out to be the high point of the day. Wantinnen declared that he was staying in, but five runners dropped out. It made sense. As the Associated Press said, their chances of winning this thing was "hopeless," and some runners were close enough to home that they'd have plenty of money left over from their travel deposit. Niels Nielson lived in Chicago, and Archie Barnes didn't have far to travel to his home in Middlefield, Ohio, and he would go on to have a pleasant life in farming. A strong, powerful man, he attracted a lot of attention for plowing his fields with two bulls. Another athlete simply declared that he was "dissatisfied with the race in general."

So dissatisfied, in fact, that several days later, runner William Meyers told the *Bismarck Tribune* in Nebraska what the reporters on the trip weren't saying, that Pyle had been ousted from control of the race. "There was nothing left in that derby for the fellows on the square, and I quit," added Meyers, who didn't add that he had been struggling with a leg injury, and that he needed 17 hours to run from Joliet to Chicago, 12 more than Salo. Whether Meyers quit or was disqualified, as the Associated Press reported, he was not long for that race.

The remaining runners were disheartened but willing to stick it out. Everyone—especially those in the lead—knew that if they were to quit the race midway and Pyle did pay, they would kick themselves for the rest of their lives.

CHAPTER 15

Football legend Red Grange (bottom row, middle) signs his contract with C. C. Pyle (right) at his side. Later, Grange would start to have doubts about committing to another contract. (Library of Congress.)

Into Indiana

Distance So Far: 2,401.5 Miles; 64 Runners

May 6, Chicago, Illinois, to Gary, Indiana, 28.4 Miles

Friendship with the devil comes at a price. After years of basking in the glow of applause and appreciation, Red Grange was finally paying his dues for his association with C. C. Pyle, who left Chicago long before the rest of his caravan did. With his business partner again gone, Grange knew he'd once more become Pyle's stand-in for spurned investors, police officers, and attorneys wielding legal summonses.

"They've been tossing attachments at me like forward passes," grumbled Grange to the press around this time. Then he unfortunately continued with inane football analogies: "The chief difficulty with them was they were offside when the ball was snapped. The race is going on regardless of interfering actions."

There had been rough patches before. Pyle was sued by a Detroit architect who charged that Pyle owed him $1,000 and $217.98 interest for drawing up plans for the theatre he and his business partner built in 1921; Grange was made a garnishment defendant and threatened to be sued as well. And Pyle introduced Grange to a cousin, whose wife became infatuated with the football star. Not long after, the cousin was including Grange in a divorce suit. Both situations ended all right for Grange, but he was continuing to rethink the idea of renewing his contract with Pyle in a few months.

Now with Arthur Duffy out of the picture, Grange was more than the race's assistant director, he was the referee. Grange was always a late sleeper, and because he had a berth in the *America*, the Bunion Derby hadn't changed that—until now. With his new duties, Grange had to wake up earlier: 6:30 a.m.

It was a 28-mile slog to Gary, so Grange had a good deal of the day to himself, without athletes complaining about the food or sleeping conditions. William Kerr was one of the worst gripers. Despite his high ranking, Kerr kept lodging grievances about the way Pyle was managing things. Each time, Grange offered assurances that he would pass along the message to Pyle, but neither he nor Kerr really believed that anything would come of it.

Grange was grateful to Pyle, but when he signed up to be a world-famous football star, he hadn't expected to be on the receiving end of lawsuits or to spend lonely days and nights waiting for weary runners to slowly traipse into town. This resentment had been building for a while. Around this time, Lyle Grange, Red's father, who had never liked Pyle, smugly told a reporter inquiring about a possible rift, that "Red said last fall that a break might come at any time."

Pyle seemed oblivious that his contract with Grange was set to expire in a few months, assuming that their show would go on indefinitely. Every time someone asked about his client's football career, the showman replied enthusiastically, "Red's trick knee has healed perfectly, and next fall, he will again be at the head of the New York Yankees in the professional football arena."

Grange kept his mouth shut.

Around this time, F. F. Gunn had a talk with the runners, insisting that they get their clothes washed. "If you haven't enough cash with you to pay for the cleaning, I will let you have some of your deposit money, and we will square up later," said Gunn. Some runners took advantage of his suggestion, and some didn't. Frank Von Flue began leaving behind dirty clothes at a town to have them freshly laundered and delivered to the next night control. The young man may have been spending money rather freely, but he was clean.

That evening, Grange received a telegram from Pyle, who was driving ahead to map out a new course from Gary to New York City. He had been making up much of the route as they went along anyway, but now the trail was being redone almost from scratch, and Pyle would have only a day or two to establish a new night control.

Pyle wrote that the next morning's run would go to Mishawaka and not South Bend, as originally planned. It was only an extra 4 miles, but the distance everyone was expected to run was already insane. Grange was glad, though, that the whole affair would be over sooner.

"There will be no more roadside picnics or fishing parties," said Grange, making one wonder just *what* he had seen during the last couple of months. "From now on the mileage will be long, and we expect to reach New York on May 27. That will make the grind plenty tough, and no weaklings will be able to carry on." He forgot to cackle maniacally and rub his hands together.

May 7, Gary to Mishawaka, 66.2 Miles

Guisto Umek was at the starting line with everyone else. He even felt almost normal—that is, until he began to run and the stomach acid began to bubble back into his throat.

In the last 10 days, Umek had traveled from 17th place to eighth. Now, on the verge of landing a respectable spot that would fill his fellow villagers in Trieste with pride, his body was failing him. It started yesterday. Umek's pace was off, halted by continual stomach cramps. His trainer and manager, following in their car, alternated between shouting words of encouragement and swearing, all in Italian, but nothing they said or did picked up Umek's pace.

Even more ill today, Umek managed to stay ahead of many men—those who were too exhausted to do much more than linger along the road, often walking and stopping to rest. But they knew their limits. Joe Wilson, from Oakland, California, ran the route hard and blistered his feet so badly that he had no choice but to quit. Gunn's strategy was working—at least a little.

Pyle joined the Bunion Derby gypsies late in the day to provide Grange and the race officials more details on the rest of the trip, now slated to end May 26. The race would be a week shorter than originally expected, thrilling Grange, but it meant making the daily runs longer.

Indeed, when Louis Perrella came into Mishawaka in first place, there were runners as far back as 40 miles.

Little wonder that sportswriters were seeing this as a race through the netherworld, repeatedly describing Pyle as a demon promoter.

GUISTO UMEK lurched into town late in the day. He was surrounded by Dr. Baker and his medical team as wild speculation gave way to a final diagnosis: Someone slipped a sedative into his food. It relaxed Umek's nervous system, when he was pushing his body harder than he ever had—exactly what his body didn't need.

There were a few not-so-subtle hints that something like this might happen. In Arizona, Umek received anonymous threats demanding that he quit the race. He was threatened again in Chicago but had relaxed his guard and accepted a dinner invitation from some well-wishers. Later,

Umek and his trainer and manager concluded that they were the ones who poisoned him.

Umek's manager Al McDonald tried to view the incident as an encouraging sign: "Umek is the real threat in this race. Someone wants him out of the way. It isn't a rival runner or trainer, but a plot that is deep and hard to fathom."

But Paolo Bruno, Umek's trainer, was enraged. "Enemies are after Guisto," he told reporters, in broken English. Bruno, who had been a Bunion Derby runner before dropping out and helping Umek, implied that he knew who was responsible and hinted that he could unleash Umek's fans on them.

"He was doped," seethed Bruno. "I can mention no names. That would be worse revenge."

EARL DILKS, an entry from New Castle, Pennsylvania, had run 36 miles that day, but 30 more seemed impossible, especially because of his heel discomfort. It had bothered him for weeks but was now painful to the touch. But Dilks wasn't giving up, not after almost 2,467 miles. And then the road faded—or was it spinning? It didn't matter. He blacked out.

When he came to, Arthur Newton was at Dilks's side. Dilks insisted on continuing, and Newton accompanied him on foot. They kept on for another 24 miles, but with 6 more to go and midnight closing in, Dilks gave up. In the old days, he could have resumed the race the next day. But the rules had finally changed. He was out.

THAT MIKE KELLY was conquering his home state of Indiana didn't matter. Neither the thought of his mother's home cooking nor crowds cheering for *him* could make his legs work any quicker. His adrenaline was long gone, maybe lost somewhere back in New Mexico. His shoes were weighed down by a continent of dirt. His body had nothing to give but repetition. Kelly shuffled along at 3 miles an hour. He was still in last place.

Near the finish line in Mishawaka, 50 Notre Dame undergraduates kept watch at Michigan Street and Indiana Avenue, waiting for their hometown hero to triumphantly trot by. The plan was to welcome Kelly with the good-natured football game cheer, "He's a man! Who's a man? He's a Notre Dame man!"

Hours later, the students gave up waiting. Almost every other runner had checked in, but Kelly was nowhere to be seen. Having jumped on the Mike Kelly bandwagon rather late, they didn't know their champion very well. True to form, Kelly hobbled past the corner of Michigan and Indiana shortly before midnight.

May 8, Mishawaka to Ligonier, 41 Miles

Shortly after dawn, fellow Hoosier Roy McMurtry roused Kelly. This was going to be Kelly's moment. In about 20 miles, he would run through Goshen. As they had been doing for those lucky enough to race into their own community, the runners would let Kelly lead the race, provided he made an effort. No one minded giving Kelly a chance at being in the lead—certainly not Pete Gavuzzi. He was more than 100 hours ahead of him. Others, like Harry Rea and Olli Wantinnen, had no qualms either because they had no strength to outrun anyone. Both wouldn't reach the finish line in Ligonier by midnight and would be summarily ejected from the race.

Kelly slipped on a pair of bright green shorts, in honor of his newly adopted Irish heritage, and headed to the starting line. McMurtry helped Kelly set the pace, but around noon he dropped behind with the others.

Two thousand people lined Goshen's streets, all shouting Kelly's name. He dashed past them, grinning, waving, and sprinting through the town as if he had been in first place for the last 2 months.

But it was an act that he couldn't sustain for long. In the last mile through Goshen, Kelly was understandably tired and not about to let an opportunity for a good time pass by. On Main Street, he slipped into the F&F Café, where he devoured lunch, rested, and chatted with old friends for the next hour.

Other racers were equally famished. Hunger pangs had even replaced Umek's stomach pains. Now, instead of being certain that he was about to die, he was merely perpetually starving. That was obvious to the thoughtful bystander who handed Umek a chocolate bar. He grabbed it, wolfing down the candy bar without bothering to take off the wrapper.

MEANWHILE, in Fremont, Ohio, Pyle strode down the sidewalk along Front Street, past the Strand Theatre advertising Clara Bow's movie *Get Your Man*. He passed telephone poles and hitching posts, and ambled underneath the awnings and fire escape balconies that jutted out from the front of the Hotel Jackson, an establishment boasting 100 rooms and dozens of chandeliers and chambermaids. It would have been a fine place to stay, but he had reserved a night with the more prestigious Hotel Fremont. His own suite, to Pyle's great interest, was somewhat recently used by Senator Frank B. Willis, a Republican who a little over a month ago died in the middle of a spirited campaign.

Pyle was accompanied by his brother-in-law, Val A. Reis. In the Hotel Jackson lobby, Pyle met Frank Buehler, the manager of the Rainbow Garden, an elegant dance hall and recreational center that he helped build. Buehler was integral to Pyle's mission: establishing another night control.

Ever since returning from World War I, where he was an army captain, Buehler had been a champion of his community. He recognized that Pyle's foot race could generate revenue and publicity for Fremont, two things the community sorely needed. Old-timers remembered Fremont as a thriving shipping port on the Sandusky River. But once the railroads became popular, river travel fell out of favor. Fremont had trains passing through, but the town never saw the growth that Toledo enjoyed. By 1928, Fremont was still stuck in 1882.

Buehler read the newspapers. He knew Pyle was looking for a new route. He sent Pyle a telegram, asking what conditions Fremont needed to meet to host the race.

But before Pyle could make his case to the chamber of commerce, he had to suffer through a meeting with Buehler and 11 other members. Fremont's chamber was newly formed, so Pyle was obliged to smile his way through mundane tasks like electing an additional director to the board and listening to the president of the chamber give a speech about the importance of helping Fremont grow as a community.

Eventually, it was Pyle's turn to speak, and he began his pitch in his usual understated way: "This is the greatest show on earth . . . "

PYLE AND REIS retired to a suite of rooms in the Hotel Fremont, quite positive that they would have an offer of financial assistance from the chamber the next morning. Moments later, reporters knocked on the door. Cheerfully ushering several scribes into the room, Pyle was soon echoing many of the sentiments in his speech with the chamber.

"This greatest show on earth before its completion will be witnessed by twenty million people. Everywhere they pass, the highways, country roads and the streets of the cities are jammed with humanity," said Pyle, adding with a sigh, "The hardest part of this is that I cannot collect a penny."

When reporters asked about his background, Pyle announced, "Well, if you want to know what's what about my birthplace, I was born right up here in Van Wert, Ohio. I'm a Buckeye pure and simple, and I lived for a great bit of my early life in Delaware, Ohio, the birthplace of Rutherford B. Hayes, who I know lived in Fremont for a great many years." The reporters' heads bobbed approvingly.

The sportswriters left the hotel entranced by Pyle's charm. One reporter, who wrote under the name "The Colonel," ladled out gushing praise for Pyle in the *Fremont Daily News* the following afternoon:

"I had the pleasure of meeting one of the finest fellows I ever came in contact with last evening, one of the most pleasant entertainers I have ever mingled with during my career as a sport writer, during which time I have met leaders in all lines of sport endeavors, some of them kings, some queens, many just mere would-be and a lot of them merely hanging onto the eyebrow of the edge, seeking publicity . . . Pyle is the champion 'take a chance' man of the world, and the greatest, versatile promoter that the world has ever seen since Nero staged his bonfire and didn't get a nickel out of it."

Even Pyle couldn't have said it better himself.

May 9, Ligonier to Butler, 41.8 Miles

In the early morning, Pyle finalized plans to bring his own traveling circus into Fremont, averting yet another disaster. Pyle's runners were due in the lonely town in 3 days.

Next, Pyle traveled to Elyria, more than 60 miles away. Accompanying the *America* was Pyle's mobile radio station, which was taking a break from promoting the Bunion Derby until near the end of the race, a decision Gunn made.

Pyle and company arrived at the Elyria Board of Trade office that afternoon to discuss the race with the center's leaders, but learned that most of the prominent businessmen in the city were at a country club banquet being held for Congressman James T. Begg, who was running for governor.

"I told the boys I'd come out and broadcast your speech for you," said Pyle, when he tracked down Begg.

"Very grateful, I'm sure," said the congressman, adding good-naturedly, "Although I'm like yourself in that I don't care so much for publicity." Then Begg asked, "Aside from the pure sportsmanship of the affair, just what is the purpose of your marathon?"

"Well, of course, I'm not a man who likes to commercialize sport," said Pyle, tongue firmly in cheek, "but I thought at the start I might make a little profit on the affair. Right now, I'm $150,000 in the red," he admitted.

"Just where will you make your money?"

"At the finish, partly, when I race the boys 10 miles around Yankee Stadium," said Pyle. "And, of course, there will be profits to be had by showing off the winner." As a businessman, Pyle knew it was important to sound confident, even if he wasn't. Chances are, being the son of a Methodist minister, Pyle was really hoping he still had some of his father's important connections to a higher authority, because at this point, divine intervention was about all that could save his reputation and the race.

THE ROAD TO BUTLER was paved, and on this sweltering day, the runners' feet began to simmer. Von Flue felt as if his feet were going to burn off. So when he spotted a small stream underneath some shade trees, he stopped, removed his shoes and socks, and waded into the stream. Many of the other runners passing by snickered and waved as they shot down the road, but Von Flue didn't care. His trainer gave him a fresh pair of socks and shoes, and several minutes later, Von Flue was back on the road, thundering down the highway at his best speed. And when he finished the race, he had energy to spare. Still, Von Flue's 12th-place position hadn't changed. His rival, Harry Abramowitz, had beaten him that day by 18 minutes and was 14 hours ahead of him in total time.

Von Flue promised himself that he would keep at it. If he could overtake Abramowitz, he could work at passing John Cronick. And if he did that, he could win the 10th-place prize money: $1,000.

But then, many of the runners in the second 10 intended to take away some sort of prize money from the first 10. Just how feasible that was, was anybody's guess.

May 10, Butler, Indiana, to Wauseon, Ohio, 44.9 Miles

With Pyle away so much, the runners understood that Gunn was in charge. To the press, however, Gunn's level of involvement was a secret. "I am not connected with the run except in the capacity of watching after my son," he insisted to a reporter. "I am not C. C. Pyle's financial angel."

Sixty runners left Indiana, easing into Ohio's dirt roads as rain turned them into muddy swill.

"The fellows have a fighting heart now that is hard to [keep] down. Speed is the thing that counts now, and all of the men know now that they will be dropped at the least sign of indifference," a half-admiring and wholly irritated Red Grange told reporters. "The midnight zero hour will be strictly enforced, and those who fail to check in will receive their hundred dollars transportation deposit and be on their way home within a few hours."

It was a challenge the runners took seriously. No one wanted to drop out at this point in the race, though for Kenneth Campbell, it couldn't be helped. The Texan's fallen arches made continuing impossible. Everyone else made it to the finish line by midnight. It was going to take more than adding miles to the daily runs to convince these guys to quit. Nevertheless, more than 2 months into the event, a weary Red Grange appreciated that F. F. Gunn was trying.

CHAPTER 16

Little was recorded of Arthur Studenroth (left) and his part in the Bunion Derby, but he made it as far as El Reno and unceremoniously dropped off the map sometime after. Mike Joyce (right), a runner from Cleveland hoping to win money for his wife and kids, was more fortunate. (Courtesy of the El Reno Carnegie Library.)

FANCY FOOTWORK

DISTANCE SO FAR: 2,623.8 MILES; 59 RUNNERS

MAY 11, WAUSEON TO FREMONT, 64.7 MILES

C. C. Pyle's advance crew of approximately 45 men invaded Fremont on a Friday morning. As they did every morning, they worked their magic. The tent city was erected at Garrison Street and Bidwell Avenue, where the rear of the Jackson Manufacturing Company's plant loomed large. Billboards featuring products—like shoe cement—were strategically erected alongside the roads leading to the finish line. American flags and banners were placed throughout the shopping district. By now the laborers were like veteran stagehands with a traveling theatrical troupe.

Unfortunately, sunlight struggled to break through the gray sky, and rain had fallen on the city for the better part of the last week, turning footpaths and lawns into swamps.

On the road to Fremont, Ed Gardner was recovering from shin splints. "I thought I was done for," said Gardner. "However, Hugo Quist brought me around, and I'll be all right in a few days, and then I'll fight my way back."

Pete Gavuzzi was not so lucky. With every step, pain jackhammered through his skull. He was still 6 hours in the lead overall, but the suffering from his abscessed teeth hadn't abated—and it wouldn't. It was evident to Gavuzzi that he didn't have the strength to last another 1,000 miles, and so there was no reason to run 23 more miles to the next night control.

In the town of Holland, 2,700 miles from Los Angeles, reporters found Gavuzzi sitting in a ditch along the road, smoking one of his trademark cigarettes. He was fighting tears.

"My teeth," said Gavuzzi. "They have been threatening me for two weeks. They finally got me. I haven't been able to eat anything but soup for two weeks. With malnutrition sapping my strength, there was nothing to do but quit."

A sympathetic sportswriter held out a bag of candy, and Gavuzzi rooted for a couple of candy mints that he could suck on.

"What will you do now?" the reporters asked.

"Bella de program, I guess," the Italian-born Englishman said, forcing a smile and explaining in his rich Cockney accent: "I guess I'll go on the program-selling crew now."

Frank Von Flue admitted later, "I was glad, yet not so glad, to see Gavuzzi go. I never did like to see any of the boys go out after getting so far." But with Gavuzzi out, Von Flue was automatically in 11th place. His odds of reaching the top 10 still seemed impossible, however. Harry Abramowitz was 18 hours ahead of him.

Abramowitz, who later changed his name to Abrams, earned his ranking in the top 10 of the race. At 21, he was already a veteran speed walker. In the Lower East Side of Manhattan, Abramowitz was an errand boy for a lithographer. His boss paid him $10 a week, plus local travel expenses, which Harry pocketed. He could outwalk the neighborhood trolley car, and he ultimately discovered the sport of speed walking, which he cultivated through the Young Men's Hebrew Association, an organization similar to the more widely known Young Men's Christian Association, or YMCA.

He started winning enough races that he wore a Star of David on his tank top, billing himself as "the Jewish champion." In this era of ethnic identification, it seemed like the way to go. He was competing against the "Italian Champion Walker," the "Champion of England," and the "German American Walking Champion." Decades later, Abrams would reflect: "You walk against people. Who cares what they are?" Back then, though, those designations mattered.

Abramowitz believed he had as good of a shot as any to win Pyle's race, and so did the YMHA, which sponsored him. Abramowitz reasoned that a runner would never actually make it across the country. A speed walker, Abramowitz thought, could walk the entire planet.

But early into the Bunion Derby, Abramowitz gave up speed walking and adopted running. He would continue running long after the race concluded. Even into his eighties, after a long, successful career in the garment industry as a manufacturer of menswear, with an office in the Empire State Building, he was still running marathons.

R. N. RUSSELL was watering his lawn at 5:30 in the evening when a luxury camper pulled into his driveway.

"This looks like a pretty good place. Guess I'll stop here," said Pyle, introducing himself.

Russell was the owner of Arrowhead-on-the-Lake in Arrowhead Beach, Ohio, a tourist town along Lake Erie, and when Pyle first suggested they set up camp on his land, he was politely rebuffed. Russell, apparently worrying about overstepping some bounds in community politics, suggested Pyle drive to nearby Painesville to arrange matters there. Pyle did, inviting Russell along, and they ate with several city officials at a tavern. Pyle had his eyes on two brothers, railroad barons Oris Paxton and Manthis James Van Sweringen. Later, Russell encouraged Pyle to ask them to put down the money for the race to visit Painesville.

"The devil with them, my business is with you, Russell," said Pyle, being able to read the two millionaires enough to know that he was getting nowhere. He also understood that he was more likely to get money from someone who wanted to be recognized than two people who already were.

At 11:45 p.m., Russell presented Pyle with a check for $1,000. After the showman left, Russell told reporters, "I'm a pretty good salesman myself, I'll admit, and . . . when Pyle pulled in, I had no idea of working with his crew, much less of paying any guarantee."

Russell was responsible for many of the duties involved in hosting the public that would converge on Arrowhead Beach in only 2 days. He had to do a lot of work in the meantime—and he had to shell out $1,000 for the privilege.

One journalist asked, "What do you get for the $1,000?"

Not much, according to Russell's shrug. With so many people coming, his property might become better known, at least in these parts. But Russell thought some more about what he had agreed to and concluded: "Oh, but that Pyle is *good*."

THAT AFTERNOON, Guisto Umek suddenly stopped to sit on a large stone next to the road. When his trainers insisted he continue running, Umek refused. He didn't explain himself, remaining quiet as his handlers begged, pleaded, and yelled at him. Umek and his trainers never really got along. Sometimes in the evening, he and his trainers argued, and Umek threw rocks at them. In return, his trainers never hesitated to push Umek to run far past his limit.

A small crowd of people gathered around Umek. The slower runners were passing him. The frantic trainers grew more frantic.

Umek remained deaf to his handlers' begging for the next 45 minutes, until he suddenly stood and began jogging. Very slowly. His trainers were infuriated.

Then 5 miles later, without warning, Umek barreled forward and sprinted all the way to the conclusion of the day's race. He came in sixth.

JOHN SALO was first past the finish line and mobbed by adoring children. Salo, beaming, now possessed the look of a winner. With Gavuzzi gone, Salo was in second place, poised to win $10,000. The eventual end to their epic odyssey never felt so real.

Every state's reception had improved upon the others, which made sense, given that the athletes kept covering so much ground.

During these moments, C. C. Pyle's vision appeared flawless. Miles from Fremont, the streets were lined with cars, with drivers and passengers all cheering for the Bunion Derby survivors. Enterprising fellows, presumably including Gavuzzi, fanned across town, shouting, "Get your official program here for 25 cents"—and what's more, people were buying them.

The crowds were overspilling into the streets. For a while, the athletes were reduced to jogging in ditches alongside the road, trying to get past the spectators.

Sheriff's deputies on horseback forced a path through the crowd. Behind Salo, a police car followed. Its siren blaring, the officer escorted him through the people-clogged streets and up to the courthouse. Salo tore through the finish line tape. The police didn't linger; they departed to repeat their performance for Andy Payne and Phillip Granville, who tied for second that day.

When Payne and Granville reached Salo, he was puffing a cigar. All of the first dozen or so athletes were given complimentary cigars and cigarettes, against the backdrop of thousands of shouting and applauding fans.

In front of the Fremont Hotel, drums were beaten and trumpets blown as the high school band greeted the runners—and not just those at the front of the pack. "That's the first time a band ever greeted me," whooped a delighted Stanley Stevano, a middle-range plodder from Canada.

Everyone was having the time of his life, save Jack Urban, a newspaper reporter traveling with the derby, who discovered that his wallet was missing. Somewhere in the crowd, a pickpocket was lurking. The runners, however, were in the money. Once their $1.50 allowances were doled out, everyone headed to a restaurant, although several detoured to the Western Union telegraph office, where money orders from family and sponsors were waiting.

In the diners and cafés, the favorite menu items were steak, potatoes, and soup, though one amused reporter enjoyed watching Sammy Robinson consume a feast that included eggs, potatoes, beans, asparagus, soup, and coffee. When asked what he would do upon returning in less than 2 weeks, "I'm going to be mayor of Atlantic City," the African American replied, tongue in cheek, given the rampant racism that infected much of the country.

Indeed, the reporter, or his editor, couldn't resist playing the race card for his readers. When the story appeared in the *Fremont Messenger* the next day, Robinson's quote was paraphrased in stereotypical, condescending fashion: "When he got back home, 'He's suah goin' to be mayoh' of Atlantic City.'"

Otherwise, the reception in Fremont was warm and encouraging. Even before the city limits, Frank R. Smith, who ran a gas station on the west side, handed out cold bottles of soda pop to each Bunion Derby participant. At the end of the race, each man received another gift from one of the local drugstores—a Christy razor and blades, a relatively new and popular brand on the market. It was an inspired gift. Most of the haggard runners resembled Robinson Crusoe and badly needed a shave.

Reporters stormed the Western Union telegraph office that night, ecstatic to have new developments to send to their editors. They sent out more than 15,000 words related mostly to the elimination of Gavuzzi earlier in the day. The Western Union manager and her assistant worked at their keys deep into the night.

MAY 12, FREMONT TO ELYRIA, 63.3 MILES

The next morning, Pyle spoke to the chamber of commerce in Conneaut, a tiny lake community on the edge of Lake Erie and right on the border between Ohio and Pennsylvania.

In the last several months, Pyle only charged towns that were hosting the runners for the night. It still bothered him that many towns benefited from the race without Pyle seeing a dime, and so this time, he tried something a little new. He proposed that the chamber in Conneaut pay him a mere $100, and then he would instruct his athletes to run *through* the town, instead of around it.

Secretary Jay C. Kiedel looked at Pyle in the way that one regards a mosquito. Kiedel pointed out that Pyle had no choice but to direct the race through Conneaut, unless he wanted to take a lengthy detour through Ohio and a significant portion of Pennsylvania, or if he wanted his runners swimming through Lake Erie. Pyle left the chamber empty-handed and drove up to Erie, Pennsylvania, where he planned on housing the runners for the night.

W. A. DOWNING, a Los Angeles clerk, sprained his ankle about 20 miles into the race and had to give up. Then John Gober, Missouri's speed machine, hurt his leg and capitulated.

Otherwise, it was a typical, if exhausting, day. Payne was still far ahead of everyone else. Salo was coming into his own, racing better than ever; nevertheless, he remained more than 21 hours behind Payne. And riding in one of the buses, Gavuzzi kept second-guessing his decision to quit the race, even though it was the only logical thing he could have done.

It must have stung to no longer be an international hero. When Gavuzzi reached Oklahoma City in second place, French newspapers reported that Pete Gavuzzi, an Englishman, was from Corsica, an island territory of France in the Mediterranean Sea. By the time he reached St. Louis in the lead, French papers were referring to him as Pierre Gavuzzi, "born of a French father from Marseilles and a mother from Brittany."

After Gavuzzi dropped out, the French headlines read, "English runner Gavuzzi quits at Toledo."

MIKE JOYCE was home.

Unlike Mike Kelly, this Mike, 35, actually was born in Ireland before coming to Cleveland. After 3 months apart, including time spent training, Mike was nearing his wife and five children, and he couldn't wait to see them. Mike was an autoworker who thought he had saved enough to take leave from the Fisher Body Company for a few months while he sought out the $25,000 prize. Before long, though, the Associated Charities of Cleveland were assisting the Joyces, and his co-workers began fundraising to help Mike get a trainer, who ended up meeting him in Claremore, Oklahoma. All of Mike's hard work was paying off—he was in fourth place.

Elyria was approximately 30 miles from Cleveland, and because Mike ran especially fast that day, he had plenty of hours available to hire a car or grab a train to see his family.

His wife opened the door and saw a bedraggled, bronze-skinned man. With dust and dirt covering him, she immediately thought he was a neighborhood rug-beater, a profession that eventually disappeared with the advent of the vacuum cleaner.

"I don't want any of our rugs beaten," she said, before Mike could get a word out.

Mike's children didn't know him either. Once he cleared everything up, his wife led him into the house. "Come over here, Peg," said Mike to his third daughter, but she burst into tears and ran away. Then Agnes and Anna began sobbing, and both dove under the bed. Later, one of his daughters ran outside to the front yard, sat on a box, and started bawling.

Joe, hardly more than an infant, was oblivious to his father as he toddled over to his brother, Mike Jr., and pulled his hair.

It wasn't the homecoming Mike dreamed of, and it lasted only a few hours before he headed back to the camp to get enough sleep before rising early. Still, after those few precious hours, his children came around, and soon even the youngest were calling him "Dadda."

Mike returned to the camp with a basket full of food, including two dozen eggs, cake, three roasted chickens, a pound of butter, cheeses, and meats. The press reported that he had a flask of alcohol, too, but stressed—a little too facetiously—that it was strictly meant for rubbing sore muscles.

May 13, Elyria to Arrowhead Beach, 51.4 Miles

Harry Sheare never saw the car.

On Sunday morning, the runners were groggy but on the go, ready to hoof through Cleveland. There were 56 runners left, and it must have looked like a mob scene to the 19-year-old kid chauffeuring Hymye Silbergeld, a successful 51-year-old junk dealer from Niagara Falls, New York.

Near the town of Ridgeville, the young driver made a split-second decision to pass an automobile, even though that meant a speedy squeeze between one car and a middle-aged runner jogging on the right side of the road.

The fender collided with Sheare's hip, catapulting him 20 feet before he somersaulted twice, crashed to the ground, and tumbled on his head. Sheare was unconscious and crumpled in a heap, with his fractured spectacles nearby.

An ambulance was called. Sheare was bleeding from his head and hip.

For yet another athlete, the Bunion Derby had ended.

Sheare was transported to the Elyria Memorial Hospital, where x-rays showed his head was fractured, and he had a possible injury to his spine. Doctors worried that Sheare's pelvis was fractured as well, and that if there was internal bleeding, it could prove to be a fatal injury.

The driver was taken to jail by the sheriff's deputy. And soon, it was determined Sheare would be fine, and his trainer informed the police that they didn't want to press charges.

Despite Sheare's promised recovery, a new sense of unease settled over the remaining runners. With less than a month to go and yet almost 1,000 miles ahead of them, it was suddenly clear, once again, that anything could happen.

Payne was especially uneasy—front-runners had a way of disappearing. Arthur Newton had been hours ahead of him, but an injury took him out. Arne Suominen looked like the chosen one until his heel cord simply snapped. Gavuzzi was unstoppable until he wasn't. Payne didn't feel invincible—far from it.

He felt especially vulnerable because Sheare was one of the better athletes remaining and an amicable fellow who regaled everyone with stories of his years driving dogsled teams in Alaska. If Sheare, a gifted and careful athlete, could be injured, anyone could. Days later, when Payne crossed into New York, he anxiously said of his chances of winning: "The only thing that can stop me is a car."

IN THE MIDST of the estimated 300,000 cars and just over 1 million residents in Cleveland, one man ran as if he were late for a train. Hardrock cheerfully shouted after him: "Hey, Mike, where ya goin'?"

"It's a poor man who can't run first into his hometown," Mike Joyce shouted back.

Mike's enthusiasm was infectious. The crowd was throwing money—collectively, almost $40—and throughout the din he could occasionally pick out an "Atta boy, Mike," and "Hooray for the Irish!" Young boys ran alongside him, trying to imitate him. Police on motorcycles escorted him, in case any fans overstepped their bounds. Everyone was waving, many people sitting in chairs that they had brought to the street curb. For the last dozen years of his life, Mike Joyce had lived in obscurity, and now, suddenly he was a star.

In the hubbub, Norman Codeluppi—at least from the media's perspective—was nowhere to be seen. Perhaps no one bothered to tell the press that he was a hometown boy, raised in Cleveland until a year before. Sports editors wouldn't have necessarily known. Pyle's program noted that Codeluppi was from Pasadena.

Little is known about what Codeluppi was up to that day. His own children wouldn't know about his involvement in the Bunion Derby until 48 years after the race. He said he never thought to tell them, and he only did when someone else brought it to their attention. Even after that, he didn't say much about it.

Codeluppi's uncle knew about the race, though they may have conspired not to tell anyone. It seems likely that Norman and Mary traded letters during the race and met somewhere in Cleveland. Gloria, his younger sister, doesn't recall seeing him pass through her city (she was only 4), but she does remember him after the race, her brother clasping her hands and giving her a gift: the piece of Petrified Forest that he had collected back in Arizona. What is without doubt is that Norman decided to abandon his original plan of ending his run in Cleveland. He had come too far to quit the race, even when on the streets of his home city he twisted his ankle and hurt his knee.

In searing pain, Codeluppi climbed to his feet and kept hobbling along, stopping every few miles to rest and pray that he could keep moving.

Right about then, Mike Joyce's biggest fans were waiting for him. His wife and children were there, dressed in their Sunday best. For the occasion, they wore new clothes, like Mike Jr.'s Irish green suit.

But this was a quick visit. Within a matter of a few minutes, Mike hugged his family, picked up his youngest child, took a few photos, and then disappeared. But he would see them later, spending the night in a warm bed with his wife. And, spreading the wealth, he invited Frank Von Flue, with whom he had become especially good friends, to spend the night at the house, too.

PYLE PULLED INTO Jamestown, New York. Immediately, a crowd gathered around his luxury camper. Pyle hastily headed into the Hotel Jamestown for a luncheon. Afterward, he scooted off to Olean. He promised he'd make a decision about the night control the next day. As it turned out, Jamestown won, promising $1,000 to Pyle for bringing in the runners. They would even set up a tent for the athletes to sleep under.

Around this time, Pyle received word from Steve Owen that there had been *another* wreck with one of the patrol cars in Cleveland, just as there had been in Arizona. Like the time before, Pyle wanted to collect the wreckage and sell it to a junk dealer, but Owen explained that the car had skidded over a river embankment. There was nothing to salvage, but fortunately, the driver had escaped a watery grave. Not long afterward, one of the Bunion Derby deputies, Bill O'Brien, noticed that Owen had far more spending money than usual.

It wasn't until much later that Pyle learned the truth—and had the good humor to laugh about it. Owen, frustrated that he wasn't being paid every day as promised, was occasionally selling these "wrecked" cars to a dealer and pocketing the money.

May 14, Arrowhead Beach to Ashtabula, 41.1 Miles

After another lengthy lap, each runner ambled to the microphone and was given the opportunity to say something to the crowd. As the hometown hero, Mike Joyce was first up to bat.

"Ladies and gentlemen," began Joyce, "it's wonderful the reception I got in Cleveland. Of course, I'm sorry I couldn't win this lap, but I was first into Cleveland."

Shortly afterward, Granville ran past the finish line, and a young boy shouted, "Say something, Granville."

Winded and ill-tempered, regardless of his condition, Granville glared at him and snapped, "Don't you know the runner is not a talker?"

Granville was right. Payne came through the finish line third. When the crowd shouted, "Say something, Andy," he took the microphone, grinned, and blurted, "Howdy." And that was it.

SHORTLY AFTER Sheare was admitted to the hospital, Red Grange dropped by, a touching gesture to Sheare, considering no one else had come by. Grange may have been grumpy, but his decency and manners hadn't left him.

"Red Grange is a pretty good sort of kid," said Sheare from his bed, sharing some details with a local reporter about the visit. "Yes, sir. Red seems pretty hard until you get to know him, but after that he's a good enough fellow. I don't know just what sort of agreement Grange and Pyle have between them, but Grange doesn't seem to take a great interest in the race."

Sheare was still processing the idea of being out of the Bunion Derby. He had come so far and even stayed in the top 25.

"I had a notion to quit twice," he said, visibly depressed. "Once in Arizona and again in Texas." But upon reaching Ohio, it was another matter. "I would not have been out of the race for $100,000," said Sheare wistfully. "I heard that Pyle was going to give every runner that reached New York City $1,000. I also heard that there would be money for the oldest and youngest runners, and I was the oldest left in the race."

The reporter asked how much training Sheare put in before embarking on the Bunion Derby. "Not much," admitted Sheare. "Just a few 50-mile runs and 10,000 miles in Alaska during the winters of 1907, 1908, 1909 when I ran along a freight-carrying dogsled."

The reporter asked if the Bunion Derby had been difficult. "Sometimes," replied Sheare. "It has taken me 16 hours to make 22 miles." And yet Sheare said he hadn't lost any weight. He kept each of his 137 prerace pounds.

He looked over for a moment at a bouquet of flowers sent by the *Chronicle-Telegram*, the paper in Elyria, where he was laid up.

"I suppose the man who struck you will take care of the hospital bill," said the reporter. The former dogsledder had no idea. "He hasn't been in to see me," said Sheare, giving a rueful smile.

The reporter said nothing, but his thought made it into the paper the next day: *That's a hell of a way to treat a fellow.*

"No, sir," said Sheare, repeating his sentiment: "I wouldn't have taken $100,000 to quit the race."

MAY 15, ASHTABULA, OHIO, TO ERIE, PENNSYLVANIA, 45.8 MILES

The next morning, a forlorn Sheare set out for New York, presumably by car or train, to catch up with the Bunion Derby runners. He had learned that Pyle was organizing a 26-hour race, to be conducted about a week after the Bunion Derby concluded, for his new superstar athletes. Sheare figured he would try that and attempt to win a little extra money.

One of Will Rogers's columns appeared in the *New York Times* that morning, urging that the country offer the runners more respect. He declared, "There is not a golf player in America that could have stood this same trip in an automobile. You will find it's the grit and the heart that's doing this more than bunions, or ingrowing toe nails, so be fair and give 'em a break."

The citizens of Erie took Rogers's advice. The crowds were even sticking around to cheer those in the back, like Codeluppi and Kelly. They shouted out questions to runners moving so slowly it was almost possible to have a lengthy conversation. One spectator asked, "Do you think you'll make it?" Another wiseacre asked if the runners were considering advertising foot medicine when they finished the race.

While recovering from another long day, Payne was asked by sportswriter Leland Lewis what he thought about his odds for winning. "I remember what happened to Gavuzzi just the other day," said Payne, far from self-assured. "He had a comfortable lead over me. Then things went wrong, and he was out. Before him, Willie Kolehmainen, Arthur Newton, Charlie Hart, Olli Wantinnen, and other great runners met misfortune. The last 600 miles are the hardest. Anything may happen."

CHAPTER 17

Andy Payne (left) runs with John Cronick (center) and William Kerr (left). (Courtesy of the El Reno Carnegie Library.)

LAST LEGS

DISTANCE SO FAR: 2,890.1 MILES; 55 RUNNERS

MAY 16, ERIE, PENNSYLVANIA, TO JAMESTOWN, NEW YORK, 60 MILES

Leaving at 8:00 a.m., the runners faced another long slog, following Highway 17 through the foothills of the Allegheny Mountains. John Salo won the day's race, chopping an hour off Andy Payne's lead. Payne was still 20 hours and 9 minutes ahead, however. But neither came in first. That honor, as far as Frank Von Flue was concerned, was going to him.

He hadn't started the race well. He was one of the last runners to leave the camp and in no hurry to get his legs moving again. He felt ill, and it was raining. But Von Flue started running anyway.

He felt better after a while, even if the muddy roads were maddening to navigate. And after several hours, he realized that he had passed about 50 runners. That meant there were just four more runners ahead of him. Encouraged, Von Flue hurried down the long stretch of countryside, passing two more runners. And as he came into Jamestown, he caught sight of the front-runner, Sam Richman, one of the three Richman brothers. Richman was just *two blocks* ahead of Von Flue.

But there were 4 miles to go.

Von Flue sped up. Unfortunately for Von Flue, Richman glanced back, saw him, and wasn't going to lose his lead without a fight.

The crowds shouted and cheered as Von Flue struggled to close the gap between them, but Richman managed to go even faster—widening the chasm between them. Von Flue kept running, but his energy started to dwindle. Richman ripped through the tape, very firmly first, finishing in 6 hours, 47 minutes, and 89 seconds. Two minutes later, Von Flue rushed across the finish line.

The timers were asleep. Von Flue and Richman may have not noticed, but Red Workman, Von Flue's trainer, did and roused Ralph Goodwin. The two men probably lost a minute of their time, thanks to the unplanned group nap, but Von Flue was too pleased to be angry. He soon learned that he was only 1 hour and 10 minutes behind 10th place Harry Abramowitz. There was still a chance that he could win some prize money.

DESPITE THEIR RIVALRY and 15-year age difference, Payne and Salo were becoming close friends, when they weren't trying to outrun the other. Many men paired off and forged friendships, and Payne and Salo managed to do what Pete Gavuzzi and Payne couldn't. They ran with each other on this day, though Payne purposely dropped back as they approached Jamestown so that Salo could enter New York alone and greet all of the well-wishers. Though Salo was from New Jersey, these were his people.

Arthur Newton, meanwhile, told a reporter, "They are coming along fine. The stamina of the entire lot is almost superhuman." Then, thinking of poor Harry Sheare, Newton implored New York motorists to use caution on the roads and give the runners the right of way. "If they show the same consideration that others have, none of the boys will be robbed of their ambition to reach their goal. Even the ones who cannot finish among the money winners want the satisfaction of going through."

As if to underscore the point, Mike Kelly came in dead last for the day, but amazingly his elapsed score was ahead of one man. The man currently in last place was Austrian runner Anton Isele, so under the radar that not only did the sportswriters generally ignore him, he didn't even have a mention in C. C. Pyle's program.

May 17, Jamestown, New York, to Bradford, Pennsylvania, 44.2 Miles

Payne and Salo were increasingly getting interview requests. The news media recognized that unless anything drastic happened, Payne would come in first and Salo second, provided they both maintained their pace and didn't give up. "I am not going to dog it either," said Payne, who was asked if he felt like he didn't have to try hard at this point. "I have run all along and will, right to the finish. If I am beaten, I will be the first to congratulate the winner."

"First place was my fondest hope," said Salo wistfully. "I have a wife and two children. My wife has worked to keep things going while I have been running so that we will have a better future than the hard sledding of the past. I may have to be content with second place, but even then I won't growl."

At the end of the long run, through a sprinkling of rain that was more relaxing than a nuisance, the high school cross-country team greeted Payne and jogged back into town with him. Then Payne promptly went off in search of food. "I'm always hungry, no matter what time, or what I eat, or how much," he confided.

Doc Payne later caught up with his son, and after their affectionate hug, rumors flew among some of the more gossip-minded townspeople. They all figured that Andy was a runaway, and that his father had just tracked him down in Bradford. There were other rumors floating about that day, too, and who knows how they got started? Several people traded the news that one of the runners was injured. Later, the hearsay was that a runner had dropped dead.

THE DAY BEFORE, the Associated Press reported that on May 17, the men would run from Jamestown to Wellsville, neglecting to mention that would mean running an inhumane 93 miles in a single day. Fortunately, Pyle came to his senses and worked out a quick deal with the chamber of commerce in Bradford, Pennsylvania. Then he stormed into the *Bradford Era* newspaper offices and informed the sports department that the Bunion Derby would be arriving the next day. Pyle then drove past Wellsville, New York, to figure out the night control after that. The Associated Press reported that the race would then head for Elmira, although it ended up in Bath. Pyle's fancy footwork was almost as intricate as his runners'.

But that was yesterday; today was today, and C. C. Pyle was in New York City, worried. Pyle didn't panic easily, but this week was probably among the worst of his life. While he had managed to keep his operation together long enough to bring an entire contingent of 55 runners across the country, and while his luck with the chambers of commerce and local governments in New York had improved, he had to face facts: Things weren't going well. Pyle's bank account was on fumes. The men would arrive in 6 days—and he had no prize money to give them.

Pyle could meet his own living expenses, which were considerable, but he was obliged to cut back, moving out of the Hotel Biltmore, which charged $50 a night, to a less expensive $30-a-night suite at the Hotel Vanderbilt—and that's not to say he didn't have a charge account that he was exploiting. He was hardly impoverished, but Pyle wasn't the wealthy man he was even a year ago, and nothing like he was in 1925 and 1926, when he and Red Grange had more money than they knew what to do with. He did, however, know one man who fit that description.

Of all the sports promoters in the country, there was only one who had more cache, credibility, and cash than Pyle. His name was Tex Rickard.

Rickard was 58 years old and on top of his game. Over the years, Rickard had been a cowboy, a town marshal in Texas, a Klondike gold rush prospector, and the owner of a gambling house. In 1906, he discovered boxing, offering an unheard-of prize of $30,000 to the victor, a huge risk until he brought in $62,000 in box office receipts. On July 4, 1910, Rickard promoted his second fight, a legendary match between Jack Johnson, who was black, and James J. Jeffries, who was white. Johnson won the $101,000 purse, infuriating whites. Riots broke out, as people began looking for the "great white hope" who could clock Johnson.

Eventually, Rickard was so successful that he bought Madison Square Garden and replaced it with an entirely new one in 1925. There, he staged boxing matches during the 1920s that brought in over $2 million in receipts. He was a rich man with an easygoing sense of humor and a generous nature, though hardly a saint. As sports columnist Westbrook Pegler said when eulogizing Rickard in 1929, he was "gullible, crafty, shrewd, generous, keen, naïve, and stubborn."

Pyle hoped to appeal to Rickard's generosity.

Once, Rickard paid for the last appeal of a complete stranger who was sentenced to death in New Jersey. Another time, he gave a friend $500 to bail out a man Rickard had never met. Like Pyle, Rickard didn't have use for authority, particularly government officials. "Of all the low down people in the world, the politicians are the low downest no damn goodest rats in the world," he growled to Pegler, who suggested those were harsh words. "Ain't harsh enough," grumbled Rickard.

Pyle went to Rickard, his hat in hand.

May 18, Bradford, Pennsylvania, to Wellsville, New York, 49.8 Miles

Exactly what Pyle and Rickard discussed may always be a mystery. All the runners knew was what the *New York Times* reported the next day—that the race would end at Madison Square Garden instead of the original destination: Yankee Stadium.

Von Flue ran alongside Payne for a while. They had gotten to know each other pretty well during the course of the race. Von Flue asked what most people were asking Payne: "Well, what do you think about your chances to keep in the lead until we finish?"

"All I have to do is keep going at a fairly steady route and, barring accidents, I will win," said Payne matter-of-factly, not maliciously. Von Flue eventually sped up, leaving Payne behind and almost catching Hardrock, who was running better and better these days. When Von Flue checked into the night control that evening, he learned that he was now in 10th place overall, 2 hours and 2 minutes ahead of Abramowitz. Von Flue was thrilled. If he had any energy left, he would have done a dance.

Payne, meanwhile, still fretted over the idea of being hit by a car. After running into Wellsville on Day 76, with eight more daily laps to go, Payne echoed his fears that he had told Von Flue and had expressed before: "I'll be in New York first—unless an automobile crashes into me. I feel fine, and I know I can keep up."

Doc Payne agreed with his son's assessment. "I'm proud of that boy, and I'm certain he'll win."

May 19, Wellsville to Bath, 52.5 Miles

Payne gave a variation of his customary greeting to the cheering crowd afterward—"Howdy, feeling fine, thanks." But Payne was not merely taciturn by nature—he was too tired to talk.

Everyone was tired, not to mention wet. It rained the previous night, and the drenching demoralized the day. About halfway through the trip, a sopping wet Frank Von Flue and Red Workman stopped at a restaurant to dry off and wolf down some sandwiches and a glass of milk. Abramowitz, whom he had just knocked out of the top 10, was there. He was friendly when Von Flue spoke to him about the race. "Let the best man win," said Abramowitz, cheerfully.

Von Flue appreciated that and headed back into the wind and rain, while Abramowitz continued with his meal. Abramowitz understood that his chance for any prize money was probably over; he was battling shin splints.

The water was warm, and Von Flue felt refreshed. He kept hurrying down the road, staying on the shoulder, because the pavement was so slippery. He came in second, an hour behind Salo, but he was now 6 hours ahead of Abramowitz and only 6 hours behind John Cronick, who was still running well but rapidly losing strength and speed. The day before, Von Flue had been 12 hours behind Cronick.

May 20, Bath to Waverly, 58.3 Miles

More rain.

Hardrock didn't care. The foot that bothered him for most of the race was healed, and for the first time, he and his trainer, Wesley "Chop Suey" Williams, had the pleasant and surreal experience of passing runners. When Hardrock passed Payne, Salo, and Seth Gonzales, all running in a pack, he knew he was having an especially good day. Then, for the longest time, Hardrock and Williams saw no other athlete on the horizon. For only the second time in 78 days, Hardrock was in the lead, and for the first time, he kept it. He finished a few minutes shy of 9 hours. Fifty minutes later, Payne, Salo, and Gonzales arrived.

Nevertheless, as one newspaper bluntly put it, Hardrock's win was "meaningless." It was clear that Payne, Salo, and Phillip Granville would finish first, second, and third, respectively. When Mike Joyce sent a telegram to his wife, letting her know that he was going to come in fourth place, he still had a week before they were due to arrive in New York City. Hardrock was in 39th place, a sure thing for the first-place prize money only if an earthquake struck and the 38 runners ahead of him all pitched into a giant crack in the ground and were then swallowed whole.

But for a brief, shining moment, Hardrock felt like a million bucks. Still, he admitted, "I do not know whether I'll keep on with pro-racing or not. I've a yearning to go back to Carolina, where the sweet 'taters grow, but, anyhow I did my stuff for one day."

There was some suspense among the other runners. Guisto Umek and William Kerr were battling for fifth place, just minutes apart. Beyond that, providing there were no mishaps or sudden upsets, it was likely that Louis Perrella, Ed Gardner, John Cronick, and Frank Von Flue would round out the top 10.

Payne was finally elated about his odds. As he ran past the finish line, relieved and delighted to be done, Andy shouted, "I'm going to win this race."

Moments later, Doc Payne greeted his boy, agreeing: "He is sure to win now."

Tom Young was currently looking like a brilliant strategist. Young wrote a letter to C. F. Godbey, the secretary of the Claremore Chamber of Commerce, in late May and described Payne as a cross between a stallion and a superman. "Andy is a wonderful bunch of flesh. He reminds me of the famous race horse (Man O' War)," wrote Young. "He goes to the starting line each morning quietly. But when he gets the word 'go,' he is off like a flash, and he don't let up until the finish. After a sixty or seventy mile run, Andy's heart beat is normal. I cannot place a limit on his endurance. He never tires. To me, there has been only one runner in this race, and he is Andy Payne, the greatest marathon runner in the world."

Young had something there. Payne was one of the few runners who had yet to have any serious foot problems.

May 21, Waverly to Deposit, 74.6 Miles

The whistle blew at 6:00 in the morning. Many runners started off slowly in the early dawn. On a day like this one, in what would be the longest run of the Bunion Derby, no one wanted to burn out too quickly.

What the men were attempting, about 250 miles away from New York City, was being greeted with more respect in some quarters across the country. "Much fun and ridicule has been poked at C. C. Pyle for his derby of foot-racers across the continent. There were few who ever thought the derby runners would get into the Mississippi Valley or to Chicago. Yet by the end of this week more than fifty men will have completed one of the most unheard of ventures that has attracted the attention of the country," stated the editorial board of the *Decatur Review*, concluding, "These men are now running because they want to finish what they started. There will be no prize money for them when they finish. They have run since March. While it was a spectacular stunt for Pyle, the determination of these runners must be admired."

FRANK VON FLUE decided to take the first 25 miles as easy as he could. After polishing off the first third of the race several hours later, he rested alongside the road for 15 minutes. Then he started to run, planning to tackle the next two-thirds of the race—almost 50 miles—as swiftly as possible. But 15 miles later, every Bunion Derby runner's worst nightmare came true.

Two cars collided on the road, just in front of Von Flue, and they were spinning out of control, right for him.

Von Flue dashed across the two-lane highway, literally running for his life. The driver of another car behind Von Flue had the same instinct—veer left. The automobile clipped Von Flue's right leg, sending the 26-year-old sprawling into a ditch.

Von Flue rolled over several times but was more dazed than hurt, though he did have a severe bruise on his leg. The drivers of the two cars involved in the wreck were also generally uninjured. Red Workman, following nearby, was able to give Von Flue a quick rubdown. When he started running again, he had lost only a few minutes.

Salo came in first, shortly after 6:00 p.m., running the 74.6 miles in 12 hours, 13 minutes, and 9 seconds, immediately setting off speculation that he had achieved some sort of world's record. He also shaved off an hour and 23 minutes and some seconds from Payne's lead. Now, he just had 18 more hours to go.

Salo often downplayed the daily runs, but not today, forcing a quick quote for reporters as he jogged up to the finish line. "Those were some hills, no fooling," he said, referring to the Catskill Mountains.

The car accident didn't faze Von Flue. He finished second, 45 minutes after Salo. If anything, the accident helped boost his adrenaline.

Payne also arrived in the evening. Afterward, he was practically long-winded and emotional about his run through the Catskill Mountains. "Believe me, boy, I stepped that trip mighty cautious," said Payne. "Those miles seemed unending, the most maddening that I've covered so far. But I'm here, and it's all over."

For others, as evening approached, the finish line was still far off. All along Highway 17 were young men lying along the edges of the road, groaning and complaining of their aching feet and tired muscles.

Around 1:00 a.m., Perrella of Albany, New York, hobbled past the finish line and told his story to sportswriter Leland Lewis. "Every mile was agony for me, especially with a bad hip," said Perrella. He wasn't understating the case. During the 70-plus-mile run, his hip was literally thrown out of place, but he kept walking and managed to get the bone back in its socket. He had also recently sprained his ankle and had fallen from fifth to sixth place overall, thanks to the 19 hours it took him to cover today's daily lap. But Perrella concluded, "Guess it wasn't any bed of roses for any of the crowd."

One hour later, at 2:04 a.m., more than 20 hours after he had started the lap, Norman Codeluppi dragged himself past the finish line. Then he stunned race officials and reporters by bursting into tears. After he composed himself, he said, "I felt my knee give way several times, and on any number of occasions I had to sit down for several minutes and rub it so I could stagger on again. Each step was agony, but I've come this far and will go on."

The tears weren't a matter of pain, however. Codeluppi thought he had been disqualified. When he learned that he was still in the race, he brightened, explaining to Lewis: "I didn't have a watch, and the knee that has held me back for days would carry me only a short distance without stopping to rest. When I found out I was still in time, it was better than any liniment that could have been put on it. I'll go through and live up to that nickname, 'Smiles.'"

The midnight rule had been eliminated again, thanks to Arthur Newton. He convinced F. F. Gunn to rescind the rule and allow any runner who made it to this day's finish line—no matter what time—to stay in the race. Gunn, a keen businessman but no monster, agreed. He likely didn't make the amends to improve the odds for his son. Harry always walked to the night controls without any major difficulty and so far didn't have one blister on his foot.

"I couldn't bear to see men, who had already gallantly covered some thousands of miles, drop out when they were so near their goal," explained Newton in his autobiography, who well after midnight located four of the last men, 19 miles away from ending their 74.6-mile trip to Deposit. One particular man was in a delirium; Newton didn't name him, but the scant information he gives seems to finger Mike Kelly.

Whoever he was, the young man "stumbled along mechanically with his mind practically a blank. Like many another, he was as thin as a rake, without an ounce of superfluous flesh . . . all of the sudden, he would realize that he was still on the road, and in a desperately exhausted condition."

Every 2 or 3 miles, Newton recalled, the runner stopped to think about his situation, hardly caring about the rain dumping over them. At one point, the man weakly asked, "How much farther is it to Deposit?"

Newton guessed that he had traveled 11 miles with them. "So that leaves eight. In a couple of hours or so, we'll be there."

"*Eight miles*," he screamed. "Then I'm going to sit down."

He did just that, squatting in the middle of the puddles on the road. Newton pulled the runner to his feet, one arm at a time, and then gave him a shove. "Once more," wrote Newton, "he was stumbling along with us, his mind dead to everything but the chronic ache of perpetual torture."

Newton's party crept past the finish line just after 3:00 a.m, meaning that they had only 3 hours to rest before they needed to wake up and run again.

May 22, Deposit to Liberty, 59.1 Miles

The good news was that a police officer on a motorcycle led the race the entire way, like a grand marshal of a weird parade, alerting the public that the Bunion Derby was coming. After Von Flue's accident and complaints from other runners about cars, the authorities decided to take extra precautions.

The bad news was that it continued to rain. Many of the men lurched toward Liberty listlessly, like the walking, wet dead.

"This sort of thing went on night after night, while I escorted men in at 3:00 and 4:00 a.m.," wrote Newton. The grind, as far as he was concerned, "killed the race so far as racing went. There wasn't a decently fit man left. Even the best of them had to do a considerable amount of walking in order to retain a trifle for the finish."

Payne couldn't keep up his normal steady pace. He started walking frequently, knowing that as long as he didn't fall too far behind he could lose an hour a day and still win. Salo gamely kept running, consistently winning the daily races, and knocking off Payne's lead from 18 hours to 15.

It was, wrote Newton, "a series of journeys . . . which were nothing less than physical torture, and which ultimately reduced the race to a pitiful struggle of listless and worn-out men." In short, Newton concluded, "It was a ghastly nightmare." But even the haggard runners appreciated what Newton was doing for them. After the race was over, the race's surviving runners pitched in and gave Newton his own prize—a race cup.

GUISTO UMEK was the first to the finish, covering the distance in 9 hours and 57 minutes. It was an impressive finish, considering the blinding, demoralizing rain. During the worst of it, runners often sat on the side of the road rather than risk slipping and falling, as several athletes had done. Eventually, they resumed some sort of regular pace, because once again race officials declared a running curfew: Arrive by 1:00 a.m., or good-bye.

Hobbled by a sore ankle and a chafed foot, Salo took longer than usual, arriving around 11:00 at night. Suddenly, a barking dog charged toward him and chased him. Several late-night spectators came to his rescue and managed to keep the canine at bay. Dogs apparently had something for Salo, either loving or loathing the guy.

Payne came in fourth, advancing his lead to more than 17 hours. Hardrock, in contrast, took 17 hours to reach the finish line. He passed it just before 1:00 a.m. Only a couple bleary-eyed race officials and sportswriters were there to greet him.

May 23, Liberty to Middletown, 38 Miles

George Rehayn was upbeat, still crooning his melodies. "I'll have a new song to tickle Broadway with Saturday," promised Rehayn to United Press special correspondent James Powers, and then he hummed a tune called: "I'm Feeling Great."

Powers observed of Rehayn that, "George, while not prominent among the finishers, is prominent for his ditties and is prominent among the unwashed element."

Pyle hadn't been seen since Gary, Indiana, and the top 10 runners worried once again that at the end of the road, they wouldn't get paid. Increasing those doubts and everyone's fury, Pyle sent word that the last portion of the race had been doubled. Once everyone was in New York City, the runners would arrive at Madison Square Garden and run not 10 more miles—but *20*.

Many athletes were furious and depressed. A few trainers contacted Pyle in New York and asked for confirmation that the money was coming.

"I'll pay the winners off in real money, not buttons," promised Pyle, referring to the nationwide pastime of collecting buttons, everything from clothing to political buttons, which especially gained traction as a hobby during his youth in the 1890s.

That simple statement placated most of the runners in and near the top 10. They ran faster, and some of the frowns etched on their faces faded. All were so exhausted that they were willing to believe anything without any evidence.

Doc Payne, not surprisingly, was onboard: "You bet Andy will finish the race by running the 20 miles required," he told reporters.

By the end of the day, Kelly scored a victory of sorts. He was the 46th runner to cross the finish line, ahead of nine other runners, a nice feat, although it had taken him 13 hours, 33 minutes, and 10 seconds. When a race official sarcastically commented on his performance, Kelly snapped, "Well, I'm here, and I'm going to finish."

MAY 24, MIDDLETOWN TO SUFFERN, 38 MILES

Upon glimpsing a sign pointing the way to Suffern, New York, one runner was overheard saying, "Well, isn't that funny? I'm suffer'n."

With 2 days to go, Salo accepted his fate for second place. "No chance of overtaking Andy now," he sighed.

Though most of the runners felt better about Pyle the day before, their worries and anger returned. No one wanted to plod an extra 10 miles around Madison Square Garden's track.

The runners were being required to perform in front of a paying audience for 20 miles. It sounded both cruel and suspicious, as if Pyle was hoping to raise prize money that he didn't have. Most of the runners—particularly the 45 of them who weren't winning money—started slowing their pace and practically snarled in front of the crowds, which did not entice people to come to the postrace carnival. There were whispers of a revolt that was, in part, spurred on by runner William Kerr, a charge he flatly denied.

"I have been blamed for far more than I am responsible for . . . I have never appeared at the nightly control meetings because my contract did not call for that. I did not wish to make an exhibition of myself in the Garden," he admitted, "but I would be foolish to destroy my chances at [being] sixth [in the] money by not competing in the race."

John Pederson was another one who was accused of trying to start a revolt.

Before the race, Pederson was as optimistic as they came about the race that lay ahead. "We'll finish in the Yankee Stadium, and I hope to carry Sunny Old Spokane across the finish line first," he assured his hometown newspaper. Pederson prepared well, having purchased 14 custom-made shoes, 300 pairs of socks, and a raincoat, and more importantly, during the summer of 1927, he had run 5,000 miles and trained throughout the fall and the winter before the race.

"I want to show you my foot," he told a Spokane reporter in January 1928, proud of his bipeds. They were muscular and simply big. He wore a size 14. At 43, he was a trim 180 pounds, confident and thrilled to be embarking on the adventure of a lifetime.

Now he was bitter and broken, having spent some nights sleeping in chicken coops, horse stables, and farm shacks full of grain. George Liebergall, a runner from Bellevue, Alberta, once wrote his sister that one morning, a rooster awakened the men at 3:00. "That was his last crow on earth," Liebergall added.

"An athlete who runs from 40 to 75 miles in a day ought to have a bath and a good rubdown," said Pederson. "But even if he doesn't get the rub, he ought to have a bath. But we have never been rubbed, except those who brought trainers with them, and the only times we got baths without going to the hotels and paying for them ourselves were in places where the YMCA invited us in."

Pyle didn't get it. He always assumed the runners' primary complaint involved the possibility of no prize at the end of the trail, never recognizing that their distress was more along the lines of not being treated like something more than pawns on a chessboard. "The runners need not worry about their money," said Pyle. "There have been only a few grievances, and they didn't mean much. One complainer was a chap who is in 47th place and wouldn't lose even if the money wasn't available."

Pederson was in 47th place.

May 25, Suffern, New York, to Passaic, New Jersey, 24.7 Miles

Pyle was tiring of promising that the money was present and accounted for: "It should not be necessary for me to state that I have funds at my disposal, with which to pay the prizes of $48,500 to the first ten runners," said Pyle in a sharply worded rebuttal sent to reporters. "However, in view of irresponsible rumors to the contrary, I do so state."

The reporters also wanted to know about the fairness of the 20-mile lap at Madison Square Garden. "The race is still my race, and any one who does not wish to run from Passaic to New York, and then run 20 miles on the board track in Madison Square Garden Saturday night is at liberty to withdraw," snapped an exasperated Pyle. "In fact, it would please me greatly if some of the discontented runners who have been trailing the field would withdraw. They have clouded a brilliant race, run for sport's sake, with sordidness."

He may have been thinking of how the night before, several runners drank at a bar, celebrating the upcoming end to the race. As they ran to Passaic the next day, they occasionally burst into song, spouting out deliriously vulgar lyrics about Pyle, which they had made up the night before.

Bill Pickens was also working the media, trying to ensure the public that the finish of the race would be worth seeing and to keep his and Pyle's reputations intact. "This race was absolutely fair," said Pickens. "We disqualified three men for cheating. It was impossible to cheat without discovery. Every runner was a detective, as his own chance to win would be lessened if a rival stole a ride."

The second-to-last stop was John Salo's hometown, and so the crowds were especially frenzied, particularly since their hero was in line for second place. It was only a 24.7-mile run, practically a leisurely walk. Cars crammed the roads, and all but one of the runners slowed down so that Salo could stride into town in first place; English runner Richard Thomas, mired in 39th place, decided to make it a race and overtook Salo at a critical moment downtown. Salo was motivated, though, and burst ahead of Thomas to cross the finish line first.

When Payne came through Passaic, he was accompanied by the police, amidst rumors that some overly enthusiastic hometown folk might try to break one of his legs or kidnap him, to put Salo in first place. The police department also allowed the runners to sleep in their newly constructed cellblock at their headquarters. Pyle gratefully accepted, since he had nothing better arranged. The police also offered Salo a job on the force when the race was finished. They had little doubt Salo would be up to the physical demands of the position.

"That's wonderful," said Salo, accepting the position before quipping nervously, "But will C. C. Pyle ask for half of my wages?"

May 26, Passaic, New Jersey, to New York City, 12.2 Miles, Plus 20 More in Madison Square Garden

The last day of the Bunion Derby was the closest thing to a day off the runners received. The whistle didn't blow until 4:00 p.m., allowing for a day to reflect on what everyone had been through. Sammy Robinson, the boxer from Atlantic City, expressed everyone's feelings: "I'm doggoned glad this is near over. My feet are so hot, they burned the blankets last night. When I get back to my home town of Atlantic City, I'm going to put little Sammy beside that old ocean and stick my feet in, and I'm going to say, 'Drink, dogs, drink!'"

There was also time to wander around, which brought some trouble to

Piu, the "female" poison snake charmer. She was behind a tent shaving—and not her legs—when an astonished and naïve sportswriter wandered by. Even more disappointing, Piu's assistant was stuffing fresh wood chips into what were supposed to be living and breathing snakes.

It was around this time that Steve Owen regretted having to tell Pyle about the destruction of another patrol car. Pyle had no time to fret over that, however, having been informed that his old nemesis, the Illinois Trust and Savings Bank of Champaign, was coming after him again. Just a few weeks after paying them $5,000, either Pyle hadn't made another prearranged payment, or the bankers figured that if he could pay the Bunion Derby runners, he could pay the bank as well. They sued him for the remainder of the money he owed, plus apparently some fees and interest: $16,626.

But Pyle couldn't worry about that either. His first objective was to get everyone into New York City and throw a party. He didn't let anyone see through his façade of self-assurance. "I could have packed Yankee Stadium," he mentioned, answering a question about the expected turnout that night. It wasn't an unreasonable statement. Oklahoma City saw 100,000 fans show up for the race; common sense suggested that New York City promised to double or triple that.

As an ever-confident Pyle told one sportswriter near the end of the race, "Sad to say, reflecting as it does upon the judgment of the great American press, my derby was treated too facetiously. It was burlesqued by the funny writers. Instead of a stunt, it was the greatest experiment in physical science ever attempted. History will give me the credit for being a great scientific pioneer, while all I get now is the dough."

And to another reporter, Pyle promised, "I'm going to give Broadway a real show. Theatrical producers who invade the great open spaces always boast of a New York east. I will say that I am presenting my own—bigger than Barnum's—with its own Mojave desert atmosphere, the blisters, the sunburn, the whiskers, and sprinkle of sand from out where men are men."

It was important that the same type of frenzy seen in Passaic recur at the finish line in New York. Pyle expected a large line of people at Madison Square Garden regardless, but the sight of the runners streaking into the arena would just make that line of customers grow even more. And thus, many of the runners came to the starting line in Passaic wearing clean running uniforms.

Pyle made certain the men had a place to shave and bathe (some of the runners still hadn't done either since the race began). Several men, wanting to do Pyle no favors or a little too accustomed to their own filth, remained unshaven, unbathed, and in the same clothes that they had worn since their journey started. Wildfire Thompson, for one, stuck with his red long underwear and bushy beard. People had taken to calling him "the bearded skeleton."

But though they were gaunt and sunburned, many of the men looked quite respectable. Meanwhile, Doc Payne, preparing for the big day, shed his farm duds and put on a white shirt and tie.

At 4:00 p.m., the whistle blew for the last time. Around that point, as cars honked and the crowd cheered, mostly for Salo, the Derby runners were confronted with a vaguely familiar sight.

Ukulele Jake.

It was as if he had never left. The young hobo had his beloved instrument, and his two dogs were with him. Cheerful as ever, Ukulele Jake ran with the men, just like old times.

The runners traversed the first 10.5 miles of Day 84 with relative ease. Their aim was to reach the ferry in Weehawken, New Jersey, and then sprint from 42nd Street in Manhattan to 10th Avenue, where they would jog into Madison Square Garden and gallop another 20 miles.

Thomas Ellis, a Canadian, was the first man to reach the ferry, with some downtime, since Pyle had made it clear that the runners would board all at once. The last one there was Sydney Morris, a 43-year-old currently in 51st place, who arrived at 6:25 in the evening. For whatever reason, the ferry didn't shove off until 8:00. Crammed with runners, trainers, race officials, carnival workers, and assorted others, including a gaggle of girls that badgered the runners for autographs, the ferry reached the other side of the Hudson River 19 minutes later. The racers filed off the boat and started down 42nd Street. A small crowd of well-wishers welcomed the ferry, but the street itself was surprisingly sparse.

As the athletes kept going, though, word of mouth preceded them, and interested bystanders ambled over to gawk, shout, and cheer.

"There's Andy," a girl from the Bronx cheered. "Ain't he the good-looking kid?"

Red Grange wanted to cheer, too. "Maybe you think I'm not glad this thing is over?" he asked a reporter on the day of the final run. "I never was so tired of anything in my life. They nearly ran me crazy in the small towns. I'm going back to Wheaton for a little rest as soon as this crazy thing is over."

The police escorted the athletes past growing crowds as they approached Madison Square Garden, and almost on cue, the car following Tobie Cotton finally broke down.

Henry Cotton's 13-year-old son, Wesley, helped push the car that had brought them across deserts and mountains, past cornfields, and into Madison Square Garden. There, Henry Cotton propped himself on the running board of the car, looking ragged in baggy and dirty corduroys, with a look of concern chiseled on his face as Tobie made his way around the track.

Wesley kept supplying his brother with water, refilling an empty bottle of ginger ale and bringing it to Tobie. Henry's son would finish no higher than 35th, but Tobie's persistence paid off for the family, anyway. According to Will Rogers, in an article he penned the following year, a contingent of African American admirers presented Ed Gardner and Tobie Cotton with $1,000 each at the end of the race. Rogers didn't mention if Phillip Granville and Sammy Robinson, both black, also received the same honor. Especially exciting for Tobie was that he got to meet performer Bill "Bojangles" Robinson, who was currently starring in a Broadway smash *Blackbirds of 1928* and would in the next decade gain much fame as the elder dance partner of child actress Shirley Temple.

The sidewalks outside were mobbed, and yet few people filtered into Madison Square Garden to see the runners cross the finish line. Nor was there interest in the carnival. Once the sideshow was in place, Tex Rickard strode into Madison Square Garden and spotted Elmer McCurdy, the Oklahoma outlaw, in his coffin.

Rickard stared at the mummy. He looked thunderstruck.

"What do you think of the outlaw, kid?" asked Westbrook Pegler.

"Think of him?" roared Rickard. "Why, he's nothing but a goddamn dead man. A hell of a place to show a dead man," he said, gesturing at his newly built Madison Square Garden. "We've got to get him out of here."

It was yet another humiliation for McCurdy, following one the night before. Someone in Passaic vandalized the Oklahoma outlaw, breaking off one of Elmer McCurdy's fingers.

The outlaw was shuttled out of the spotlight, and McCurdy would remain in the darkness of obscurity for the next 48 years, until December 1976, when it was discovered that the petrified thief was working on the set of *The Six Million Dollar Man*. While filming a fun-house scene, someone bumped into what was supposed to be a wax dummy, and when the arm fell off, a protruding bone revealed another story altogether. McCurdy was finally buried and put to rest.

And it was soon clear that C. C. Pyle's amazing foot race needed to be put to rest. For starters, it didn't help the runners' morale that most of the public hadn't bothered to show up at the finish line. Few people had the appetite to shell out $1.65 for the privilege of going into Madison Square Garden to visit the carnival and watch the runners circle the track for a couple hours, considering that the actual winners were easy to spot as far back as Ohio. It was enough for the public to stand on the street and watch with fascination as the haggard runners hobbled past them into the stadium—and then go home.

Those who came saw interesting things—but nothing resembling athletics. Wildfire Thompson puffed on a cigarette and downed gulps from his whiskey flask, ambling along the track, 500 hours behind Payne. George

Jussick, who had numerous hours added to his time because he was drunk in Illinois, was chain-smoking. Rehayn broke out into what one writer called "insane snatches of song." Many of the runners were bandaged from injuries sustained along the way, including dog bites.

Thomas Goodwin, a Californian who finished in 12th place, was in particular agony. The day before, he had broken his foot. This close to his destination, he couldn't bear the thought of quitting, and so he hobbled along, dragging his foot. The race was torture to run and torture to watch.

Pyle could see that. These didn't look like the superhuman athletes who were going to make Pyle millions. Who would want to pay to see a bunch of invalids shuffling at a snail's pace?

"Come on, you fellows," shouted Pyle, as they struggled onto a slippery, concrete track at Madison Square Garden. "Streak it, boys, streak it! Show 'em what I've brought to New York."

Many of the runners automatically sprinted, but that only lasted a few minutes. Injury, resentment, and maybe a bit of gravity took over. Soon the runners returned to shuffling along, and several men pulled out bananas and sandwiches from their pockets. Others drank bottles of pop, as they moseyed forward.

"Show your mettle, boys," shouted Pyle, looking panicked.

The seats at Madison Square Garden were filling, but the attendance did not live up to Pyle's hopes. There were fewer than 2,000 people in an arena that sat 15,000, and some were friends and family members of the runners. Hardrock, for one, had several cheering him on at the finish. Several college students and his older brother drove up to see him, leaving Burlington, North Carolina, the day before.

The spectators with no personal connection to the runners likely regretted their decision immediately. Eugene Germaine, for one, was painful to follow. The French Canadian had the dubious distinction of being the first to sign up to be in the race, and now his left leg, from the ankle to below the knee, was swollen to almost twice its normal size. Germaine was in

46th place, moving at the speed of molasses, but he had run across the entire continent. He felt good about that.

Salo was giving a good show, running like his life depended on it, while Payne cruised at his usual rate. But most of the runners were closer to Germaine's state of health. Umek was still weak from stomach pains that developed about 2 weeks earlier, apparently unrelated to his poisoning in Gary, Indiana. Abramowitz was nursing shin splints, Perrella had his wrenched hip, and Codeluppi had calloused feet and an especially sore knee.

The press wasn't impressed. The *New York Sun* called the race as a whole "the flop of the century," and the *Newark Evening News* described the runners as "emaciated scarecrows, unshaven, unshorn, caricatures."

"The affair could hardly be dignified by calling it a sporting event," cracked the paper in Dunkirk, New York.

Sportswriters were everywhere, in fact, taking notes, interviewing and writing articles. Most of the reporters' faces were a blur, but Hardrock, years later, would see one of them on television and suddenly make a connection to the Bunion Derby. Ed Sullivan, host of the longest-running variety series in television (1948–1971) was a sportswriter for the *New York Evening Graphic*.

In the audience, a bored and wealthy man showed off $100 and offered it to whomever could win a mile sprint. Several men tried it—Oregonian Allen Currier won, happily scampering away with his only prize money after running more than 3,400 miles.

And then, it started to end. Salo crossed the finish line first, running 32 miles in 3 hours and 46 minutes. He was so happy, he ran another lap. When Payne finished 45 minutes later, the remaining spectators broke into a huge cheer, and it was official. Andy Payne from Foyil, Oklahoma, a 20-year-old with little money and prospects, won.

Pyle rushed forward, hustling his new meal ticket to face a swarm of camera bulbs. Doc Payne lost his reserve. According to a United Press reporter, Doc was "the happiest man in the garden. He jumped up and down in a frenzy, unable to control his joy."

Andy's mother was also thrilled. She was thinning the corn crop in Foyil when her third cousin rushed over to see her. He was the secretary of the state market commission and received word of Payne's win over the telegraph wire. Mrs. Payne wasn't wearing her glasses and asked George to read the news to her. After he finished, she fell to the ground, where she lay crying, a puddle of happiness and relief.

"Ain't it wonderful? It's all over," said Zona Payne. "I'm so glad it's all over. You don't know what a suspense it has been. Two and one half months it has been . . . with Andrew running every day, without Sunday off. I was afraid he would get hurt, or his heart would break down."

All of the runners were thrilled. Granville summed up his physical accomplishment accurately, if immodestly: "Lindbergh only sat down and drove an engine for 36 hours. I ran 84 days, on my feet."

For the next 10 minutes, photographers surrounded Payne, one of the most famous men in the country, and for once, he didn't seem to mind the attention. After Payne ran a grand total of 3,421.5 miles, there was a lot of laughter and animated conversation as he jockeyed to answer questions from sportswriters, race officials, and well-wishers.

But Payne had two questions of his own: Would Vivian allow him to call on her, and would Pyle cough up his prize money?

He knew the first answer would have to wait until he returned to Oklahoma. The second question wouldn't be answered for at least another week. In the meantime, Payne tried to make the best of it. He and his father celebrated the victory the next day by taking a sightseeing excursion of New York City—a walking tour.

CHAPTER 18

Andy Payne's father (left) in his earlier years and (right) in his later years. (Courtesy of the Vivian S. Payne collection.)

WAITING GAME

TOTAL DISTANCE: 3,421.5 MILES; 55 RUNNERS

MAY 26 (6 DAYS UNTIL JUNE 1), NEW YORK CITY

Late that night, discussing the race with a reporter in his suite at the Hotel Biltmore, C. C. Pyle was stoic, even upbeat. "The papers all spelled the name right, which is the important thing. You know," he added, "you have to have a sense of humor in this promotion business, and most important of all, you must keep it working overtime. I'm not only satisfied with the outcome of this year's race but also plan to re-stage it next year. In my next cross-country race, the entrance fee will be $250 instead of the $125 demanded this year. The runners will be required to feed and house themselves as well as taking care of their trainers. This will eliminate innumerable squawks regarding the cuisine."

Pyle interrupted the interview to answer the telephone. It was an ex-runner, Sydney Morris, who placed 51st. The runners had been calling ever since the race ended. Pyle told Morris to drop around the hotel the next morning to collect the $100 deposit money. "Is one hundred all I get?" thundered Morris on the other end of the phone. "Think what I suffered in this race, Mr. Pyle. Shouldn't I get a little something extra for my suffering?"

"What do I get for *my* suffering?" Pyle retorted. "I've suffered, too, Morris. I have wrinkles in my trouser pockets from digging and writer's cramp from signing checks to bring you from Los Angeles to New York. See me in the morning, and get your $100."

Pyle hung up the phone, pivoting back to his interviewer with a remark that could simultaneously be interpreted as sympathy toward Morris and as a plea for respect for himself: "Yes, this pioneering a sport is a tough racket, but you can't hang a guy for trying."

SYDNEY MORRIS hung up the phone and, in all likelihood, realized that he wouldn't be sleeping in a hotel. The runners who had no place to go and were too sleepy, exhausted, and broke to find lodging were offered another option.

They were given permission to sleep in the basement of Madison Square Garden, where the visiting animals were kept.

Sunday, May 27 (5 Days until June 1)

The next morning, the overnight guests in Madison Square Garden were kicked out. Many of the men spent the next several nights sleeping on New York City sidewalks.

Wildfire Thompson was one of several runners who couldn't stand still. He was still wearing his long underwear and lengthy beard—and found himself jogging up and down the block and playing catch with kids on a street near Madison Square Garden.

"I believe in tapering off," explained Thompson, who had checked into a nearby hotel. "When you've been through torture like this, it is a dangerous thing to stop agony all at once. A little while ago, I got kind of scared.

I said to myself, 'I miss something.' Then I said, 'Oh, yes, I miss those stabbing pains.' When all the misery's gone you feel kind of lonesome and lost. A lot of the boys are feeling terrible and don't know what's wrong with them. The thing they are suffering from is a lack of pain."

Several runners rented rooms on the same hotel floor as Pyle. Every chance they got, they asked whether Pyle could pay the prize money. The press wanted to know about the money, too, and Pyle stalled reporters with a lengthy speech.

"The human foot is going to come into its own," said Pyle. "I have made such a study of the ailments of the human walking mechanism as has never been equaled, and I claim to know more about toe trouble, heel trouble, instep trouble and ankle trouble than any man living. I can tell you exactly what to do for anything that goes wrong from the knee down. I am going to write a treatise on chiropody in English, which he who runs may read, and I am going to give away one copy with every purchase of C. C. Pyle's Patent Foot Box, which will contain remedies for every one of the 3,000 maladies of the human foot. I will make vast sums out of this because the country is going marathon mad," said Pyle, who suddenly seemed a little mad himself.

"We are just entering the golden age of the foot," continued Pyle. "There are going to be more marathons, more 26-hour footraces, more 6-day footraces and more transcontinental footraces than anybody would have dreamed to be possible. All along our route, children who could hardly walk were out trying to keep up with my transcontinental runners. Schoolboys were organizing cross-country runs and marathons. We are going to have hundreds of thousands of distance runners in this country, and every one of them will naturally buy C. C. Pyle's Patent Foot Box. All that I hope is that the present rage for traveling great distances on foot does not go too far. Some of my best friends are in the automobile business."

Pyle looked regretful for a moment, as if he hated to bring down Henry Ford's empire, before he continued, saying: "But I will not have to wait for profits to accrue from the miraculous foot fixer in order to pay my athletes their prizes. They will get them immediately after the 26-hour foot race, which will begin on Friday at 9 o'clock and end on Saturday at 11 o'clock. My contract does not stipulate that I pay them at any particular time," he noted, "and I am perfectly within my rights in paying them then. As to worry whether I can pay the $48,500 in prizes or not, that is absurd. That is all attended to. It is true that we are in the red at present. It is impossible to say how much, but we expected to lose money on the race. That is under the head of promotion expenses. I will race the 10 winners that I have under contract in marathons and 26-hour races in all the big cities of the country and hold bigger annual transcontinental derbies every year. We are in the early stages of the thing."

Pyle wasn't finished. When asked about the poor conditions that the athletes faced on the trip, he said, "Those fellows are *men*. They're not crying. Of course, they've been through a lot. A transcontinental race is no kissing bee. It's done 'em a world of good, a world of good. All those boys are in marvelous health—from the ankles up."

Bill Pickens was, for possibly the first time ever, not optimistic. Around this time, in an interview, he expressed the opinion that the country had been "over-thrilled."

Monday, May 28 (4 Days until June 1)

Thomas Goodwin was in a hospital. He had taken his $100 from Pyle and used that to have his broken foot treated. Later, when his doctor bills were paid, Goodwin purchased a shoe-shining kit, planning to work his way back to California. When a Pennsylvania newspaper profiled him in August 1928, Goodwin's hope was that he would make it home by Christmas.

Tuesday, May 29 (3 Days until June 1)

Will Rogers wrote another missive to the *New York Times*, expressing his affection for the Payne family. He noted that his childhood pal, Doc Payne, named his youngest Will Rogers Payne. "I am certainly going to try and keep him from running down to Buenos Aires, or up to Alaska or somewhere," wrote Rogers. "If Andy don't get this prize money this certainly ought to be a lesson to never run that fir unless he is sure. If I was him from now on I would just enter some short sprints of maybe just 1,050 or 2,000 miles."

Andy Payne flew that day to Washington, D.C. He was scheduled to meet with President Calvin Coolidge, who turned out to be too busy. But Andy's congressman, who called him "America's greatest runner," introduced him to much applause in the House of Representatives.

Pyle tried to remain positive. By the way he spun things to one journalist, he sounded glad the newspapers were reporting how broke he was. "If I tell everyone I've got plenty of money to pay off, that makes only one story," said Pyle. "But if they think I can't pay, that makes a lot of stories. And, besides, when they put in the paper that you're broke, that cuts attachments and suits down to about one third."

One would hate to see what happened if the papers reported that Pyle was rich. Before the day was over, he was notified that he was being sued by Jay Peters, owner of the mobile radio station. Pyle still owed him $3,183, which included $228 in incidentals, $480 in railroad fare for the men to return home, and $2,475 in back rent for the station. Pyle also learned that star client Red Grange was named as a defendant in the ongoing lawsuit by the Illinois Trust and Savings Bank of Champaign. Grange was now just as responsible for the remaining $16,626 that Pyle owed. And in the next few weeks, one Mrs. Susan Retherford, an enigmatic figure in Pyle's life, would sue him for $28,543.89. She had done work for him in Illinois and New York, where for a time she oversaw his daughter's education. The suit involved a home he had purchased for her in Danville, Illinois, which he had stopped paying the mortgage on, and he was supposed to be paying her rent in New York City.

Wednesday, May 30 (2 Days until June 1)

Pyle released a statement to quell growing suspicion of his ability to pay out the prize money. "To quiet rumors that have persisted in connection with the possibility of a failure to pay in full and in cash the $48,500 I offered to the first ten to finish in the transcontinental foot race from Los Angeles to New York, I now declare that amount will be placed in the hands of Tex Rickard Thursday afternoon and will be paid to the winners in the arena of Madison Square Garden at 8 o'clock Friday night, one hour before the start of the 26-hour team running race." (The winners of that race would also get some cash prize money.)

Pyle had another fire to put out. He learned that he and F. F. Gunn were being sued by five employees of his race, including Steve Owen, who felt obliged to "crash" cars to earn his back pay. Neither Owen nor Pyle took umbrage at the other's conduct, however: The following year, Owen worked for Pyle again. Neither man had hard feelings because they both understood what everyone who came to know the sports promoter understood: To know Pyle was to eventually sue him.

Why was Gunn being sued? As gifted a businessman as he was, he wasn't omnipotent. The contract for their partnership was signed in Gary, Indiana, and because they hadn't sent their paperwork to the state, by law they were considered general partners. To know Pyle was to sue him—or to be sued with him.

Thursday, May 31
(The Day before the Big Day, June 1)

On Thursday afternoon the *New York Times* reported breathlessly, if facetiously, on Pyle's every move. Word for word, here's its timeline:

5:35 p.m. *Mr. Pyle just left the Hotel Vanderbilt with the $48,500 to give to Mr. Rickard.*

5:45 p.m. *Mr. Pyle is still at the Hotel Vanderbilt but is just about to leave with $48,500 for Mr. Rickard.*

5:55 p.m. *Mr. Pyle actually hasn't been at his headquarters at the Hotel Vanderbilt for two hours and nobody knows where he is.*

6:05 p.m. *Pyle left his headquarters twenty minutes ago with a suitcase full of money to give to Mr. Rickard.*

6:15 p.m. *Mr. Pyle has not been here since early this morning and nobody knows where he is.*

6:25 p.m. *Mr. Pyle has just arrived at the hotel and will leave for Madison Square Garden with the money.*

6:40 p.m. *Pyle left for Madison Square Garden two hours ago and everybody is very much worried about what happened to him. Are there any hold-up men still operating in New York?*

6:50 p.m. *Mr. Pyle has been hunting for the vice president of a bank who has to sign the draft.*

7:00 p.m. *Through the error of a bank in California, the money was sent to the wrong New York bank, and it is too late to rectify the error today, so that the draft-presentation ceremony must be delayed until tomorrow morning.*

Pyle's struggle to collect the prize money from the bank certainly seemed to suggest he raised the money himself, but as Payne told a historical group at Oklahoma Christian College years later, Tex Rickard more or less bailed him out. Besides, if the money was coming from Pyle, why on earth, after 80-odd days on the road, would Rickard be the one presenting prizes to the runners?

Friday, June 1

Pyle announced on June 1 that the winning runners would receive their money right before the 26-hour race at 9:00 p.m., Saturday night, not on Friday, as originally planned. "I'll have the money, and in greenbacks today," promised Pyle.

Meanwhile, the winner of the Bunion Derby received a welcome surprise on Friday when a telegram from the Oklahoma City Chamber of Commerce informed him that the $5,000 that had been planned for Pyle—until he went to court saying that the money wasn't owed to him—would instead be given to Payne. The telegram said that he would receive $4,097.20—expenses for the race apparently subtracted. "We have felt a moral obligation to pay," the telegram stated.

SATURDAY, JUNE 2

Mike Kelly must have been crushed to learn he wouldn't be running the 26-hour marathon or working for Pyle. Earlier in the week, he returned to Goshen, Indiana, to wait for word from Pyle and enjoy some hometown glory. But Pyle naturally chose the 40 men he thought were the best of the runners, even if they hadn't reached New York City. Arthur Newton and Pete Gavuzzi accepted invitations to run the race. Even Italian runner Joe Conto, who excitedly hugged Hardrock after each day's race and had bailed early in California, was there.

Hardrock came in 36th, a respectable finish considering all of the aches, pains, bruises, blisters, charley horses and shin splints he endured. Hardrock was not asked to run the 26-hour race and, in view of his condition, may have been grateful. Earlier in the week, he returned to Burlington, North Carolina, whose residents lavished him with attention; he was quickly recruited to perform in the local vaudeville theatre.

Harry Sheare, the Alaskan musher hit by a car in Ohio, was also not on the team roster. He was an excellent runner and chased the Bunion Derby with the sole purpose of entering this valedictory race, but Pyle had only a certain number of slots to fill for his runners. Pyle wasn't one to carry a grudge, but Sheare had been a troublemaker in Texola, Oklahoma, and Pyle may well have decided he didn't want to be working with the guy for 2 more years.

That evening, the runners jogged into Madison Square Garden, and something went wrong immediately. Payne collided with a pillar, knocking himself out for a few moments. He was otherwise unhurt, but he hadn't been paying attention, going through the motions of running. He was weary. The last thing he felt like doing was running off and on for 26 hours. He just wanted his check.

Shortly before 9:00 p.m., a brass band blared, and Payne, Newton, Gavuzzi, and 37 other runners stood in the middle of the track, staring at their surroundings. They expected Madison Square Garden to be filled with 15,000 or more people, and, granted, they were just at the start of a 26-hour race, but things didn't look good. Two hundred people were in attendance.

C. C. Pyle kept smiling, nevertheless, as if his reputation wasn't falling apart before him.

Aside from the $48,500 for running the Bunion Derby, there was $5,000 in prize money at stake for the top runners in the 26-hour foot odyssey, and the event would be conducted in a way similar to the then-popular 6-day bicycle races. The men would run in relays, like the cyclists, relieving each other whenever someone needed a break. That way, over the 26 hours, at least one man on a team could sleep—rather humane by Pyle's standards.

The runners were in the middle of the arena along with two rows of iron beds. Each cot was equipped with two chairs, and in the middle of the floor was a rubbing table for any athlete who needed a massage. Next to that was the brass band. That was it, giving the place a rather barren look, especially with so few spectators there to watch.

Pyle, his hat off and gray hair showing, stepped into view. He joined Tex Rickard, in a dark suit and bright green hat. Both men walked across the arena, as if they hadn't noticed the dearth of clapping and cheers.

Rickard was even more of an egomaniac than Pyle, and he strode onto a stage before motion-picture cameras to present the top 10 Bunion Derby runners with bank drafts. His voice echoed in the empty arena—one observer pointed out that he sounded like a small boy shouting in a tunnel.

There was an announcer who in godlike tones spoke through an amplifier, his voice bouncing off empty seats. He used words like "greatest" and "most extraordinary" and "in the history of the world" to describe the race, only heightening everyone's embarrassment.

Finally the announcer called Andy's name, and Payne received a check for $25,000. Seconds later, Rickard grabbed it back, and Payne tensed up, looking as if he was going to slug the famous promoter. Rickard quickly explained that a photographer had gotten there late and asked if they could repeat a shot of the check being handed over. They did, and then John Salo received his $10,000. Phillip Granville won third place and $5,000. Mike Joyce came in fourth, earning $2,500. Umek was in fifth place, and took away $1,000, as did the runners who finished sixth through 10th: William Kerr, Louis Perrella, Ed Gardner (who also received a large bouquet of pink and white flowers from his admirers), Frank Von Flue, and John Cronick.

Payne had run the entire distance in 588 hours, 40 minutes, and 13 seconds. For comparison's sake, Wildfire Thompson came in 50th and had traversed the country in over 1,000 hours.

Minutes after the checks were handed out and Andy gave his to his father for safekeeping, the 26-hour race began at 9:00 p.m. The runners, half of them, broke out into a run; the others stood near their cots.

It was, as advertised, a long race. Most of the men's muscles were still stiff and tender, and they moved as though they were wearing lead boots. They were quite literally going through the motions.

Not to be deterred, Pyle enthusiastically shouted, "C'mon, boys, show 'em what you've got!"

The men had little left, but they all ran at various points during the 26 hours. Conto collapsed the next day at 5:30 p.m., unconscious for an hour until he managed to get up and continue running off and on until the end of the race that night. (He later said that his doctor blamed the collapse on overeating and insufficient rest.) Of the 20 teams, four wouldn't complete the 26-hour race, saddled by fatigue. Payne ran the 26-hour race apathetically. Inside, however, he was anything but. When he finished running,

Payne knew that he finally had more than enough money to help his family's farm, and he hoped that Vivian had begun to notice him. Maybe she would even consider breaking up with the man she was supposedly dating. Now all he had to do was go home and find out.

Throughout the 26-hour race, Pyle refused to admit defeat. "There'll be more today," he said, referring to the attendance. "And what's more, next year, the transcontinental race will be the big event. Next year, I won't let them in for $25 a piece, and I'll make them feed and house themselves en route. I may have lost money, but I'll get it back next year."

"Next year, next year," Pyle kept repeating throughout the race.

The next morning, as dawn splashed across the city, all 20 cots were filled with exhausted, mostly bearded skeletons with skin; the men running on the track looked no better, and there were still over 12 hours to go. The runners on the cots wiggled their sore toes, rinsed their throats, and spit water on the floor. They made themselves at home: Open suitcases and wet, crumpled newspapers lay next to the beds, and clothes hung over the backs of chairs. In the stands, 50 bleary-eyed spectators were wondering what the hell they were watching.

Later that day, as the race ended, Pyle was borne out as being corrected. Attendance had climbed; in fact, the stands had swelled to 150 people, who all watched Granville and Von Flue finish first, splitting $1,000. Newton and Gavuzzi split $750 for their troubles. Payne collected another $350, to divvy up with August Fager, who had angrily quit the race back in Chandler, Oklahoma. Not one to hold a grudge, Pyle brought him back nevertheless.

And from the moment he entered to the moment he exited Madison Square Garden, Pyle looked positively delighted. If the race hadn't turned out how he envisioned it, maybe it didn't matter: Pyle delivered. He brought the runners across America; staged a parade of sorts for dozens of towns; publicized Highway 66, whether the highway officials appreciated it or not; and he made 10 runners wealthier than they were before. Because of his race, Charles Cassius Pyle had changed lives, some even for the better.

As an ecstatic Mike Joyce told him several days earlier, after signing a deal with a vaudeville theatre that agreed to pay him $350 a week, "Why, Mr. Pyle, you made me famous. I'll never forget you. My five children have nothing to worry about now, and all because of you."

Perhaps the showman in the midst of Madison Square Garden was thinking along those lines because he seemed so pleased. He didn't know that Mike would return to his welding job before the year was up. During thc 26-hour race, C. C. Pyle sat in the center of the ring, grinning while he watched his runners do their laps, continuing to look as if he had discovered the fountain of youth or the cure for tuberculosis. He kept that smile even when the race finished and Rickard's cleaning crew began sweeping up. He was, as one newspaper put it, "the Peter Pan of optimists."

Epilogue: End of the Line

Despite all of his troubles during the Bunion Derby, Paul "Hardrock" Simpson, shown here much later in life, was a lifelong runner. (Courtesy of the Simpson family.)

June 3, 1928, New York City

"Well, I seem to have made a mistake," admitted C. C. Pyle, watching the bubbles rise in his beer as he talked with sports columnist Westbrook Pegler. "I felt certain that after those 55 fellows of mine had run all the way across the continent, the customers would come out to see them finish indoors," said Pyle, his voice tinged with regret. "But they didn't. That is, we got about $4,000 that night last week, but you know what the rent of the Garden is, with ushers and lights and all. I was expecting more."

Even Pyle's plans for having his superhuman athletes under contract weren't working out. William Kerr enlisted a lawyer to represent him and several other runners who wanted nothing more to do with Pyle. Kerr's attorney said that while the runners may have signed contracts stating that they would basically be a marathon's equivalent of indentured servants for the next 2 years, Pyle violated the terms in his own pact so many times that he stood little chance of enforcing his document in front of a judge.

"I thought a 26-hour race between the best runners in the transcontinental field would draw them," Pyle continued. "But there weren't more than 300 people in the house across the way there, even at the finish. So I will just admit that C. C. Pyle has taken one on his chin this time. I think I will go to Europe for the summer. I need the rest, and, anyway, I want to go to the Olympic games and have a look and a long laugh at those amateurs who call themselves distance runners. But New York isn't the world," said Pyle, suddenly looking cheerful.

Pyle continued to expound on the aftermath of the Bunion Derby: "That boy Stanley Payne, or Andy Payne, or whatever his name is—the one I paid $25,000 last night for winning the cross-country race—will be worth some money in Oklahoma," concluded Pyle. "I'm going to take him down there and do a Lindbergh with him at the county fairs. We'll get some money yet. Then Europe for the summer. But I'll be back. I'll have something new."

And roughly 2 weeks later, C. C. Pyle was ready to make good on his promise.

"When I was out on the Hopi Indian reservation, signing up some runners," he told a reporter, "I complained about being too fat. The chief gave me some pills to take, and they reduced me in a week. I bought the patents on the pills, and when I get around to it, I'm going to give it to the public. I'm going into every town in the country, hire the fattest woman I can find and put her in the drug store window," promised C. C. Pyle. "I'm going to feed her those pills and let the public see her fade away. And I ask you, will the public buy those pills!"

Pyle never did actually market weight-loss pills. He would try something else, though, something vaguely familiar.

1929

Pyle discussed making the Bunion Derby an annual event from the beginning. What no one expected was that Pyle would go through with it, particularly after the financial drubbing he took. Sure enough, though, Pyle organized a *second* international transcontinental race the following year.

From the start, the second race looked more promising. The event began in New York City, so the men wouldn't have to endure the blistering heat of the desert at the very beginning, which Pyle hoped would preserve runners at the start. Will Rogers gave the race a lot of respectability by firing the starting gun, though he declined to travel with the Bunion Derby.

Various chambers of commerce across the country seemed thrilled to bring the Bunion Derby to their towns and were more than willing to pay Pyle for the privilege. Truly striking was the number of repeat runners: John Salo and Pete Gavuzzi returned, as did Ed Gardner, Guisto Umek, Roy McMurtry, Harry Abramowitz, Morris Saperstein, Mike Joyce, Arthur Newton, Hardrock, and many others. Maybe most surprising was the inclusion of Patrick De Marr, thrown out during the first race for hitchhiking. He had his entry fee; all had been forgiven.

Contract or not, Payne ignored Pyle's entreaties to defend his title. Payne became the assistant director of the race, filling Red Grange's old role, crossing the country not by foot but in a Ford sedan.

Rather than the carnival, Pyle brought in a vaudeville troupe, which had eight dancing ladies, some comics, a few actors, and a lot of actresses. Payne also did lasso tricks that Will Rogers taught him. They were to perform once every afternoon and evening during the race.

Pyle also upped the prize money from $48,500 to $60,000, with the first 15 runners entitled to prizes.

Russ Newland of the Associated Press went along again and concluded a couple years later, "It was like seeing a movie for the second time. The kick was gone."

Good point, though in many ways there was even more drama during the second race. What doomed the idea of a third race was the second Bunion Derby's unhappy ending. In the days after everyone ran from New York to San Diego, it soon became apparent that this time, Pyle couldn't pay the runners. They ran all that way—and got nothing.

Everyone, particularly Salo and Gavuzzi, in first and second place, was furious. Pyle was sued, and a few months later, the police put a warrant out for Pyle's arrest and took him in. Humiliated, the showman declared bankruptcy and finally uttered a sentence to the media that had never passed his lips before: "Boys, I'm flat broke."

Everyone scattered to different parts of the country and led their lives.

THE ENDURANCE CONTESTS hung on for the next couple of years. One week after the Bunion Derby fizzled out, promoter Milton Crandall organized a dance marathon at Madison Square Garden, and 11 Bunion Derby participants signed up, midrange obscure plodders who couldn't quite figure out what else to do. What they got themselves into, though, was a doozy. The courts stopped the marathon after 481 hours (20 days) because too many people were dancing past what their bodies could take.

Catalina Island also-swam Norman Ross, a.k.a. Big Moose, for the last few weeks had been talking up an idea that sounded like the Bunion Derby in a river. He envisioned a swimming race stretching from Chicago to New Orleans, or Pittsburgh to St. Paul, Minnesota. It didn't happen.

The Noun and Verb Rodeo, on the other hand, did. Also known as the World Champion Gabfest, it began in December 1928. A staff of nurses, doctors, and dentists were all ready to help out, in case anyone talked him or herself into oblivion. Crandall was once again the organizer, and he offered a $1,000 prize to the 30 men and women who could talk the longest without stopping.

The Great Depression, which began clobbering the country in October 1929, effectively ended endurance competitions, though some forms held on throughout the 1930s. Dance marathons continued into the Depression, when people were even more desperate to win big stakes in prize money, and tree sitting seemed like a nice, safe, and inexpensive diversion. It was an endurance fad that became popular with children for a brief time in 1930, inspired by flagpole sitting.

There was no big money, just bragging rights among neighborhood kids. The beginning of the end came in August 1930, though, when tragedy struck in Ashland, Kentucky. After 496 hours of sitting in a tree, 16-year-old Nelson McIntosh was waiting for his mother to bring him his lunch when he lost his balance. He fell a distance of almost 50 feet and was killed instantly.

Tree sitting suffered another blow later in the year, when a 21-year-old Austrian was shot and killed—a game warden testified that he thought the young man was a wildcat.

OVER THE YEARS, Andy Payne and Vivian kept a scrapbook of mementos from the days gone by of the Bunion Derby. As the rest of the world slowly forgot about the amazing and surreal foot race across the country, the participants couldn't possibly resist looking back, from the early months after the event to many years later. Harry Gunn sent a postcard to "Dear Andy, No 43," during the Christmas season of 1928. Around the same time, Mike Kelly wrote. The letter wasn't saved, but Andy hung on to the envelope, amused because there is a *photograph* of Kelly on the left-hand side. Kelly was quite the self-promoter, even if he risked looking like an egomaniac.

During the 1950s, Dr. Arne Suominen wrote to say he was doing well and was a physician in Hollywood. And in the early 1960s, Antonio Constantinoff, a native of the Soviet Union who was living in Toronto when he ran the Bunion Derby, wrote to Andy, sharing poignant details of his life during World War II, and in a second letter asked, "If possible, send me some photos of that race in 1928. They would be a fine memory to me. Everything I had was lost during the late war."

That the race was a fine memory to Constantinoff may be a testament to how challenging the years were for him afterward. Ten days into the Bunion Derby, the 21-year-old Constantinoff's legs were overcome with boils. He slowed to a steady walk, to give them a better chance to heal. It took 3 weeks until he conquered them. Constantinoff came in 17th place.

In 1977, 49 years after the race, Joe Spangler, a runner from Los Angeles, wrote Payne to reminisce, clearly wishing to revisit their bygone age one last time.

> Dear Andy Payne,
>
> I was indeed thrilled to hear your voice again after all these years. Very nearly a half century has passed since we ran the hills of Elysian Park in Los Angeles. Today the park has been bisected by freeways, roads leading to the Dodger's baseball stadium, etc. Part of the terrain we covered in our six mile or so running jaunt now harbors dwellings, apartment houses, etc.
>
> Several years ago, I tried to map out our old training terrain. It was a nigh impossible task. Today, we would have to cross new boulevards.
>
> As for Ascot Speedway, where Pyle pitched his tents prior to the start of the 1928 race, it is now non-existent. The car line to the north of Ascot is gone. The orange trees that lined the boulevard, El Monte on eastward, are gone, have been replaced by urban blight.
>
> U.S. 66 is now a score of different streets and names. Segments of the route going through Cajon Pass have been replaced at three different times, relocated as a matter of fact.
>
> Confusion results from the fact that there is another Ascot Speedway, this latter day one located about 30 miles away. Naturally, when I speak of Ascot Speedway, there is a lot of confusion. There seems to be no recollection of the one east of Lincoln Park, located on Valley Boulevard. Incidentally, the carousel in Lincoln Park is no more. The park itself is a continuing victim of vandalism.
>
> I have been driving all over southern California, checking out both the 1928 and 1929 routes of the transcontinental marathons. I have been to Arizona with the same purpose in mind.

In another letter, Spangler revealed that he was trying to write a book on the race, and what a book that might have been, from the point of view of one of the actual runners. Which is what he wanted it to be, a story that would focus on the race from the "standpoint of the participants, not from the vantage view of ignorance, as displayed by those who have deprecated the event. Too much emphasis has been placed on Pyle's peccadilloes," he griped, "and not enough on the insurmountable difficulties . . . mental, physical, terrain and weather wise, faced by the runners. I can go on and on, but you know as well as I do what I am talking about." Spangler added, "Believe me, even a slight sweep upward in the road, sometimes for miles, was more tiring and time consuming than similar stretches downhill."

As an alumnus of the Bunion Derby, Spangler may have passed the years feeling frustrated at how the race was remembered, but he led a long and apparently fruitful life. He was among the fortunate.

William Hickman Pickens

C. C. Pyle lost his right-hand man the following year. Pickens declined to participate in the second Bunion Derby and continued in the promotions business. In 1930, Pickens represented two pilots who were going after a world refueling record, but he declared bankruptcy in 1931, citing $500 in assets and debts worth $31,000. By 1933, Pickens was back in automobile racing and, when he was 60, staged a successful 500-mile stock race in February 1934. But Pickens couldn't enjoy his comeback; he stepped on a rusty nail while inspecting the grounds. The wound became infected. He lost his foot, then his leg, then his life.

Red Grange

Weeks after the Bunion Derby, a very weary Grange politely ended things with Pyle and mentioned to the press that he was going to pursue a career in films. "I was the target for three years for the guys who were getting dough out of me. They gave me plenty of beatings, and I'm through with it. I can get four thousand a week in the movies, and that's pretty good. I haven't got the half million the papers say I have, but I don't have to take a beating every Sunday to get groceries."

Before the year was up, Grange's movie career didn't happen, nor did a brief attempt at vaudeville, and he was arrested in connection with a paternity suit. The woman claimed that Grange fathered her 7-month-old baby daughter, whom she named Haroldine. Grange settled for a reported $900.

In 1929, he went back to the Chicago Bears for 5 more solid, if not spectacular, years. Later in life, he became a popular sports announcer. A genial figure until the end, he lived a long and evidently happy life until he passed away in 1991. Despite all his reasons not to, even in old age, he defended Pyle's character, at least publicly. But it's safe to say that of all the years he wouldn't have wanted to relive, 1928 probably ranked first.

Mike Kelly

Over the next few years, Kelly turned to his past career as a professional painter and later became a furniture mover.

During the Great Depression, he channeled C. C. Pyle's business acumen and sold Mike Kelly's Bunion Derby Liniment for 35 cents a bottle. The packaging promised relief from ailments like charley horses, stiffness, cramps, and sprains, and Kelly showed up at local drugstores almost every day to see if anyone had bought his product. He was usually disappointed.

Kelly kept trying to find his niche. He was a trainer at a dance marathon and ran against horses at the fairgrounds. Once, as a publicity stunt for a dairy, he handcuffed himself to a bicycle and rode 55 minutes every hour for 2 weeks. "I rode with him all night once," Kenneth Bickel told the *South Bend Tribune* in 1980. "He was sound asleep riding that bicycle."

Despite his numerous acts of derring-do, or because of them, the locals eventually came to think of Kelly as "a pathetic character," as Goshen sportswriter Dale Peffley told the *Tribune*. Kelly lived with his mother until her death in 1949. "He had a lot of friends," added Peffley, "but he was bashful and backwards—a likeable devil, though."

Like so many people whose personalities were defined by an endurance competition, Kelly couldn't shake the idea that he was still meant to do something big. In the last act of his life, Kelly had a show called "The Great

Kelly—Ride of Death." His advertising promised it would be "the world's greatest suicide thrill act," and he performed it at state and county fairs, mostly in Iowa, Michigan, Ohio, and Texas.

Kelly was truthful in his advertising. On July 4, 1955, when Kelly was 50, he was at a fair in Hillsboro, Oregon, a booking he secured through his talent agency in Chicago. Kelly performed a motorcycle stunt that he had done many times: He would careen down a steep ramp and crash through a solid wall of glass before soaring over two cars and touching down at the other end of the ramp.

On this occasion, Kelly smashed through the glass at 60 miles per hour, losing control of his motorcycle. He failed to clear the second car and landed on his head.

Dr. Arne Suominen

Suominen, an avid runner who made national headlines in 1940 for almost beating a horse in a 27-mile race, returned to the spotlight in 1956. He organized a foot race between smokers and nonsmokers . . . to the top of Pikes Peak—and back.

Eleven other nonsmokers accepted the doctor's challenge to race him up 14,100 feet in an oxygen-starved climate, but only three smokers were willing, one of whom was Lou Wille, a hospital maintenance man from Laramie, Wyoming, who won two Pikes Peak races in the 1930s, albeit at a time when he was in his twenties and a nonsmoker. By 1956, Wille was puffing two packs a day.

As it turned out, Wille was the only smoker to reach the peak, and he beat Suominen to the top by 20 seconds. However, Wille didn't run to the bottom. One newspaper story, 10 years after the fact, said that Wille wrenched his knee upon reaching the top; another account states Wille actually gave up and asked for a cigarette and a ride back down the mountain. Regardless, Wille didn't care that he hadn't raced down the mountain or that he was 12 years younger than Suominen. He bragged about his 20-

second victory over Suominen, who calmly retorted, "Just think how good he could be if he didn't smoke."

A decade later, when Suominen was 66, he tried to repeat the stunt, challenging the Air Force Academy in Colorado Springs to send three of their most fit cadets who also smoked, and vowing to outrun them up Pikes Peak. "I will beat them all up the mountain," promised Suominen. "I will outwrestle them all. They would have a chance against me only in the boxing ring, if they are young and fast." Perhaps thinking they were dealing with a cracked nut, the Air Force politely declined.

Brother John

In October 1928, Brother John ran into the streets of New York City. The prophet with the long flowing beard and wild hair finally finished the race. Brother John arrived on the heels of another Bunion Derby casualty. A couple weeks earlier, Adam Ziolkowski arrived in New York, despite the fact that he dropped out 7 days into the race in Danby, California, after severely cutting his foot on a jagged shard of glass. He worked peeling potatoes on a nearby ranch until his foot heeled. Then, he began running again.

But Ziolkowski didn't cause any commotion when he arrived, unlike Brother John, who made his entrance sporting a robe and wearing a lot of signs, one announcing his support for presidential candidate Alfred E. Smith. He was at a Herbert Hoover rally and caused quite a commotion. Brother John was arrested and brought to the court, where he proudly displayed papers alerting people that he had been in seven insane asylums. When he was released, he blew his long fish horn and walked off.

Tobie Joseph Cotton

The young boy who had wanted to help his paralyzed father finished the Bunion Derby in 35th place. Perhaps inspired by his son, once back in

California, Tobie's father resumed working, but as a blacksmith, a job in which he could sit down. He lived a good, long life, passing away in August 1953. Tobie moved to Harrisburg, Pennsylvania, where his paper trail ends.

Norman Codeluppi

Codeluppi finished the race in 27th place and soon returned to Ohio. Two years later, he and his sweetheart Mary married. Before long he had his own garage, where he worked on cars, and he lived in Cleveland for years, until retiring to Rio Rancho, New Mexico.

John Salo

After running across the country for the second time in 1929 and receiving nothing, Salo bought a house for his wife and two kids and settled into his crime-fighting career. During one incident, two men and a woman attacked him, mistaking Salo for another officer who arrested a member of their family. They beat him savagely, though Salo managed to escape without lasting injuries.

Later that year, he was diagnosed with diabetes. He was sick through the winter of 1930 and then was able to return to his job. Not long after, Salo was assigned to work crowd control at a baseball game. During the seventh-inning stretch, several overly enthusiastic fans raced onto the field near third base. Salo ran out to reel them in just as a player threw a ball from left field.

It hit Salo right behind his ear.

He fell to the ground, but a few moments later, he climbed to his feet. He refused medical treatment and continued watching over the crowd and directing traffic until he suddenly collapsed. He was taken to the hospital, where he died. He was only 38.

Norma Jean Payne remembers that years later, she and her father were on a trip to New York City, and they stopped to visit Salo's widow, and they had a nice, long talk about the good times the two men once shared.

FRANK VON FLUE

Von Flue happily paid Red Workman 10 percent of his ninth-place winnings, leaving him with $900 to show for running across the entire country. He still had to get back home, and he had to settle with F. F. Gunn for having his clothes laundered and delivered to him at towns along the race route in the last couple of states, but none of this took anything away from his prize money. He had his $100 travel deposit and $500 from winning the 26-hour race with Phillip Granville. Von Flue spent the next couple of weeks traveling back to his home in Kerman, California, where he had a future waiting for him as a farmer, a husband, a parent, and a generally happy person. By all accounts, he lived a long and pleasant life.

But not right away. A couple weeks after the Bunion Derby ended, on a Saturday evening, Von Flue stopped for the night in Sacramento. An elderly gentleman struck up a conversation with him, and before Von Flue knew it, he was with two aging con men at the corner of Fifth and M Streets, playing bunco, a coin-matching game that involves dice. Von Flue later claimed he had a feeling they were out to hustle him, but he thought he could outwit them.

He lost $900.

PAUL "HARDROCK" SIMPSON

Hardrock married his college sweetheart, Ruby Maude Braxton, in December 1928.

His adventures in athletics continued in the 1930s, with more running and walking competitions, a dance marathon, and even a boxing match. He was in a brutal fight when his waistband snapped, and for the remainder of a round, Hardrock held onto his trunks with one glove and fought with the other as the crowd laughed. In 1934, Hardrock attempted to win a dance marathon that has been said to have lasted 1,498 hours—62 full days. Two years later, Hardrock decided to try to crash the Olympics, since he had disqualified himself by becoming a professional runner—a bit of a joke, since he hadn't collected more than $1,500 of the $5,000 he won over the years. Hardrock sent in an application, using his own name, Paul Simpson, but putting down a Florida address.

He got to Boston the night before the trials, which were held nearby. In disguise—he grew a handlebar mustache—Hardrock tried out, but he had skipped breakfast, thinking he'd have time to eat before the trials. He didn't and ran on an empty stomach, which may have helped doom his chances.

When he was 52, Hardrock ran his own personal marathon, going a mile for each of his birthdays, continuing that tradition annually until he was 60. Meanwhile, baseball fields hired him—beforehand the crowd guessed how many laps he could run, and Hardrock would run around the diamond as the players did their thing.

In 1958, Hardrock entered a race with Bunion Derby alumnus Roy McMurtry and a 37-year-old policeman. They were racing a horse for 157 miles. McMurtry stopped after 27 miles, concluding, "This'll be my last run. At 62, I think I'm just a bit too old." The policeman dropped out after 118 miles. His legs were aching, and his toenails were worn off.

Hardrock kept going. Even after the exhausted horse won, he kept running. Finally, race officials convinced Hardrock to stop, 35 miles from the finish line.

Hardrock slowed down in his seventies, leaving Burlington on July 3, 1978, after a massive stroke at the age of 74. His death invited genuine grief from his friends, family, neighbors, and strangers. He was always well-liked. For years, children followed this beloved man around their neighborhood every day, because they knew he would give them chewing gum and tell them a story. Even now, he isn't forgotten: At the historical Burlington depot, there's a mural on the wall, where generation after generation can spy a young-looking Hardrock in his running trunks.

He and Ruby had five kids, and early on, Hardrock realized he couldn't support his family as a runner or endurance competitor forever. So in the 1930s, after a short, miserable job as a salesman at a clothing store, Hardrock found the lifelong career that made him happy, in part because it utilized his gift for covering a lot of territory on two feet. He became a mail carrier.

Andy Payne

When Payne stepped off the train a few weeks after the race, alone at the station in Vinton, Kansas, 124 miles from his family's house, he did what came naturally. He started walking.

Twenty miles into his journey, a driver offered him a ride, and Payne took it the rest of the way. The driver had no idea who his passenger was, and Payne was fine with that. After being dropped off in Foyil, he started walking home but stopped when he saw some friends playing baseball in a vacant lot. Without saying a word, like he had never left, he joined in the game.

Pyle kept in touch with Payne, but little came of the showman's plans for races. Later in the year, Payne ran a 26-mile marathon against an Olympian marathon runner known as El Ouafi. Payne quit when he developed stomach cramps. He had run 10 miles.

Payne paid off his family's farm and bought his parents and siblings a new home. He married Vivian. He went to college. About 2 months after the race, he bought a nice car. The Great Depression didn't help his finances a year later, nor did his attempt to drill for oil on his family's farm. By 1930, he was broke again.

Andy and Vivian had a daughter, Norma Jean, and Payne was pushing a plow on his father's farm—until late March 1930, when he became a sportswriter. Vivian went back to teaching. Later, they would have a son, Jim. But in 1934, Payne decided to enter another race—he ran for office. With few funds to spend on campaigning, he drove around in an old car, talking to people and newspaper editors, trying to gain support. Eventually he was elected to the position of clerk of the Oklahoma State Supreme Court.

He was reelected numerous times, until the position became an appointed one; even then, he remained in the job until his retirement in the early 1970s, with the exception of a 2-year stint when he volunteered to join the army during World War II. During that time, Vivian was sworn into office as his replacement.

After Payne turned 40, he earned a law degree. His financial acumen increased, and throughout most of his life, Payne was quite affluent. That he quickly spent his Bunion Derby windfall didn't make him bitter. "Oh, I should have saved more of it," admitted Payne in 1940. "But I haven't anything to regret. I'm a lot better off than I was before the race."

Andy died in 1977, and Vivian spent her remaining years in Oklahoma City. She died in August 2004, at the age of 96.

In Foyil, a bronze statue of Andy Payne stands in a lonely greenspace, and he is also immortalized in a sculpture at the Cherokee Heritage Center in Tahlequah, Oklahoma. Additionally, every May, Oklahoma City hosts the Andy Payne Bunion Run marathon.

C. C. Pyle

One year after his disastrous second Bunion Derby, it must have pleased Pyle to learn that he was being lionized on the stage. Comic legend W. C. Fields conceived a stage musical about a sports promoter named Q. Q. Quale. *Ballyhoo* debuted in December 1930. It was directed by legend-in-the-making Oscar Hammerstein and produced by his famous uncle, Arthur Hammerstein.

The musical's story line featured Q. Q. Quale organizing a foot race that traveled from one hick town to the next, and along the way he swindled everyone he came in contact with. As a nod to Pyle's traveling carnival, the stage was filled with fire-eaters, dancing girls, acrobats, tumblers, and tap dancers. But as if Pyle needed another insult, the biographical *Ballyhoo* was a flop, closing after 2 weeks. It was Fields's only unsuccessful show in 15 years on Broadway.

On December 23, 1930, Pyle took a taxi from Tijuana, Mexico, to San Diego, and then refused to pay the fare. The driver drove an intoxicated Pyle to the police station. When they searched his things, they found 20-odd dollars in cash, an expensive watch, and several papers, including writs of attachment.

But C. C. Pyle's lot in life improved. In 1933, Robert L. Ripley of *Ripley's Believe It Or Not!* fame hired him to manage his exhibit at the Chicago World's Fair, which lasted until 1934. He was master of ceremonies for a freak show featuring attractions such as a woman who looked like a mule. A registered nurse was hired to offer smelling salts to any faint-hearted customers who didn't see the value in that.

Pyle left Effie for good on November 2, 1934, and moved to Santa Rosa, California, where his brother, sister, and mother lived. A court granted Effie a divorce in 1936. Pyle tried to fight paying financial support, but once again, the court didn't side with him.

Without missing a beat, Pyle married the following year. By now, he was the president of a radio transcription company and, by all accounts, he mostly stayed at home with his 32-year-old wife Elvia Allman, a radio comedienne. He even reportedly paid off some of his debts, though some things didn't change. He was sued by a comedian and musician, Bob "Bazooka" Burns, who didn't want Pyle airing some of his old radio material.

Interestingly enough, like Payne and Hardrock, who each became well-known local figures, one could argue that Elvia Allman also achieved far more enduring fame than C. C. Pyle. She transitioned from radio to television, forging a long career as a character actress. The public may not know of her role on *Petticoat Junction* as Selma Plout, but virtually everyone has seen her guest turn on *I Love Lucy.* In the famous chocolate factory scene, Allman is the forewoman who shouts, "Let 'er roll," just before the assembly line overwhelms Lucy and Ethel.

Pyle never saw the episode. He died of a heart attack in February 1939, a week after his ailing mother passed away.

PYLE WAS MOURNED by the sportswriters who both scorned and admired him. Bill Henry, a columnist for the *Los Angeles Times*, explained Pyle this way: "Charley no doubt had his faults—as haven't we all, but how many of us had the virtues that were his? We all dream dreams but few of us can couple with the hazy wishfulness the initiative and the courage that makes dreams come true. Charley Pyle could do that. He overreached himself at times but that failing was not unique with him. It's the penalty that is paid—and rather gladly—by those who refuse to be shackled by conservatism, custom and willingness to let well enough alone. Nobody could ever accuse Charley Pyle of that. He never quite found things so satisfactory that he was willing to quit trying to do something bigger and better."

Henry summed up Pyle this way: "I liked Pyle for his nerve and courage. This world full of cry babies could use a little of it."

Westbrook Pegler also eulogized him in a column. "We saw him come, and we saw him go, the gay gray optimist who quit the small-town nickelodeon business to become the most spectacular and least hate-worthy man of his type and time, which was the American era of wonderful nonsense. Charley Pyle . . . was goofy. Not crazy, but goofy. He had big ideas and a casual, inefficient, careless ability, and he would have been a Barnum if he had had in his makeup a little bit of that ingredient you might call balance."

Pegler added that Pyle may have been a schemer, but at least most people knew it. "Charley would show you his hole-card," wrote Pegler, referring to a common term used in poker, "and bet 'em high as a cat's back and didn't care much whether he won or lost, just so he got action. He liked to win, naturally, and no kid with a new red wagon was ever happier than Charley, when he found himself pocket-rich for the short spell."

IT WAS OFTEN SAID in the 1930s by friends and associates and Pyle himself that of all the sports, stunts, games, and gimmicks the showman-entrepreneur-agent was involved in, it was the Bunion Derby that he felt most deeply about. The Bunion Derby was forgotten within a generation or two, and C. C. Pyle just as quickly, but he leaves a legacy. For good or bad, he practically created the high-stakes, money-laden culture of professional sports.

The Bunion Derby, the way Pyle organized it, is an event that will probably never be repeated again in a litigious society, and in many ways, the endurance fad of the 1920s needed to end. These competitions were, after all, a chancy way to live. But as Pyle himself pointed out, as difficult as his amazing foot race was, for all the car collisions and nervous breakdowns involved, calling it the Bunion Derby was never quite accurate. As winter turned to spring in 1928, the runners suffered blisters, bruises, boils, shin splints, charley horses, sore toes, broken and fallen arches, corns and calluses, but not one of them developed a bunion.

About Notes and Resources

During the summer of 2004, I spoke to Pauline Bean, the sister of Andy Payne. She was only 10 years old when her brother ran across the country, and so she couldn't remember much about the Bunion Derby. But she did recall that her brother "would write letters home, saying that he could win. He said he ran with the best in the world, and he could beat them."

"Letters home?" I was suddenly thrilled beyond belief.

"They saved all those things," said Pauline. *Yes*, I thought, until Pauline continued: "But a man from around here came and said he was going to write a book, and he asked if he could have the letters, and they gave him all of the letters, the newspapers, the pictures—everything that they collected. He never did write a book."

My heart sank. "Do you know this guy's name? Maybe I can track him down."

That's when Pauline informed me that they had given away everything shortly after the race—back in 1928.

"Do you know anything about this man?" I asked, weakly, hoping against hope that I could still find his descendents . . .

"I understood that his wife and kids lived here, but he was a school-supply salesman who traveled a lot. I heard he had two families," said Pauline, chuckling. "I don't doubt it. He might have sold the letters, too. Who knows?"

I made a mental note to be on the lookout for a century-plus-old bigamist carting around letters that were more than 70 years old.

I have no doubt that letters to loved ones are out there, hidden away in someone's attic, but I was unable to find any from runners to family members from the time of the race. Fortunately, some letters to home were published in newspapers like the Burlington, North Carolina, paper, which has had a number of names over the years, but is now the *Times-News*. Paul "Hardrock" Simpson was front-page news in Burlington's paper. Issues from May through the summer of 1928 seem to be lost forever, but I combed every word of Burlington's articles in January through April. They also covered Hardrock extensively over the years, and it became an invaluable resource on Hardrock and in providing interesting details about the race.

In July 1928, the *Fresno Bee* ran a series of articles over 2 weeks, covering the race from the perspective of Frank Von Flue and offering gems of information about the Bunion Derby.

Arthur Newton's autobiography, *Running in Three Continents*, published in 1940, was a fantastic source of information. As was Maxwell Stiles's slim but helpful book published in 1959, *Back Track: Great Moments in Track and Field*. It was here that I learned some key information about Ukulele Jake, like his arrival near the end of the race. Other books with some interesting nuggets of information include *Red Grange and the Rise of Modern Football* by Lewis Carroll and Benjamin G. Rader (it had some helpful biographical information on Grange, of course, as well as some nice Pyle moments that I incorporated into the book—his coin trick, Ed Healy's comment about deciding not to work for Pyle—and it's a must-read for Red Grange fans). Another fun book about a marathon that a Bunion Derby alumnus wound up in is *America's Ultimate Challenge: The Pikes Peak Marathon* by Harald Fricker. *Man on the Flying Trapeze: The Life and Times of W. C. Fields*, a great book by Simon Louvish, provided the information that Fields once performed in a show inspired by Pyle. And Michael Wallis's incomparable *Route 66: The Mother Road* was a must-read for me, and should be for anyone who wants to learn more about the fabled and famed highway. Most of the important items in this book about Elmer McCurdy's life and afterlife came from Mark Svenvold's whimsical, wonderful book *Elmer McCurdy: The Misadventures in Life and Afterlife of an American Outlaw.*

Bill Crawford's article "The Bunion Derby" in the May–June 1998 *Oklahoma Today* is essential reading.

I took a look at as many court cases as I could find that involved Pyle, particularly from the Circuit Court of Cook County and the Superior Court of Cook County. I read the divorce papers between Charles C. Pyle and Effie R. Pyle, as well as between Effie Arnold and her former husband, Howard.

Jefferson Hospital in Philadelphia sent me the report that Dr. Gordon and Dr. Baker compiled when studying the Bunion Derby runners.

But most of all, I've looked at hundreds of articles from dozens of newspapers, many of which I was able to find online, which helped, though I still made numerous trips to the microfilm machines at an incredible institution, the Public Library of Cincinnati and Hamilton County. Still, a sampling of the papers I pored through, includes the *New York Times*, the *Los Angeles Times,* the *Washington Post,* the *Chicago Tribune*, and the *Oklahoman.* I also came to depend on the *Decatur Review*, the *Charleston Daily Mail,* the *Oakland Tribune*, the *Port Arthur News,* the *Reno Evening Gazette*, the *Ogden Standard-Examiner* (with a lot of F. F. and Harry Gunn info), the *Charleroi Mail*, the *Olean Times*, *Manitoba Free Press*, the *Goshen Daily News-Times* (lots on Mike Kelly), *Oxnard Press-Courier, Indiana Evening Gazette*, the *Zanesville Signal*, the *Rolla Herald*, the *Joplin Globe*, *St. Louis Post-Dispatch*, the *Los Angeles Examiner, Hollywood Daily Citizen*, *Albuquerque Journal*, *Amarillo Daily News*, *Maroon and Gold (*Hardrock's college newspaper), *New Castle News*, the *Arizona Republican*, the *Coconino Sun*, and many, many more.

Acknowledgments

I owe my agent, Laurie Abkemeier, a debt of thanks for believing that I could transition from writing magazine articles to a book, and for being a fan of the Bunion Derby story from the moment I told it to her. I'll always be grateful for her enthusiasm and pragmatic advice. She's a great cheerleader, a gifted editor, and a good friend. I owe many thanks to Brian DeFiore of DeFiore and Company for believing in me as well.

Laurie also put me in touch with Pete Fornatale, my editor at Rodale—gifted, smart, and simply a heck of a nice guy. I also appreciate that when it came time to point out some sophomoric writing in my first draft, he never used the word "sophomoric." I feel lucky to have him in my corner, not to mention everyone at Rodale. In fact, I should profusely thank Rodale's editorial staff—in particular, Karen Neely and Emily Williams, who are both extremely meticulous wordsmiths.

Before I even found a publisher for this book, I contacted Norma Jean Roupe, Andy Payne's daughter, and she was so supportive of this project. She didn't have to be. She has been approached by quite a few writers over the years. Some books were written; other projects disappeared into the ether. But she acted as if I were the first journalist to approach her, letting me call and ask questions as often as I needed. And when I finally went to Oklahoma City to do research, she invited me to stay in her guest house—where Andy Payne and his wife Vivian spent their golden years.

I talked to Vivian briefly on the phone during the summer of 2004, about a month before she died. She was very accommodating and said I was welcome to visit her when I came out to Oklahoma City. I was sad that we didn't get the chance to meet, but knowing we talked, and that I had another connection to the past, made working on the book all the more special. Andy's cousin, J. R. Cook, drove me around Oklahoma City and shared stories about Andy; Andy's son, Jim Payne, was also gracious with his time; and Andy's nephew, Gerry Payne, showed me where Andy grew up and drove me around Foyil. I should also thank Terri Tyree, another cousin of Andy's who sent me some thoughts on her relative.

Locating C. C. Pyle's great-granddaughter was a thrill, and Gina Laitinen is as good a person as they come. She only knew of Pyle through her grandmother, Kathrine, who spoke highly of him until the day she died. I deeply appreciate Gina's moral support throughout my writing of the book.

I also need to thank Fred Saperstein, the son of runner Morris Saperstein. Fred was a big champion of this book.

But then, everyone was: Tammy Hata, who introduced me to Fred; Marguerite Brandgard, daughter of Norman Codeluppi; Gloria Armitage, his sister; some of Norman's cousins, George and Jean Codeluppi; and George's mother, Lois Codeluppi. Dorothy Gunn Bryant, daughter of Harry Gunn. Dale Adams and Anne Jennison, daughters of Harry Abrams. Guy Gavuzzi, grandson of Pete Gavuzzi—and simply terrific about sending me, a complete stranger, key information and photos about England's greatest runner. Hardrock's daughter, Marjorie "Joann" Barnwell, was also helpful, as was her caregiver and friend, Susan Stewart. I also owe a debt of thanks to Leland P. Torliatt, historian and amateur sleuth in Santa Rosa, California, where Pyle once lived. I found Frank Von Flue's grandson, Scott Von Flue, very late in the writing process, and he, too, was very supportive of this project.

Thanks also to F. Michael Angelo, university archivist at Scott Memorial Library at Thomas Jefferson University; Michael Salmon at the AAF Sports Library in Los Angeles, who was kind enough to send me material from Arthur Newton's biography, which is sadly not only out of print but almost impossible to find; Dottie Patterson, Delray Beach Historical Society for some information that she gave me on Dr. Arne Suominen; Kevin Hill, assistant reference librarian at the Amarillo Public Library; the archives staff at the Office of the Clerk of the Circuit Court of Cook County; Terri M. Anderson of the Needles Branch Library; the Victorville Branch Library in Victorville, California; Nancy Sherrill at the Vigo County Public Library in Terre Haute, Indiana; Carolyn Richardson of Oldham County Library in Vega, Texas; Jason D. Stratman, assistant librarian at the Missouri Historical Society, who provided a lot of material to me; David E. Hubbard, a librarian at the Curtis Laws Wilson Library at the University of Missouri–Rolla; Jean Vickey, a librarian at the Erie County Public Library; David A. Smith, a research librarian at the New York Public Library; the archives staff at the Office of the Clerk of the Circuit Court of Cook County for providing some helpful details on two lawsuits against C. C. Pyle. Many thanks to Jeramy Eiken, a reference library at the Joplin Public Library in Joplin, Missouri; Dr. Bob Blackburn, director of the Oklahoma Historical Society; and Chad Williams, manuscript archivist at the Oklahoma Historical Society. Debbie Elmenhorst at El Reno Carnegie Library in El Reno, Oklahoma, also really came through for me, especially in helping me get some of the photos for this book.

I need to spotlight Dan Bigbee Jr. and Lily Shangreaux, whom I contacted midway through my research, and who were very enthusiastic about the book. They produced, directed, wrote, and researched *The Great American Foot Race*, a wonderful PBS documentary primarily about Andy Payne's involvement in the race. They have an invaluable and thorough Web site, www.itvs.org/footrace, that's all about the Bunion Derby, and if it's still up, and you want to learn more, you should check it out. It was an incredible help to me.

I'm also extremely grateful to Millie Barnhart and Connie Minor of the Delaware Historical Society in Delaware, Ohio. This was where C. C. Pyle grew up, and Connie drove me around Delaware, showing me landmarks and taking me to places where I could dig up local government records—and then Millie was like a magician when it came to research. I'd search fruitlessly for a fact, ask Millie, and if an answer existed, she found it.

Paul "Hardrock" Simpson was a very minor character in the book until I met up with Katie Nash, the archivist and special collections librarian at Belk Library at Elon University; she sent me numerous articles, the photo of Hardrock, and a lot of supportive e-mails. I'm also very grateful to Theresa St. Romain, who during my writing was working on her own book on Pyle's first sister-in-law, the silent era actress Margarita Fischer. I'll be first in line to buy her book; she was very generous with her knowledge of the Fischer family.

Since I was stranded in Ohio, Julie Harris let me use her Los Angeles Public Library card, so I could do some extensive research in the *Los Angeles Times* newspaper archives, saving me an unknowable amount of money and time.

And in the beginning of the writing process, I often went to John Senatore, DPM, chief of podiatry at Union Memorial Hospital in Baltimore. He's also a marathon runner. He was great at answering my foot-related questions. I also came to depend on the wisdom of Cynthia R. LaBella, MD, medical director for the Institute for Sports Medicine at Children's Memorial Hospital in Chicago.

Many of my friends and family motivated and encouraged me as I wrote the book, and I'd like to thank all of them, but I know I can't. So let me just express gratitude to Eileen Kailholz, Stu Rubinstein, Brian Kieffer, Teresa Ciulla, Patty Onderko, my grandmother Mary Wellinghoff, Pat Scorti, Angela "Tootsie" Scorti, Theresa Muthert, Larry Wellinghoff, Joe Wellinghoff, and my brother and sounding board, Kevin. And I may never be able to thank enough my parents, Jim and Rita Williams, whose emotional, and sometimes financial, support has been unwavering. Even when I was eating peanut butter out of a jar for my meals, my mom (usually) didn't suggest that I find another line of work. Nor, in later years, did my lovely wife, Susan, even during the numerous occasions when our mortgage was late. And thanks to my two wonderful young daughters, Isabelle and Lorelei, who both—let's go with an analogy apropos to this story—have made the road of life even more meaningful and special than I ever imagined it could be.

INDEX

Boldface references indicate photographs.

A

Abramowitz, Harry
  about, 236–37
  May 9, 11th place overall, 233
  May 11, 10th place overall, 236
  May 16, Von Flue trying to catch, 251
  May 18, drops in standings, 255
  May 19, further behind, 255–56
  May 26, last day of race, 272
  returns for 1929 race, 288
  supplied with shoes by YMHA, 108
  watches movies, 146
African Americans
  Gardner and Cotton awarded money, 269
  Ku Klux Klan intimidation, 147–48
  racist sports reporting and, 61
  runners (*see* Cotton, Tobie Joseph; Gardner, Ed; Robinson, Sammy)
Albuquerque, New Mexico, 134–35
Allman, Elvia, 301
Amarillo, Texas, 151–52
American Legion, 107–8, 146
Anderson, Frances, 176–77
Anthony, Nick
  April 6, after the blizzard, 153
  April 27, out of race due to feet, 200–201
  runners' mental states observed by, 88
Arnold, Effie B., 211–12. *See also* Pyle, Effie
Arrowhead Beach, Ohio, 237–38
Ascot Speedway, 31

B

Bagdad, California, 78–79
Baker, John, 43, 84, 120, 121, 122, 146, 190, 200, 227
Baker, Roy "Bullet," 95–96
Barefoot runners, 72
Barnes, Archie, 222
Barney, Charles Lloyd, 86–87
Barry, Edwin D., 122
Barstow, California, 71
Bath, New York, 253
Bathing, 79, 82, 264
Baze, Mike, 167, 172
Begg, James T., 232
Begg, K. H., 3
Belly dancers, 59
Bennett, Gordon, 23
Bircher, Butch, 117–18
Blisters the dog, 126, 149, 167, 191
Blizzard, in Oklahoma, 150–51
Bloomington, California, 62
Boredom during race, 145–46
Boston Marathon, 5
Bowling endurance contests, xii
Boxers in the race, 45
Bradford, Pennsylvania, 253
Bray, James A., 219
Bristow, Oklahoma, 174
British runners. *See* Gavuzzi, Pete; Hart, Charles Walter; Newton, Arthur; Thomas, Richard
Brother John (John Nash)
  description of, 74–75
  life after the race, 91
  March 12, out of the race, 91
  ultimate fate of, 294
Bruno, Paolo, 47, 228
Buckley, Ted, 146
Buehler, Frank, 230–31
Bunion Derby. *See also* Carnival
  Americans' lack of excitement about, 193–95
  boredom of crew, 145
  corporate sponsorships, 37–38
  daily life, **41** (*see* Living conditions)
  discrimination (*see* Racism)
  dropout rates, 73, 84, 113, 140
  eve of race, 49
  finances (*see* Finances of race)
  first proposed, xiii
  inspiration for, 17
  medical criticism of, 122
  night finish rules, 178, 179, 234, 260, 262

Bunion Derby *(cont.)*
noteworthy days
last day, 266–73
longest leg, 257–61
most grueling climb, 64–66
starting day, 50–59
worst weather, 149–52
official name of, 6
origin of nickname, 5–6
poor organization of, 188
prizes (*see* Prize money)
publicity (*see* Publicity)
Pyle's police force for, 95–96
race route, 226, 227
race vehicles, 54, 103
runners (*see* Runners)
saved by F. F. Gunn, 218–19
songs, 215
staff and officials, 41–42, 43
unpredictability of, 244
Bunions, 5
Busch, Billy, 106, 125, 153

C

Cajon Pass, 65–66, 73
Campbell, Kenneth, 234
Canadian runners. *See* Cronick, John; Germaine, Eugene; Granville, Phillip; Metcalfe, Osmond
Carnival
attractions
animals, 59
belly dancers, 59
Dolly Sisters, 116
McCurdy corpse, 59–60, 90, 177, 270
musicians, 59
snake charmer, 59
stunt pilots, 115–16
circus nature of, 59–60
as money-making event, 58
robberies during, 121
shutdown in Rolla, 193
Car(s)
collision with, as Payne's fear, 244, 255
Gavuzzi's near collision with, 204
motorists urged caution, 251–52
poor visibility of, 81
runners hit by
Frank Von Flue, 258–59
Harry Sheare, 243
Olli Wantinnen, 222
Pat Mahoney, 84
Carthage, Missouri, 186–87
Catalina Island swimming race, **xi**
C. C. Pyle's Patent Foot Box, 276
Chavez, Frank, 152, 154
Chelsea, Oklahoma, **158**
Chicago, Illinois, 199, 221–22
Chiropodists, 1
Claremore, Oklahoma, 27–28, 34–35, 178–79
Clarizo, Giacomo, 112
Clark, Grover L., 8
Clothes, race, eccentric, 52, 75
Codeluppi, Norman, **117**
March 27, sandstorm, 137
May 13, decides to continue, 245
May 21, day of agony, 259
May 26, last day of race, 272
reasons for running, 123–24
ultimate fate of, 295
Colorado River, crossing, 92–93, 95
Comstock, Gus, xii
Conneaut, Ohio, 241
Conrad, A. F., 24
Constantinoff, Antonio, 290
Conto, Joe
March 8, out of the race, 77
one of best Italian runners, 47
in postrace marathon, 281, 283
sportsmanship of, 63
Cook, Staley, 35, 124–25, 129, 154
Cooks for the race, 117–18
Cooley, Mrs. Frank, 16
Corns, 5
Corpse, in carnival. *See* McCurdy, Elmer
Cotton, Tobie Joseph
March 8, finishes last, 76
March 22, struggles, 125
March 27, sandstorm, 137
May 26, last day of race, 269
racial prejudice and, 149
reasons for running, 76–77
ultimate fate of, 295
Coward Good Sense Shoe for Bunions, 5
Crandell, Milton, 22
Cronick, John, **250**
March 11, wins leg, 89
March 17, considered top runner, 116
April 17, sprints to finish, 179–80
April 28, tied for eighth overall, 202
May 9, 10th place overall, 233

May 19, Von Flue on heels, 256
May 20, in top 10, 257
reasons for running, 46
receives $1,000 prize, 283
Currier, Allen D., 166, 272

D

Danby, California, 82
Dance marathons, xi, 24, 289
Dean, Walter C., 163
DeMar, Clarence, 3
De Marr, Patrick
as a boxer, 45
April 3, wins leg, 151
April 21, out of the race, 191
April 22, tries to reenter, 191
returns for 1929 race, 288
Dilks, Earl, 119, 121, 228
Discrimination against foreigners. *See* Racism
Dr. Scholl, 1–2
Dolly Sisters, 116, 167
Downing, W. A., 241
Drinking competitions, xii
Dropouts
after first 4 days, 73
after 7 days, 84
by Day 11, 113
by Day 27, 140
reasons for dropping out, 146
why dropouts stayed, 174–75
Duffy, Arthur, 41–42, 86, 106, 191, 192, 200, 203, 218

E

East St. Louis, Illinois, 199
Eating competitions, xii
Elevation gain, grueling, 113
Elks Club as party host, 205
Elliott, William T., 116
Ellis, Thomas, 50, 268
Ellsworth, Rod, 83, 111, 115
El Ouafi, 299
El Reno, Oklahoma, 92
Elyria, Ohio, 232–33
Endrizzi, Billy, 136
Endurance competitions
addictive nature of, 174–75
flourishing, 181–82
Great Depression and, 289
medical criticism of, 122
risks of, 23–24, 33
in the Twenties, xi–xiii
types of, xi–xii
English runners. *See* British runners
Erickson, Nestor
March 7, moving up, 73
March 30, trainer fired, 140
April 12, wins leg, 166
April 14, out of the race, 173
predicted to win, 47
quits on principle, 172
Erie, Pennsylvania, 248
Estoppey, Eugene
about, 51
logging boots and, 50, 52, 53
March 4, starting day, 56
March 9, out of the race, 79
ultimate fate of, 80
Evans, Owen, xii

F

Fager, August
March 30, trainer fired, 139–40
April 13, in Oklahoma City, 167
April 14, out of the race, 173
places third in marathon, 284
quits on principle, 172
Faucette, Owen, 8, 9, 10
Female runners, 16–17
Fenton, Bob, 177
Filipino runners. *See* Rivera, Teodocio
Finances of race
fees charged to towns, 207–9, 216
high costs of, 37–38, 128
in jeopardy, due to dropouts, 73
lack of money for final prizes, 253
monetary benefits of, for Pyle, 38
profitability questionable, 232–33
Rickard bails Pyle out, 253–54
Finn, Alex, 139–40, 173
Finnish runners. *See* Erickson, Nestor; Kolehmainen, Willie; Suominen, Arne; Wantinnen, Olli
Fischer, Dottie, 69–71
Fischer, Margarita, 69, 95
Fisher, Nicky, 157
Flagpole sitters, xii, 20–21, 24, 175
Flagstaff, Arizona, 115–16
Flaherty, Ray "Red," 95–96
Flying Yank. *See* Seiler, John J.

Food
breakfast, 146
eaten by vegetarian runners, 146
quality of, 117–19
Football in the 1920s, 42, 86–87
Foot problems
bruised heels, 105
early podiatry and, 1–2
hot toes, 170
loss of toenails, 105
primitive shoe design and, 1–2
Pyle claims expertise in, 276
as reason for dropping out, 146
Foot race, second, in 1929, 287–89
Foyil, Oklahoma, 179
Francis, Walter, 132
Freeman, Leroy "Doc," 83
Fremont, Ohio, 230–32, 235, 239–40
Frost, Dick
about, 44–45
March 11, contender despite age, 88
April 28, ejected from race, 203
May 1, still running, 213
Frost, R. Lucien. *See* Frost, Dick

G

Gallena, Charles, 88, 142–43
Gallery, Tom, 77–78
Galloping Ghost. *See* Grange, Red
Gallup, New Mexico, 135
Gardner, Ed, **144**
March 5, finishes second, 61
March 7, wins leg, 72
March 9, wins leg, 78
March 18, wins leg in tie, 119
March 27, sandstorm, 136
March 28, wins leg, 137
April 3, wins leg, 147
April 4, Ku Klux Klan, 147
April 10, running first, 160
April 11, harassed, 161
April 13, Oklahoma City, 166
April 18, runs with Payne, 180
April 23, wins leg, 191
April 26, finishes fifth, 198
April 27, wins leg, 199
May 2, wins leg, 215
May 4, ranked fourth overall, 220
May 11, shin splints, 235–36
May 20, in top 10, 257
May 26, last day of race, 269
often treated to dinner, 146
as postrace entertainer, 58
racist incidents, 147, 161–62
receives $1,000 prize, 283
returns for 1929 race, 288
supported by black community, 161
Gauvin, Alfred E., 106
Gavuzzi, Pete, **25**, **181**
about, 97–98
March 4, sings to crowd, 58
March 6, elevation gain hard, 66
March 12, boat crossing, lost, 96, 97
March 16, Hart drops out, 113–14
March 20, running strong, 121
March 25, wins leg, 132
March 26, wins leg, 133
March 27, sandstorm, 136
March 28, arrives with Payne, 137
March 31, wins leg in tie, 141
April 8, as threat to Suominen, 156
April 11, wins leg in tie, 162
April 12, overtaken by Payne, 162
April 14, as Payne rival, 173
April 15, beats a train, 173
April 15, first place overall, 174
April 16, Tulsa, 176
April 17, lead slips, 179–80
April 18, wins leg, 180
April 19, bad water, 182
April 20, harassed, wins leg, 186
April 23, finishes 11th, 191
April 25–29, first place overall, 195, 199, 202, 204
April 30, dodges car, wins leg, 204
May 2, Payne catching up, 216
May 4, wins leg, 220
May 8, allows Kelly the lead, 229
May 11, out of the race, 236
May 12, fallen hero, 241
marketability of, 195–96
in postrace marathon, 281, 284
returns for 1929 race, 288
shaves his beard, 213, 216
teams up with Hart, 47
threats against, 186, 189
Gemmell, Andrew, 116, 153
Germaine, Eugene, 271–72
German runners. *See* Rehayn, George
Gleason, James F., 46
Gober, John A., **144**
April 13, finishes second, 166
April 19, wins leg, 183–84, 185–86
April 20, passed by Gavuzzi, 186
April 22, wins leg, 191

May 12, out of the race, 241
wins in home state, 183–84, 191
Gonzales, Seth, 133, 205
Goodwin, Ralph, 41, 57, 166
Goodwin, Thomas, 271, 277
Gordon, Robert Burgess, 32, 43, 84
Goshen, Indiana, 229–30
Grange, Red, **224**
about, 42–43
branding of, by Pyle, 38
during the Bunion Derby
assistant race director, 43, 51
emcee at carnival, 58
postrace emotional state, 269
as Pyle's spokesperson, 213–15, 217–18, 224–25
serves as referee, 225
sought for Pyle's debts, 205–6, 278
visits Sheare in hospital, 247
as crowd attraction, 42
Pyle as promoter of, 2–3, 22, 225
ultimate fate of, 292–93
Granville, Phillip
March 7, finishes 27th, 73
April 4, fifth place overall, 148
April 13, in pain, 172
April 23, wins leg, 191
April 27, in top 10, 198
May 5, Chicago, 222
May 11, finishes second, 239
May 14, speech, 246–47
May 26, last day of race, 273
mistaken kinship incident, 103–4
predicted to finish second, 116
race strategy of, 99–100
receives $5,000 prize, 283
threats from Ku Klux Klan, 148
wins 26-hour marathon, 284
Grimmett, Harry, 45
Gunn, Freeman Fremont (F. F.)
about, 100
insists on clean clothes, 226
loans money to save race, 218–19
rescinds midnight rule, 260
Gunn, Harry
postrace letter to Payne, 290
shoes, 149
speed walking and, 100

H

Hadge, Hammouch Ben, 16
Haldeman, George, 182
Hall, Asa, 174
Hardrock (Paul Simpson), 7, **286**
about, 105
March 6, stops writing, 66
March 13, finishes second, 106
March 20, shin splints, 120
March 21, joined by reporter, 124–25
March 23, struggling, 129–30
March 24, keeps going, 130–31
March 26, feeling better, 133
March 27, sandstorm, 137
April 5, blizzard, 152
April 6, falling behind, 153–54
April 7, hobbling, 155
April 9, hoping to finish, 159
April 10, running slowly, 160
April 16, trainer arrives, 176
April 19, finishes late, 184
April 23, finishes late, 191
April 30, finishes late, 205
May 20, makes comeback, 256
May 22, finishes last, 262
May 26, last day of race, 271
pens memoirs, 35–37, 49, 63
races with a pony, 8–10
reasons for running, 6–10
returns for 1929 race, 288
returns to hometown, 281
shoes worn by, 50, 106
scoffs at trainer idea, 32
travel to the race, 29–30
ultimate fate of, 297–99
writes letter to mother, 134
Harrison, Morton, 187
Hart, Charles Walter
March 4, starting day, 56
March 6, Cajon Pass, 65
March 7, passes younger racers, 73
March 8, second-to-last, 76
March 11, finishes 13th, 89
March 14, making up miles, 111
March 16, out of the race, 113
as oldest runner, 47, 88
Hayden, Kathleen, xii
Haynes, Elton, 61
Healy, Ed, 168
Hedquist, Arthur, 207–9
Highway 66. *See* Route 66
Hubbell, John Lorenzo, 116
Human Dynamo, 39–40
Hurry Up Yost, 86

I

Isele, Anton, 252
Israel, Jonas. *See* Brother John
Italian runners. *See* Bruno, Paolo; Clarizo, Giacomo; Conto, Joe; Umek, Guisto

J

Jamestown, New York, 246
Jensen, Clarence H., 142
Joachim, Alex, 192
Johnson, Frank
  bathing and, 79
  complaints about the food, 118
  interview at home, 139
  letter home, 134
  perils of slipping behind, 74
  race chronology
    March 4, starting day, 56
    March 14, trailing badly, 109–11
    March 15, almost quits, 111–12, 113
    March 16, runs again, 113
    March 20, shin splints, 120
    March 22, struggles, 125
    March 25, trainer arrives, 132
    March 26, Indian dances, 133–34
    March 27, sandstorm, 137
    March 29, out of the race, 138–39
  reasons for running, 11, 19
  scoffs at trainer idea, 32
Joliet, Illinois, 207–9
Joplin, Missouri, 183
Joyce, Mike, **235**
  March 13, in the desert, 106
  April 2, describes typical day, 146
  April 27, in top 10, 198
  May 12, visits family, 242–43
  May 13, in hometown, 244–45
  May 14, speech, 246
  receives $2,500 prize, 283
  returns for 1929 race, 288
  thanks Pyle, 285
Jussick, George, 205, 271

K

Kelly, Alvin Aloysius, xii, 20–21, 175
Kelly, Mike
  March 4, starting day, 56
  March 27, sandstorm, 137
  April 1, shoes worn out, 142
  April 6, after the blizzard, 153
  April 21, in last place, 190
  April 23, naps to cope, 191–92
  April 24, gets trainer, 192
  May 7, still in last place, 228–29
  May 8, in hometown, 229–30
  May 16, finishes last, 252
  May 21, day of agony, 260
  May 23, set on finishing, 263
  postrace letter to Payne, 290
  reasons for running, 12–13
  returns home to Goshen, 281
  scoffs at trainer idea, 32
  ultimate fate of, 293–94
Kelly, Shipwreck, xii, 20–21, 175
Kerr, William, **250**
  March 13, sleeps in hotel, 107
  April 8, disgusted with Pyle, 157
  April 23, finishes 11th, 191
  April 28, finishes eighth, 202
  May 6, gripes about conditions, 225
  May 20, battling for fifth, 257
  May 24, accused of revolting, 263–64
  receives $1,000 prize, 283
  special treatment and, 107–8, 146
Kingman, Arizona, 104–5, 107
Kolehmainen, Willie
  about, 48
  March 4, starting day, 53, 55, 58
  March 5, wins leg, 61, 62–63
  March 6, pulls groin, 65
  March 7, out of the race, 71–72
Ku Klux Klan, 147, 148

L

Laguna, New Mexico, 134
Larsen, Karl, 146
Lenglen, Suzanne, 196
LeSage, Dick, 141–42, 154–55
Levett, the Human Dynamo, 39–40
Lewis, Leland, 65, 98, 151, 249, 259
Lindbergh, Charles, 18, 194–95
Living conditions. *See also* Food
  during race, 109–11, 162
  sleeping, 113, 121–22, 193
  at training camp, 35–37
Lloyd, Harold, xii
Lossman, Juri
  April 13, in Oklahoma City, 167
  April 14, out of the race, 173

expected to be in top 10, 47
quits on principle, 172
Lowry, Paul, 66

M

Madison Square Garden, 269–73, 282–85
Mahoney, Pat, 84, 87
Marathon, 26-hour, 281, 283–84
Margarita Fischer Company, 69
Mascot, unofficial, 126
McCurdy, Elmer (corpse), 59–60, 90, 177, 270
McLean, Texas, 155
McMurtry, Roy
about, 44
April 27, in St. Louis, 198–99
April 28, tied for eighth, 202
May 8, in Indiana, 229
returns for 1929 race, 288
on starting day, 56
McNutt, Harold, 190
Medical conditions of runners
cursory exams given, 32
by last day, 271
at the marathon, 283–84
after 1 week of running, 84
before the race, 46
runner expelled due to feet, 200–201
Mental breakdowns, 88, 103, 111, 143
Metcalfe, Osmond, 111
Meyers, William, 222–23
Mojave Wells, California, 74, 76
Moriarty, New Mexico, 138
Morris, Sydney, 268, 274–75
Motorcycles as hazards, 112
Motor home, Pyle's luxury
in the gully, 159–60
police try to seize, 204
reclaimed, 219–20
seized, 209–10, 212
Munitz, Morris, 142

N

Nash, John B. *See* Brother John
Native American runners. *See* Payne, Andy; Quamawahu, Nick
Needles, California, 79, 89, 90
Nelson, Hans, xii
Newland, Russ, 145, 288
Newton, Arthur, 25
about, 25–26
as Bunion Derby staff member
appreciated by runners, 261
cares for runners, 136, 141, 193, 228
midnight rule changed, 260
snowstorm memories, 150
urges motorists to be careful, 251–52
in the postrace marathon
chosen to run, 281
places second, 284
returns for 1929 race, 288
as runner in the Bunion Derby
Kolehmainen as main competitor, 48
March 4, starting day, 56, 59
March 7, fourth place overall, 72
March 8, sunburn, 76
March 10, wins leg, 82
March 11, finishes second, 87, 89
March 12, wins leg, 97, 101, 102
March 13, wins leg, 106
March 14, wins leg, 109
March 16, struggles, 114, 115
March 17, first place overall, 115
March 18, swollen ankles, 119
March 19, out of the race, 119–20
observations on the runners, 44
reasons for running, 25–26
speech, 48–49
was well prepared, 47
New York City
lodging for runners, 275
Madison Square Garden, 269–73, 282–85
more miles added, 262, 265
no prize money, 253
Nezareno, Cadarino, xii
Nielson, Niels, 222
Night control, xiv
Nilson, Gunnar, 53, 55, 58, 62–63, 72
Normal, Illinois, 215–16
Northcott, Stewart Gordon, 56–57
Noun and Verb Rodeo, 289
Nurmi, Paavo, 41, 47

O

Oatman, Arizona, 101–2
O'Brien, William, 32, 128
Oklahoma City, Oklahoma, 162–69, 281

Oklahoma Outlaw. *See* McCurdy, Elmer
Oldfield, Barney, 4, 23
O'Leary, Dan, 32–33
Orr, Charles C., 135
Overholser, Edward, 169, 171
Owen, Steve, 95–96, 103, 111, 246, 267, 279

P

Palmer, Al J., 215
Payne, Andrew "Doc," 99, 151–52, 255, 257, 263, 268, 272, **274**
Payne, Andy, **127**, **158**, **181**, **250**
about, 26–28, 99
childhood, 122–23
postrace
given money from Oklahoma City, 281
introduced in House of Representatives, 278
places third in marathon, 284
receives $25,000 prize, 283
scrapbook of memories, 289–92
written about by Will Rogers, 277–78
during the race
evening diversions, 146
family's finances publicized, 197
father joins him, 151–52
financial backing for, 26–27, 34–35
friendship with Salo, 251
interview, 184–85
predicted to win, 116
Pyle considers marketability of, 196
race strategy, 98
shoes worn by, 50
total hours run, 283
trainer, 32, 34
race chronology
March 4, starting day, 55–56
March 6, Cajon Pass, 66
March 7, sixth place overall, 73
March 10, motivated, 84
March 11, second place overall, 89
March 12, river crossing, 96
March 16, feeling fine, 114
March 17, second place overall, 115
March 20, tonsillitis, 121
March 25, finishes third, 132
March 26, finishes third, 133
March 27, sandstorm, 136
March 28, finishes with Gavuzzi, 137
March 31, wins leg in tie, 141
April 3, running conservatively, 147
April 5, finishes third, 151
April 8, as threat to Suominen, 156
April 11, wins leg in tie, 162
April 12, finishes 10th, 162
April 13, in Oklahoma City, 162–65, 167
April 14, friendships, 173
April 15, beats a train, 173
April 17, hometown run, 176–77
April 18, reverts to pace, 180
April 19–20, first place overall, 183, 186
April 23, finishes 11th, 191
April 25, way ahead, 195
April 26, playing catch-up, 198
April 27, in St. Louis, 199
April 28, second place overall, 202
May 2, trims Gavuzzi's lead, 216
May 4, still trailing, 220
May 11, first place overall, 239
May 12, still far ahead, 241
May 13, in first, but uneasy, 243
May 14, short speech, 247
May 15, in first, but uneasy, 248–49
May 17, interview, 252
May 18, fear of being hit by car, 255
May 19, tired, 255
May 21, runs cautiously, 259
May 22, walks in rain, 261
May 25, sleeps in jail, for safety, 266
May 26, wins, 272–73
reasons for running, 14–16, 19
returns to 1929 race as staff member, 288
ultimate fate of, 299–300
Payne, Zona, 273
Peach Springs, Arizona, 110
Pederson, John E.
March 4, runs in business suit, 52
March 18, repulsed at dinner, 117
April 8, disgusted with Pyle, 157
May 24, accused of revolting, 264
Pern, Bill, xii
Perrella, Louis
April 28, finishes eighth, 202
May 7, wins leg, 227
May 20, in top 10, 257
May 21, day of agony, 259

May 26, last day of race, 272
receives $1,000 prize, 283
Peters, Jay, 127–28, 135
Pickens, William Hickman
brings stunt pilots, 115
career of, 22–23
comments by, 4, 277
on the fairness of the race, 265
as part of race staff, 51, 145
predicts Payne will win, 116
promotes race to Chicagoans, 199–200
ultimate fate of, 292
Piu, 59
Pletcher, Dean. *See* Kelly, Mike
Podiatry, early, 1–2
Pollard, James, 125–26, 137, 166
Powers, Joe "Hold 'Em," 24
Prize money, final
handed out, 283
provided by Rickard, 280
promised existence of, 262–63, 265, 277
for top 10 finishers, xiii–xiv
Prizes, daily
denied on Day 6, 80–81
not offered first 5 days, 49
unfulfilled promise of, 116
Programs, race, 38, 57–58
Prouty, William F., 23–24
Publicity
on the last day of the race, 272
Levett writes instead of runs, 39–40
prerace, 37–38
on race day, 53
waning, by Day 8, 86
Puente, California, 54, 56–57
Pyle, C. C., **1, 50, 224**
biography in race program, 57–58
the Bunion Derby
luxury camper, 54, 209–10
mistakes admitted, 286–87
monetary benefits of, 38
organization problems, 188–89
race proposed, xiii–xiv
runners' dislike of Pyle, 172–73, 13–15
career of, 67–71, 93–95, 129, 211–12
childhood and family life of, 55, 131–32
death of, 302
divorces, 211, 301
as father of professional sports, 303
getting out of tight spots, 170–71
heroes of, 86–87
lawsuits against, 168–69, 177, 188–89, 204, 220–21, 267, 278, 279, 288–89, 301
lionized in Broadway musical, 300
marriages
Dottie Fisher, 69–71
Effie Arnold, 211–12
Elvia Allman, 301
Martha Russell, 210–11
money management and, 128–29, 171
physical attributes of, 2–3
as promoter, 2–3, 42–43, 196
racism and, 147–48
Red Grange and, 42–43
second race planned, 287–88
as showman and entrepreneur, 18
Pyle, Dottie, 69, 70–71, 95
Pyle, Effie, 55, 210, 211–12, 301
Pyle, Kathrine, 55, 70, 95
Pyle, William, 131–32

Q

Quamawahu, Nick
March 4, starting day, 55, 58
March 7, injury, 72
March 8, back in race, 73
March 11, greeted by band, 89
March 16, out of the race, 114
multiple trainers for, 31–32
racist sports reporting and, 61
receives money from Hopi, 116
wins practice race, 34
Quist, Hugo, 41, 115, 133, 200, 235

R

Race of 1929, 274, 284, 288–89
Racism
fear to eat in restaurants, 148
Ku Klux Klan intimidation, 147–48
sportswriters' coverage and, 61, 240
Radio station, mobile, 127–28, 232, 278
Rea, Harry
March 13, accidental shortcut, 106
March 28, wins leg, 137
April 13, Oklahoma City, 167
April 17, sprints to finish, 179–80
May 8, out of the race, 229
Rebou, Euphemia. *See* Pyle, Effie
Referee, race, 41–42, 225

Rehayn, George
April 14, singing, 173
March 26, still singing, 133
May 23, still upbeat, 262
May 26, last day of race, 271
water can incident, 83–84
Rice, Grantland, 2
Richman, Sam, 65, 153, 184, 251
Rickard, Tex
bans McCurdy corpse, 270
final prize money and, 279, 280
makes deal with Pyle, 254
as successful promoter, 22, 254
Ricketts, Walter, 81
Rivera, Teodocio, 84, 216–17
Roberts, Wynn, 173
Robinson, Sammy
as a boxer, 45
May 11, dining in Fremont, 240
May 26, last day of race, 266
racial prejudice and, 148, 240
Rogers, Will
fires gun in 1929 race, 288
offers prize money in Claremore, 178
as race supporter, 158–59, 269
urges respect for runners, 248
writes about Payne family, 277–78
Rolla, Missouri, 192–93
Roller-skater pursuing runners, 174
Route 66
good name besmirched, 217
Highway 66 Association, 217
as race route, 38
as unpaved, new road, 4
Runners. *See also specific names*
athleticism of, 44, 46–47
biographies of, 57
colorful characters, 44, 74–75, 79–80
complaints by, 169–70, 264–65
dislike of Pyle, 173, 213–15
first to drop out, 61
harassment by fans, 189–90
last surviving participant, 85
lodging in New York City, 275
medical problems of, prerace, 46
number that started, 51
occupations represented, 45–46
older runners, 47, 88
perils of slipping behind, 74
rebellions by, 156–57, 172–73, 263–64
top contenders, 47
vulnerability of front runners, 244
Running
as new sport, 5
race hazards
being hit by a car, 76, 81
mental breakdowns, 88, 103, 111, 143
running in the dark, 76
Russell, Martha Lindsay, 210–11
Russell, R. N., 237–38

S

Salo, John
about, 126
March 7, moving up, 73
March 22, befriends dog, 126
April 5, wears out shoes, 149
April 13, in Oklahoma City, 167
April 17, midnight rule, 179
April 18, back on track, 180
April 23, dog missing, 191
April 25, third place overall, 195
April 26, stomach problems, 198
May 5, wins Chicago leg, 222
May 11, second place overall, 239
May 12, coming into own, 241
May 16, friends with Payne, 251
May 17, interview, 252
May 21, wins longest leg, 258–59
May 22, slows down, 262
May 25, in hometown, 266
May 26, last day of race, 272
receives $10,000 prize, 283
returns for 1929 race, 288
ultimate fate of, 296–97
Sanchez, Eli, 62
Sandsberry, Roy, 146
Sandstorm, in New Mexico, 136–37
Saperstein, Morris
life after the race, 85
March 4, starting day, 56
March 10, out of the race, 84–85
oldest race survivor, 85
reasons for running, 11–12, 19, 84
returns for 1929 race, 288
scoffs at trainer idea, 32
Sapulpa, Oklahoma, 176–77
Scherck, George, 37–38
Scherrer, August, 133
Schoemmel, Lottie Moore, 182
Scott, Lon, 169, 193, 217
Scott, Ralph V., 168, 171–72

Seiler, John J.
about, 39, 102–3
March 11, begins running, 87–88
March 12, abandons quest, 102
throws down challenge gauntlet, 39
Seven Springs, New Mexico, 137–38
Shaddox, Vivian, 14–16, **20**, 299–300
Sheare, Harry
food complaints, 118, 119
March 10, water scarce, 83
May 13, hit by car, 243–44
May 14, in hospital, 247–48
not chosen for marathon, 281–82
as rebellion leader, 156–57
Shin splints, 120, 235–36
Shoemaker, official, 142
Shoes
as cause of aching feet, 5
as Hardrock's undoing, 106
poor design of, 1
variety of, worn by runners, 50–51, 105
wearing out of, 149–50
Simpson, Paul. *See* Hardrock
Singing Dutchman. *See* Rehayn, George
Slayton, Luther, 181
Sleeping conditions, 35–36, 59, 113, 121–22, 155, 193
Smallwood, Percy, 62
Smith, Paul A., 149
Snyder, Burt, 192
Songs about the race, 215, 222
Sonney, Edward, 177
Spangler, Joe, 290–92
Speed walking, 99–100, 101
Sponsorships, corporate, 37–38
Sportswriters racist reporting, 61, 240
Stevano, Stanley, 240
Stinson, Eddie, 115, 167, 182
Studenroth, Arthur, **235**
Study of runners, medical, 43
Stunt pilots, 115–16
Sullivan, Frank, 187
Sunburn, 76, 82
Suominen, Arne
about, 64
March 5, interview, 63–64
March 6, finishes 10th, 64
March 20, finishes well, 121
March 25, finishes second, 132
March 26, passed by Gavuzzi, 133
March 27, sandstorm, 136
March 28, still first overall, 137
March 31, first place overall, 141
April 3, first place overall, 147
April 5, finishes second, 151
April 8, out of the race, 156
postrace letter to Payne, 290
ultimate fate of, 294
Suratt, Valeska, 220–21
Swabey, Henry, 162
Swimming endurance races, xi, **xi**, xiii
Swiss runners. *See* Scherrer, August

T

Tarahumara tribe, 16–17
The Sheik. *See* Gardner, Ed
Thomas, Richard, 266
Thompson, Wildfire
attire of, 45, 52
May 26, last day of race, 268, 270
May 27, tapering off, 275–76
never bathed, 79
number of hours run, 283
Tilley, Hope, 211
Tingley, Clyde, 134–35
Topock, Arizona, 92–93
Toste, Anton, 150, 153
Towns
Albuquerque refuses to pay, 134–35
fees paid for race to enter, 38, 209, 241
hometown leads, arranged, 229–30
night control scouting, 237–38
Trainers
benefits of, 31–32, 34, 83, 109–10
share prize money, 35
Training camp
benefits of, for Pyle, 31, 36
benefits of, for runners, 31
cursory medical exams given, 32
ethnic groups at, 37
lectures given, 32–33
living conditions at, 35–37
practice races, 33–34
Tree sitting, 289–90
Truckimowicz, Frank, xii
Tucumcari, New Mexico, 144–45
Tulsa, Oklahoma, 176–77

U

Ukulele Jake
March 4, begs for racing fee, 52
March 5, unofficial, but runs well, 62

Ukulele Jake *(cont.)*
March 6, cheerful, 66
March 7, in good health, 73
March 11, doing well, 88
March 12, Pyle ends his running, 91
May 26, runs last day of race, 268
Umek, Guisto
March 4, starting day, 51
March 7, finishes 21st, 73
March 13, sleeps in hotel, 108
March 16, bad knee, 113
March 17, finishes 12th, 115
May 7, food poisoning, 226–28
May 8, always hungry, 230
May 11, reluctant runner, 238–39
May 20, battling for fifth place, 257
May 22, wins leg, 261
May 26, last day of race, 272
one of top Italian runners, 47
receives $1,000 prize, 283
returns for 1929 race, 288

V

Vegetarian runners, 146
Victorville, California, 65
Villa, Pancho, 211
Virden, Illinois, 203–4
Von Flue, Frank, 202
March 3, hardly sleeps, 49
March 4, starting day, 56, 58
March 6, Cajon Pass, 64–65
March 10, bath, sunburn, 82
March 13, almost quits, 105–6
March 14, 16th place overall, 109
March 15, miserable night, 113
March 22, struggles, 125
March 23, meets dentist, 130
March 24, reenergized, 130
March 25, finishes fourth, 132
March 27, sandstorm, 137
April 14, forms alliances, 173
April 20, sick, 186
April 23, finishes second, 191
April 24, buys new shoes, 192–93
April 27, in St. Louis, 198–99
April 29, finally has trainer, 202
May 6, clean clothes, 226
May 9, 12th place overall, 233
May 11, 11th place overall, 236
May 13, stays in Joyce's home, 245
May 16, battle with Richman, 251
May 18, 10th place overall, 255
May 19, gaining on Cronick, 255–56
May 20, in top 10, 257
May 21, hit by car, keeps running, 258–59
prerace foot injury, 30
reasons for running, 12–13
receives $1,000 prize, 283
shoes worn by, 50, 90, 149–50
trainer idea scoffed at, 32
ultimate fate of, 297
wins 26-hour marathon, 284

W

Walking, endurance, 32–33, 140–41
Wantinnen, Olli
March 5, interview, 63
March 7, first place overall, 73
March 9, cheered on, 78
March 28, finishes second, 137
March 30, trainer fired, 139–40
April 11, wins leg, 147
April 13, fifth place overall, 166
May 5, hit by car, 222
May 8, out of the race, 229
Warner, Dare Devil, 182
Weston, Edward Payson, 140–41
White, James, 155
Williams, Arizona, 114
Williams, Meredith, 163–64
Williams, Wesley, 29, 176, 184, 256
Wilson, Elmer, 135
Wilson, Joe, 227
Witt, Bill, 160–61, 193
Workman, Red, 202, 258

Y

YMHA, 108, 237
Yost, Fielding, 86
Young, George, xiii, xiv, 175
Young, Harry, xii
Young Men's Hebrew Association (YMHA), 108, 237
Young, Tom, 34, 98, 167, 184–85, 257

Z

Ziolkowski, Adam, 295